THE ROUGH GUIDE to

Philip Pullman's

HIS DARK MATERIALS

by
Paul Simpson

www.roughgu

D0090130

CREDITS

The Rough Guide to Philip Pullman's
His Dark Materials

Text editor: Paul Simpson
Design: Sharon O'Connor
Cover design: Peter Buckley, Chloe Roberts
Proofreading: Lesley Turner,
Martin Rosser, Ian Cranna
Writing: Paul Simpson, Tom Bullough
Thanks to: Philippa Mathers, Simon Kanter

Rough Guides Reference

Series editor: Mark Ellingham
Editors: Peter Buckley, Duncan Clark,
Tracy Hopkins, Sean Mahoney,
Matt Milton, Joe Staines, Ruth Tidball
Director: Andrew Lockett

PUBLISHING INFORMATION

This first edition published September 2007 by
Rough Guides Ltd, 80 Strand, London WC2R 0RL
345 Hudson St, 4th Floor, New York 10014, USA
Email: mail@roughguides.com

Distributed by the Penguin Group:

Penguin Books Ltd, 80 Strand, London WC2R 0RL
Penguin Putnam, Inc., 375 Hudson Street, NY 10014, USA
Penguin Group (Australia), 250 Camberwell Road, Camberwell, Victoria 3124, Australia
Penguin Books Canada Ltd, 10 Alcorn Avenue, Toronto, Ontario, Canada M4P 2Y3
Penguin Group (New Zealand), Cnr Rosedale and Airborne Roads, Albany, Auckland,
New Zealand

Printed in Italy by LegoPrint S.p.A.

Typeset in Morpheus, Gill Sans, and Adobe Caslon Pro

304 pages; includes index

A catalogue record for this book is available from the British Library

ISBN 13: 978-1-84353-920-9
ISBN 10: 1-84353-920-9

1 3 5 7 9 8 6 4 2

Contents

PART III THE WORLD OF HIS DARK MATERIALS

··†··

INTRODUCTION

"Stories are vital. Stories never fail us because, as Isaac Bashevis Singer says, 'events never grow stale'. There's more wisdom in a story than in volumes of philosophy."

Philip Pullman

His Dark Materials is a trilogy of novels that wants to be read. That, in itself, is something of a novelty for a work of contemporary fiction. The fiction universe today consists of many novels that are written to be admired; some that are written merely to make the author and the publisher rich – in the same way that Heinz might decide to make a new variety of baked bean – and some that are barely written at all. Then there are those novels written in pursuit of an artistic, intellectual or philosophical goal so lofty that we mere readers begin to feel irrelevant and slightly disadvantaged, like people who have been invited to a party by a friend of a friend and are consequently unsure of their welcome when they arrive.

Philip Pullman's trilogy is not like any of those novels. The books – *Northern Lights/The Golden Compass*, *The Subtle Knife*, *The Amber Spyglass* – are rich, complex and intellectually ambitious. But they never forget that they need us, the readers. That may explain why, although the books have sold millions of copies, most readers feel, in some way, that the trilogy belongs to them. This sense of ownership – as if we have nearly as big a stake in the story as Pullman does – probably explains why the books' rocky road to the big screen has been so anxiously monitored and why so many fans scan the online forums and Pullman's own website for any revelations, no matter how small, about the long-promised companion to the trilogy, *The Book Of Dust*.

There are many reasons why *His Dark Materials* work so well. You can even list them. They have a compelling central narrative, derived from one of the greatest stories the human race has ever told itself: the journey from innocence to experience. They use the guise of fantasy to raise such topics as honour, courage and personal responsibility, all relevant to the way we live, yet too often ignored by "adult" novelists. Lyra and Will are up there, in the pantheon of immortal characters, alongside Alice in her wonderland, Dorothy in Oz and Holden Caulfield in a state of existential angst.

For some, the real secret is Pullman's writing. I must admit I didn't get that. Judged purely on the magic of words on a page, he didn't seem quite up there with the writer who is – in my eyes – the undisputed master, F. Scott Fitzgerald. Yet as I pressed on through the books, I found myself having strange, haunting dreams that were obliquely related to something I had just read, as if Pullman's words had inexplicably opened a secret passage into my subconscious. That had not happened to me when reading a novel since D.M. Thomas' *The White Hotel*. This seems to me the true source of the books' real power. They have many qualities, and a few flaws, but they pack an emotional punch that is all too rare.

I had the good fortune to be able to interrogate Philip Pullman and discuss a few "unopened questions" for this Rough Guide. He is unusually helpful for such a famous author but then hopefully he understood that this book's sole purpose is to increase everyone's enjoyment of the novels. I hope you feel it does that.

Paul Simpson, Shepperton

ACKNOWLEDGEMENTS

This book would not exist without the enthusiasm and imagination of Tom Bullough and designer Sharon O'Connor; the indefatigability of Lesley Turner, Martin Rosser, Ian Cranna, Andrew Lockett, Mark Ellingham, Ruth Tidball and Matt Milton; a conversation with my son, Jack; the generosity of photographer Catherine Ashmore and the grace of Philip Pullman.

···†···

PART I
HIS DARK MATERIALS

His Dark Materials
The Origins

Light fantastic: the Aurora Borealis, often likened in *His Dark Materials* to a magic curtain, has a pivotal role as a bridge between worlds for Asriel and John Parry

WHERE it ALL BEGAN

How *His Dark Materials* emerged from childhood tragedy, epic journeys and a lifelong passion for *Paradise Lost*

"You'll never make it. You'll never earn a living. Get a decent job and forget all about it. There's no future in it." That is what **Philip Pullman** was told when he was starting out as a writer. For much of his career, that advice proved sound. The bank once refused him an overdraft, prompting Pullman's wife Jude to write back assuring the bank manager that one day her husband would be a famous author. When he was 47, her husband took the giant step that would prove his wife right. The idea came to him, a bit vaguely at first, that he wanted to write something "large", an idea that would, over the next seven years, change his life.

In most accounts of the making of *His Dark Materials,* Pullman started out wanting to recast *Paradise Lost*. But interviewed for this book, he said: "The realization that I was telling the same story as *Paradise Lost* came a little way after I consciously knew that I wanted to recreate the atmosphere of books one and two – or rather wander about in the landscapes of Hell."

The decision didn't seem especially propitious. He would have to write his large story as three separate novels – partly because that felt artistically appropriate and partly to keep the money rolling in. The fruit of his labour was the *His Dark Materials* trilogy, a truly remarkable, intricately crafted, hugely controversial, bestselling work of fiction whose epic scale can be judged by the fact that it manages, with not too much strain, to encompass Plato, The Bible, John Milton, Dante, Carl Jung, William Blake, quantum physics, *The Magnificent Seven*, the occult historical investigations of Frances Yates, *The Alteration* (one of Kingsley Amis's lesser-known novels), the Aurora Borealis, an essay on marionette theatre by Heinrich von Kleist and the remote Norwegian island of Svalbard.

The trilogy – which starts with *Northern Lights* (*The Golden Compass* in the US), continues with *The Subtle Knife* and climaxes with *The Amber Spyglass* – is almost impossible to squeeze into a nutshell. But, in essence – shorn of its religious, scientific and philosophical dimensions – *His Dark Materials* revolves around a pair of pre-adolescent children, **Lyra** and **Will**, who are literally from different worlds. Both have lost parents (Will's father has disappeared; Lyra's parents, **Lord Asriel** and **Mrs Coulter**, are remote and mysterious). Both possess a piece of technology that gives them privileged access to very special knowledge: Will has a subtle knife which can cut a window from one world to another, Lyra a truth-telling oracle called an **alethiometer**. They become crucial to the holy war raging throughout the trilogy between God and Satan. Pullman, inspired by Milton's sympathy for the devil, recasts the conflict so that many readers regard Asriel as heroic, not satanic.

> "I REALIZED I WAS TELLING THE STORY OF *PARADISE LOST* WHEN I DECIDED TO WANDER IN THE LANDSCAPES OF HELL."

So where did this story – arguably more ambitious than the fictional sagas by **J.R.R. Tolkien** and **C.S. Lewis** it is inevitably compared to – come from? One obvious answer is the author's own life. Given that the novel crosses many parallel universes, touches heavily on The Bible and Milton and encompasses dæmons, spies as small as dragonflies and armed polar bears, huge swathes of *His Dark Materials* cannot be regarded as autobiographical. But Pullman's own life, until he became a prosperous bestselling author, was strange enough to belong to one of his characters.

In most photographs, Pullman peers out at the rest of the world like a quietly self-confident Oxford don who is privately debating whether a full-blown smile would be appropriate. Albert Camus said that every man over forty was responsible for his own face, but Pullman's photographs give few clues to the

Face value: Philip Pullman does his best not to look like "the most dangerous author in Britain"

vicissitudes of his life, many of which are refracted in *His Dark Materials* and may explain why the story, for all its epic sweep and intellectual ambition, has a rare emotional intensity.

An Unfinished Life

"I mistrust the biographical way of interpreting novels, as many writers do, because we know how much we make up for the sake of making a pretty pattern in the story," Pullman once cautioned a writer. Keeping those words in mind, let's quickly review his life.

On his website (*www.philippullman.com*), **Philip Nicholas Outram** (as he was born – he became Pullman later in honour of his stepfather) sums up his early life with the dry observation that "I was born in Norwich in 1946 and educated in England, Zimbabwe and Australia, before my family settled in North Wales. I received my secondary education at the excellent Ysgol Ardudwy, Harlech, and then went to Exeter College, Oxford, to read English though I never learned to read it very well." The autobiographical sketch on his website shows that this paragraph obscures as much as it reveals. The sketch is full of minor and major revelations. "I always liked girls. At one point I even wanted to be a girl myself, and picked a name: I was going to be Margot," he admits. Recalling the day, when he was just seven, he was told that his father had died, he says: "I suppose my brother and I cried, though I didn't feel really sad".

You can stretch a point only so far before it snaps, but it seems valid to connect the books' vast geographic span and his own epic journeys as a child. When he was six, the Outrams – Philip, younger brother Francis, mother Audrey and father Alfred – moved to what is now **Zimbabwe**. Pullman's father, a fighter pilot in the **RAF**, had been assigned there, and his son warmly recalls that "Africa was full of strange things." Among those things were the haunted school (where pupils had to wear trilbies), boxing matches (where the smell of corn on the cob was so powerful – and so evocative of his father – that when he encountered it in London years later he was moved to tears) and the theatre where his mother acted out drawing-room plays.

After Alfred Outram's tour of duty in Zimbabwe ended, the rest of the family returned to Drayton, near Norwich, to live with his wife's parents. But then, when Pullman's mother married another airman in the 1950s, the family sailed for Australia. Pullman says now, "How grateful I am to have lived at a time when, if you made a long journey, you travelled across the surface of

A FEW OF PULLMAN'S FAVOURITE THINGS

Philip Pullman's enthusiasms are too vivid and varied to be condensed into the kind of questionnaires you find in glossy magazines. But here is a brief rundown of stuff – apart from books – he has admitted to admiring.

Food Cheese, ginger cake.

Colour Green.

Movies *Ask A Policeman* (a 1938 Will Hay comedy in which Hay plays a police officer in a village with no crime), *The Magnificent Seven*, almost any film with Cary Grant in it, Jacques Rivette's *Celine And Julie Go Boating* (a 1974 movie in which two women either meet or imagine ghosts in a house).

Musical instruments The piano, which he plays badly, the saxophone and guitar.

Music The piano sonatas of Nikolai Medtner (1880–1951). The Russian composer's *Sonata Reminiscenza* in A minor from *Forgotten Melodies* (Opus 38) is the work he would most like to take to a desert island. The only pop record he listed as on *Desert Island Discs* was Dean Martin's "Memories Are Made Of This". He also owns several CDs by the Madagascan band Tarika.

Soap opera *Neighbours*. "It's all pure story: one thing following another", said Pullman once. The Australian soap is part of his daily routine.

Superhero Batman (before he became dark and post-modernist). The caped crusader superseded Pullman's first superhero love, Superman.

Comic *Eagle*. The most popular comic for British boys of a certain age in the 1950s, *Eagle* specialized in sci-fi. and its most memorable character was Dan Dare, chief pilot of the Interplanet Space Fleet. who was brave, honest, and only resorted to violence when absolutely necessary.

Possession "A bronze Byzantine ring given to me by my wife."

Tipple Whisky.

Unfulfilled ambition To present his own woodwork programme on daytime TV.

the earth." As a child, he learned how big the world was, knew the difference between the hemispheres as a physical sensation and, from the precision and passion with which Lyra's expeditions are described, he never forgot it.

THE ORPHANED AUTHOR

Pullman's reaction to his father's death can sound cold. "It was a drama but we were offstage… so we felt that something rather important and grand happened to us, that we were almost orphaned," is how he recalled his sudden

Man of Harlech: if Pullman hadn't read poetry at school here, he might not have become a writer

bereavement on the BBC Radio 4 show *Desert Island Discs*. The family were told that Alfred had died in a plane crash, fighting the Mau Mau rebels in Kenya. They went to Buckingham Palace to receive the **Distinguished Flying Cross** he had been posthumously awarded. Philip was, he admitted later, preoccupied by the mystery of his father, "a hero cut down in his prime, a warrior, a man of shining glamour". His father's glamorous aura was complicated – "a blend of, among other things, cigarettes, beer, leather armchairs". The mystery may have preoccupied him because he sensed something wasn't right. Nearly four decades later, after his mother's death, the mystery was solved in a rather shocking way.

"He hadn't been shot down in battle, he'd been drinking and he'd crashed while practising for an air display," said Pullman. "It was generally known among his friends that he'd crashed his plane on purpose. He'd **committed suicide**. That had been covered up so that he could be awarded the medal and my mother could receive a widow's pension. He'd been in all kinds of trouble, he'd borrowed money he couldn't repay, his affairs with other women were beginning to get out of control and he'd had to agree to a separation from my mother. I knew none of this while my mother was alive."

Later, when Pullman was in conversation with the author Peter Dickinson, "this subject came up and we both agreed how strange it was that so many

THE TRILOGISTS

Pullman and Tolkien have much more in common than having their work optioned by New Line Cinema.

Philip Pullman may not be a massive fan of J.R.R. Tolkien's fiction – and the creator of *Lord Of The Rings* would certainly have disapproved of Pullman's theology – but for two boys born more than half a century apart in different hemispheres, their lives have some odd similarities.

Both spent part of their childhood in southern Africa: Tolkien was born in **South Africa** in 1892, Pullman lived in **Zimbabwe** as a child for a few years. Both returned to England to live with their maternal grandparents, leaving their fathers in Africa, where they would die prematurely.

Both turned to clergymen as surrogate fathers: Philip to his grandfather, a Church of England priest with, so Pullman said, "a big soul" and Tolkien to the Catholic parish priest **Father Francis Xavier Morgan**.

They would study at the same Oxford college – **Exeter** – though Tolkien had his first poem printed there, while Pullman read a lot of thrillers. They have both become, in different ways, so synonymous with the city of dreaming spires that tours are named after them or their characters. And both, finally, have written epic multi-million selling trilogies, peopled with fantastic creatures, which have been filmed by New Line Cinema.

children's authors had lost one or both of their parents in childhood."

The mystery of **Alfred Outram** has obvious echoes in *His Dark Materials* – the most glaring being Will's quest to find his heroic father in *The Subtle Knife* – and the theme runs so deep it is explored separately in a box on p.18.

After Alfred Outram's death, Philip's maternal grandfather **Sidney Merrifield** became, Pullman said, "the sun at the centre of my life." From his grandfather, a parish priest in the Church of England, he learned the power of storytelling. How, for example, an ordinary tree could be transformed by the old man's remark that Robin Hood had once hidden there.

Their grandfather's attentiveness distracted the Pullman brothers from the fact that their mother was working in London at the BBC. His mother was, Pullman told *New Yorker* magazine, considered difficult by her family, and the milieu of her life in London sounds similar to the disturbing, yet enticing, grown-upness of **Mrs Coulter**'s chic London life in *His Dark Materials*.

When Audrey married a friend of her late husband (Philip suspected they'd been having an affair before his father's death), the family moved again, to **Australia**, where the young Pullman fell in love with comic books, superheroes and radio. After reading **Superman**, he said later, "I was sure that I would write stories when I grew up.

IN THE NAME OF THE FATHER

How Pullman's enigmatic dad influenced *His Dark Materials*.

If you read all of Pullman's novels, you'll find enough bereaved children to fill a medium-sized orphanage.

Sally Lockhart has just become an orphan at the start of *The Ruby In The Smoke* (and in *The Tiger In The Well* her own daughter is without a father); Roger, the main protagonist in *I Was A Rat*, knows nothing about his parents; Ginny in *The Broken Bridge* and the title character in *The Firework-Maker's Daughter* have both lost their mothers; *Count Karlstein* centres on two orphaned girls, and at the heart of *His Dark Materials*, **Lyra** wrongly believes she is an orphan and **Will** is obsessed by finding his missing father.

Pullman has himself suggested there is a link between his life and all these absent parents, discussing how many children's authors had lost a parent in childhood. "My father died in a plane when I was seven," he recalled, "and naturally I was preoccupied for a long time by the mystery of what he must have been like."

Lyra is equally mystified by her often absent father, **Lord Asriel,** a character who owes much to the cliché of the Byronic Romantic hero.

For years, Pullman imagined his father Alfred Outram as a hero. And it was hard to shake that habit, even after he had discovered that his father's life ended, not in heroic combat, but scandal and suicide. He once admitted: "Sometimes I think he's really alive somewhere, in hiding, with a different name. I'd love to meet him."

Asriel, ultimately unknowable, geographically and emotionally remote from his child, defying categorisation as good or evil, brave and reckless, is to Lyra – and to many readers – as mysterious as Pullman's father must have been to him.

Among the images or threads that prompted Pullman to write *His Dark Materials* was the idea that a boy called Will would search for his father. **John Parry** had, like Alfred Outram, been in the services (albeit the Royal Marines, not the RAF). Parry and Outram both made mysterious exits. Will's father vanishes while on an expedition in Alaska; Pullman's died thousands of miles away in circumstances that were, for many years, shrouded in secrecy.

John Parry does prove to be alive somewhere, in hiding, under a different name (Stanislaus Grumman). He does finally meet Will, but he's dying, killed because of his fidelity to his wife (is this a deliberate contrast to the womanizing of Pullman's own father?). Yet his ghost is around to help his son out in time of need. Whatever hopes Pullman might have entertained, there could be no such comeback for the late Alfred Outram or his son.

What I enjoyed most was the sense of the storyteller, of this eye that zoomed in and chose this bit of action and then moved out to a panoramic picture of Metropolis late at night."

In the last move of his childhood, the family relocated to **Llanbedr**, a small town a few miles from Harlech on the North Wales coast, where Pullman's stepfather kept a chicken farm for a while.

Here, finally, Philip settled, making friends at the local school after his grandfather had shown him how to box. He was inspired, by a teacher called **Enid Jones**, to discover Wordsworth, Milton and the metaphysical poets. (He and Enid are still friends. He sends her copies of each of his books.) He discovered art, too, and began sketching obsessively. He saw his first dead body (lying peacefully on a grass verge) when he was 11, adjusted to an expanded family (acquiring a new sister and brother and making room for a stepbrother) and thought he might become a poet.

> "I WENT THROUGH OXFORD LIKE A NEUTRINO. I SPENT MY TIME PAINTING, DRINKING AND READING TRASHY THRILLERS."

That seemed, to him, a high calling, a bit daunting, but writing verse – initially inspired by the metaphysical poets and Dylan Thomas – taught him to appreciate rhythms and cadences. He later regretted not going to art school but, as he wanted to write, the logical thing to do was study English – which he did, with no great diligence, at **Exeter College** in Oxford (1965 to 1968). He admitted: "I went through the place like a neutrino. I spent my time painting pictures, drinking and reading trashy thrillers." He graduated at Oxford with a third-class degree in English but, the day after he left, started writing a novel. And he got stuck, trying to decide which point of view he was going to write it from. "I couldn't help noticing that I'd learned more about the novel in a morning trying to write one than in seven years of trying to write criticism."

THE MAKING OF A STORYTELLER

His real education started later, in London, while he was working for Moss Bros, the clothes rental chain, and writing **rondeau**, a stylized form of French verse, in a nearby churchyard in his lunch hour. Nineteen seventy was an annus mirabilis for Pullman. He married **Judith Speller**, a teacher, and felt a "jolt of recognition" when he discovered **William Blake**'s illustrations to Dante's *Inferno*.

He later reread Blake while writing *His Dark Materials*, believing it helped him maintain his vision. He gave up Moss Bros, worked in a library and then, following his wife's example, became a teacher and polished his storytelling skills, recounting **Homer**'s *Odyssey* and *Iliad* to his students. He also began, through school plays, to explore the subtleties of plot.

He must have been a good storyteller. Once, during a family meal on holiday, his son Tom got so excited about his father's retelling of the *Odyssey* that he bit a chunk out of a glass he'd been holding. Pullman learned, he said later, that he wasn't good at making people laugh out loud but he could "evoke an atmosphere, paint a picture in the mind's eye." When *New Yorker* profiled him, he seemed happiest when discovering that someone had written to him, addressing the envelope to "Philip Pullman, the storyteller, Oxford".

In 1972, Pullman won his first literary prize, the New English Library's young writers award, and wrote his first novel *The Haunted Storm*, published under the name of Philip N. Pullman. The middle initial made him sound American, like Philip K. Dick. The novel was, Pullman says, "completely terrible", although it has earned this glowing review on Wikipedia: "It is wonderful and involves lots of people doing karate."

His next novel, *Galatea*, blending fantasy, sci-fi and magic realism, was published in 1978. Reviewers didn't know what to make of it but didn't damn it out of hand. Pullman insists he's still proud of "my last adult book". Questions of religion, sexuality and morality recur in both his early novels, and in *Galatea*, some menacing ecclesiastical characters threaten to put the flautist hero to death – a harbinger of clerical villainy to come.

Adapting a story he had first done as a school play, Pullman turned to children's literature with the novel *Count Karlstein*, which was published, to decent reviews, in 1982. This is a good point at which to ask the question: why, in his early twenties, did Pullman become a children's author?

It certainly wasn't because he felt inferior to other novelists. In 1995, after the first volume of *His Dark Materials* had won the **Carnegie Medal**, awarded by British librarians to the year's best children's book, he proclaimed, in a speech, that: "There are some themes, some subjects, too large for adult fiction; they can only be dealt with adequately in a children's book." He assailed contemporary adult fiction on two counts: that it lacked moral seriousness and that "in adult

THE REST OF PULLMAN: ADULT NOVELS & PLAYS

The adult novels

The Haunted Storm (1972) An odd story of murder, incest, Gnosticism and existential angst that Pullman would prefer us to forget.

Galatea (1978) An intriguing sci-fi/fantasy novel in which a flautist, searching for his wife, becomes embroiled in surreal adventures. Not perfect, but worth reading. Some of the motifs – angels, the dead becoming zombies, the mysteries of matter – recur in *His Dark Materials*.

The plays

Frankenstein (1990) Pullman's accomplished adaptation of Mary Shelley's classic comes complete with a section on genetic engineering.

Sherlock Holmes And The Limehouse Horror (1993) Though some Holmes purists were left unmoved, this affectionate spoof, inspired by a "giant rat of Sumatra" mentioned in one of Sir Arthur Conan Doyle's original stories, is an appealing blend of parody and suspense.

fiction, stories are there on sufferance". Present day would-be George Eliots were more interested, he alleged, in style, technique and literary knowingness.

Pullman remarked scathingly: "In a children's book, you can't put the plot on hold while you cut artistic capers for the amusement of your sophisticated readers. They've got more important things in mind than your dazzling skill with wordplay, they want to know what happens next."

"CHILDREN HAVE MORE IMPORTANT THINGS IN MIND THAN WORDPLAY. THEY WANT TO KNOW WHAT HAPPENS NEXT."

This provocative speech, a personal manifesto for Pullman, struck a chord with almost anyone who had given up on a work of adult fiction. The "artistic capers" in his earlier "adult" novels, some of which were akin to the effects Angela Carter was known for, often misfired. The manifesto gave him an intellectual rationale to move on and concentrate on what, as a writer, he was good at.

His argument that storytelling is of massive import to children in particular ("'Thou shalt not' is soon forgotten, but 'once upon a time' lives forever" he said once) and the human race in general has been spectacularly endorsed. Millions of adults now buy "children's novels" with a strong narrative drive – a description that could apply to the novels of Pullman, J.K. Rowling and, with the smallest stretch, Dan Brown.

His reference to George Eliot was deliberate. Pullman is fascinated by the 19th century – its literature, its German Romanticism, even the seedy allure of London's old East End. In the 1970s, he bought two sentimental Victorian postcards in London. "I kept them on my desk for years without thinking about them until one day I found myself wondering about the people in them and about the other important person, the one who isn't visible: the photographer." Out of that curiosity – and years of research – came *The Ruby In The Smoke* (1985) the first of four novels starring the adventurer **Sally Lockhart**.

These novels are, Pullman cheerfully suggests, "old-fashioned Victorian-blood-and-thunder historical thrillers". He says: "I wrote each one with a genuine cliché of melodrama right at the heart." The trick worked. These novels made his name. He would dearly love to return to this milieu because "there are many more such hackneyed situations awaiting my attention".

The Victorian backdrop continued in his two **New Cut Gang** novels, *Thunderbolt's Waxwork* (1994) and *The Gas Fitter's Ball* (1998). These were intended to be the first two in a series of six, but his commissioning editor at Puffin left and the series was abandoned. A modified version of the Victorian world provides the setting for much of *His Dark Materials*.

Giving up full-time teaching when the Lockhart series started, Pullman became more prolific. Two contemporary novels for a teenage audience – *The Broken Bridge* (1990) and *The White Mercedes* (1992) – dwell on the importance of stories in their characters' lives, a theme that flowered magnificently in *His Dark Materials*. Both books were, he says, attempts to write "realistic stories about the way we live now", something he hasn't done very often as a novelist.

Paradise and Daemons

Sometime in 1993, the idea that he had to write something "large" became, for Pullman, a personal mission. He told his publisher **David Fickling** that he had in mind a very long story that would take three books to tell. Even more audaciously, at some point in time, it became clear that this long story would, in some way, be a reworking of *Paradise Lost*.

Looking back, Pullman can make the creation of his trilogy sound almost too cut and dried. "I knew the kind of thing I wanted to do – I knew the length, I knew it was going to be in three volumes and I knew it was going to be big and ambitious and enable me to say things I'd never been able to say in any other form," he recalled once. But these formal goals were accompanied by

Philip Pullman, out of the shed, reflecting on the success of his trilogy

artistic inspiration, a series of vivid, detailed pictures that somehow felt, he says, loosely connected: "Lyra hiding in the wardrobe and overhearing something she wasn't meant to; two bears fighting to the death; a window to another world appearing in mid-air – and so on."

But when he started writing the first volume in his shed in the garden of his house in Oxford, he got stuck, redrafting the first chapter sixteen or seventeen times. And then, mysteriously, an image came to him. "I don't know where the idea came from – it just emerged as I was trying to tell the story. I suddenly realized Lyra had a dæmon and it all grew out of that."

Interviewed for this book, Pullman explains: "This made a big difference in that first chapter because Lyra had to have someone to talk to and argue with, which introduced a dynamic into the narrative. If you are just describing someone's thoughts and feelings it tends easily towards the static. Then I realized what else I could do with dæmons and, as a matter of fact, I'm still discovering more things. There is a scene I wrote for *The Golden Compass* film in which something entirely new happens between a character and a dæmon. And I didn't think of that until the need for the scene arose."

After a bit of a struggle, Lyra came to him with the image of a dæmon, and when he first glimpsed Will he knew the boy already had a mission: to find his missing father. Other characters emerged slowly and more mysteriously. Asked, for this book, how he first envisaged the fantastically ambiguous Lord Asriel and Mrs Coulter, he replied: "I had a sort of apprehension of them as large figures in the misty darkness nearby and then, as I wrote about them, I discovered more and more."

THE REST OF PULLMAN: CHILDREN'S NOVELS

The Sally Lockhart series

The Ruby In The Smoke 1985

Orphaned Sally is a very uncommon heroine – pretty, able to run a business, shoot a pistol and ride like a Cossack, with a useful grounding in military tactics. It's easy to see why, having invented her, Pullman decided she was too interesting to be discarded after one novel. This marvellously atmospheric thriller may start with a Holmesian conceit (a man dies from a heart attack induced by the remark "Have you ever heard the phrase The Seven Blessings"?) but it is soon clear that Pullman has, with this heroine and novel, found his voice.

The Shadow In The North 1988

The second Lockhart novel – in which Sally and her friends investigate the collapse of a British shipping firm – may be even better than the first. This is a riveting yarn of fraud, murder, corrupt power and the supernatural.

The Tiger In The Well 1990

Pullman was intrigued by what Sally might be like as a young woman. In lesser hands this could have gone wrong, but Pullman starts with a compelling premise – Sally is sued for divorce by a man she's never heard of – and never really puts a foot wrong.

The Tin Princess 1994

This is the Lockhart novel Pullman enjoyed writing most – and many people enjoyed reading least. Sally has only a cameo role in this swashbuckling tale

of former prostitute Adelaide (who appeared in The Ruby In The Smoke) who becomes queen of a mythical central European kingdom. There's much to enjoy here, but the story is unfortunately hampered by too many places, twists and names, and it struggles under the weight of research.

The New Cut Gang series

Thunderbolt's Waxworks 1994

In this fast-moving comic caper, plucky Victorian street urchins have to free a pal's dad and protect their waxwork from villains.

The Gas-Fitter's Ball 1998

More wry humour as the urchins are pursued by the homicidal owner of a hoard of counterfeit gold sovereigns.

One-off novels

Count Karlstein 1982

In this precise Gothic farce, which draws on such tales of derring do as Anthony Hope's The Prisoner Of Zenda, a girl and her tutor foil the titular villain's plot to sacrifice his young nieces to a demon huntsman and become rich.

How To Be Cool 1987

This modern dry run for the New Cut Gang books, this story – in which kids discover the government runs a National Cool Board – is a tad dated.

Spring-Heeled Jack 1989

As a boy in Australia, Pullman loved Batman comics, and this rip-roaring adventure pays homage to the Caped Crusader. Its titular hero, from the Victorian penny dreadfuls, comes to the aid of three orphans. David Mostyn's fine illustrations add flavour.

The Broken Bridge 1990

The emotional truths in this novel may be so raw because it is obliquely autobiographical. Teenage heroine Ginny, who must unearth family secrets to rebuild her world, lives in the kind of small North Wales village where Pullman spent part of his childhood. Like her creator, she discovers she has a half-brother. And Ginny's image of perfect happiness is, Pullman admits, based on an idyllic memory of his mother hanging sheets on the line and singing to herself on a bright blue day.

The White Mercedes 1992

Republished as The Butterfly Tattoo, this novel divides readers. For some, the tragic tale of a boy who unintentionally betrays and kills the girl he loves, is bleakly compelling. Others, like the Books For Keeps reviewer, just find it "profoundly cruel".

The Wonderful Story Of Aladdin And The Enchanted Lamp 1995

The brilliance of Pullman's retelling of this children's classic is matched by David Wyatt's astonishing illustrations.

The Firework-Maker's Daughter 1996

In this exciting, mythic tale, feisty Lila, having almost finished her apprenticeship as a firework maker, embarks on a quest of self-discovery, accompanied by a white, talking elephant covered in graffiti, and journeys into the lair of the Fire-fiend.

Clockwork 1998

This Faustian tale of the clockmaker's apprentice was inspired by an old clock at the Science Museum and is as brilliantly constructed as an old-fashioned timepiece. Amid the quirky characters, spine-chilling tension, asides about clockmaking and nods to the brothers Grimm is a serious message about responsibility.

Mossycoat 1998

Pullman's rhythmic variation on Cinderella is one of the highlights in this series of fairy tales retold by contemporary writers.

I Was A Rat 1999

In this beguiling inversion of Cinderella, a scruffy little boy doesn't revert at midnight to his rodent form after escorting a woman to a ball. In desperation, he turns to his adoptive parents, the tabloid press and a princess for help. A brilliant, playful – and thought-provoking – spoof.

Puss In Boots 2000

Pullman turned this classic children's tale into a play and then, with the aid of illustrator Ian Beck, into this superb picture book.

The Scarecrow And His Servant 2004

A charming tale for younger kids of a likeable, if pompous, scarecrow who has all his body parts replaced.

His application for a grant to visit **Svalbard**, the remote Arctic island where much of the first novel was set, was rejected. This wasn't, he maintained, too much of a blow. He researched it in local libraries instead. He pressed on, convinced, he said later, that: "Everything I'd done, read and written in life had been in preparation for this book."

When his publisher suggested that the first novel might have illustrations at the beginning of each chapter, Pullman volunteered to do them himself. He went to the park, drew a sketch of pine twigs (which later became the picture for Chapter 17, The Witches), and a polar bear's head (used in Chapter 10, The Consul and the Bear). For the second volume, *The Subtle Knife*, he drew symbols to alert the reader as to which world the action was taking place in. In the final volume, *The Amber Spyglass*, he started all 38 chapters with an appropriate quote from some of his favourite authors.

The quotations ease appreciation of the books but they were an improvised solution. He had intended to illustrate the third volume, too, but said, in an email: "The publishers were in such a hurry to print the books, and get it out into the shops that there wasn't time. Each of these little pictures takes me a day, because I'm not an illustrator, so I have to go about it laboriously. But for the later edition, I could finally do the illustrations I wanted and *The Amber Spyglass* has pictures as well as the quotations I found."

> "I HAD AN APPREHENSION OF ASRIEL AND MRS COULTER AS LARGE FIGURES IN THE MISTY DARKNESS NEARBY. AS I WROTE, I LEARNED MORE AND MORE ABOUT THEM."

The first novel, *Northern Lights*, was published in the UK in 1995 (and in the US, under the title *The Golden Compass*, in 1996). Pullman's American publisher **Alfred A. Knopf**, deciding the alethiometer on the cover looked a lot like a compass, wanted to call the book *The Golden Compass* – which had been one of the first titles Pullman had in mind for the trilogy – and Pullman could not change their minds.

Nor could he convince them, in the first American editions of the trilogy, to include his illustrations or quotes. Knopf felt the illustrations made the books feel too childish and would deter adults who might enjoy them.

Pullman had pessimistically predicted *Northern Lights* would "be read by about 500 people at most". The first novel wasn't, as selective quotation from the best reviews might have us now believe, praised to the skies by every critic, but it earned Pullman easily the best notices he had enjoyed in his steady rise to global fame, and a couple of children's literature awards.

REVIEWERS AND DEAD SQUIRRELS

The Guardian hailed *Northern Lights* as an "eye-widening fantasy, a scorching thriller and a thought-provoking reflection on the human condition", while *New Statesman* magazine called it "the most ambitious work since *Lord Of The Rings.*" The *New York Times* thought the novel "very grand indeed" but offered the caveat that "it doesn't quite achieve the majestic poetry of Tolkien's powerful sagas, or the sinewy gravity of **Ursula K. Le Guin**'s *Wizard Of Earthsea*, or the wit of **Russell Hoban**'s fable *The Mouse And His Child.*" The *Complete Review*, which took exception to the "feeble and obvious" device of the alethiometer, damned the novel with faint praise, calling it "worthwhile as a fun, light read but not exceptional".

Luckily for Pullman, the first book in the trilogy left hundreds of thousands of readers across the world hungry for the next instalment, *The Subtle Knife*, which duly arrived in 1997. This novel was acclaimed – especially by the *New Statesman* and the *Times Literary Supplement* – though some critics grumbled about Pullman's allegedly two-dimensional characterizations and his habit of jumping between storylines. Rachel Pastan, in *Salon*, caught the general mood best when she asked: "How can I wait two years to learn whether the rebel angels will triumph over the Authority, and at what price?"

Her impatience was shared by many Pullman fans. One girl famously sent him a picture of a **squirrel** and a note saying "Release your book or the squirrel dies". He finished *The Amber Spyglass* (which might have been called *The Lacquer Spyglass* until Knopf said the title might be misheard as "lack of spyglass") in 1999. While promoting the book in 2000, Pullman met the squirrel-threatener Sophie and was delighted to be presented with the knifed, plastic rodent.

Some admirers – such as the American novelist **Michael Chabon** – felt *The Amber Spyglass* was the weakest novel in the trilogy. Yet the critic Charles de Lint, author and devotee of the fantasy genre who had not enthused about the first two novels, praised *The Amber Spyglass*'s "remarkable depth", saying the trilogy had, on the strength of this volume, become one of his favourite series.

Most judges agreed with De Lint. The book was longlisted for the Booker Prize and, in January 2002, made Pullman the first children's author to win the UK's prestigious **Whitbread Book of the Year** award. By then, a handful of shouts of acclamation had been replaced by a chorus of praise, with the likes of Chabon, Robert McCrum, Monty Python member Terry Jones, and the acerbic political journalist Christopher Hitchens publicly extolling the trilogy's virtues.

Infamy and Fortune

Not everyone was so impressed. Hitchens' brother – and fellow journalist – Peter spoke for many when, soon after the Whitbread award, he thundered, in a Sunday newspaper, that Pullman was "**the most dangerous author in Britain**". Perhaps incensed by Pullman's remark that "my books are about killing God", Hitchens portrayed the novelist as a sinister propagandist. Even as this professional controversialist laid into Pullman, he had to admit that he had found the first two novels to be "captivating and clever". But *The Amber Spyglass* was, Hitchens felt, a "disappointing clunker… too loaded down with propaganda to leave room for the story". Comparing the trilogy unfavourably to C.S. Lewis's **Narnia** novels, Hitchens dubbed Pullman "the anti-Lewis, the one the atheists would have been praying for, if atheists prayed."

Hitchens was merely the most eloquent of many commentators, some sincere, others with sinister agendas of their own, who attacked *His Dark Materials* and the trilogy's creator for something that sounded remarkably like the terribly old-fashioned offence of **heresy**.

"PULLMAN is the anti-Lewis, the one the atheists would have been praying for, if atheists prayed."

Leonie Caldecott, in the *Catholic Herald*, said the books were "far more worthy of the **bonfire** than Harry Potter". Caldecott's point – that *His Dark Materials'* systematic anti-clericalism posed a much greater threat to Christianity than the adventures of a boy wizard – was soon lost as the media exaggerated the review first to imply – and then to declare – that the *Catholic Herald* had recommended the novels be chucked on the bonfire. Pullman, who behaves as if such attacks are a badge of honour, replied: "If you find that you inadvertently become a satanist, you can write to the publisher and get your money back."

Expectation of a backlash from Christian fundamentalists may have complicated the trilogy's progress to the big screen, but such fears were less

THE ART OF WRITING

To write *His Dark Materials*, Pullman needed A4 paper, coloured pens, discipline and imagination.

Philip Pullman doesn't believe in writer's block. Or, to put it another way, he believes in writing through it. The discipline to write three pages a day – long-hand on A4 paper – is, he thinks, a better cure for this malady than whisky or opium.

Writing fiction as ambitious as *His Dark Materials* posed special problems. In an email, he gave some insight into the effort required to ensure that the trilogy's infrastructure didn't collapse halfway through.

"I was compiling a big file of notes all the time – on A4 paper exactly like the stuff I write on – but I number the notes in the top centre of the page instead of at the top right, where I number the text, so I can distinguish them. I also colour the paper. Each book has a different colour or combination of colours at the top right-hand corner. I usually run a coloured pencil across so there's a little sliver of colour there, and the paper is dedicated to that book."

Even so, he admits, the procedure wasn't flawless. He admitted in a recent discussion of the movie that there were things in the first novel that, as he wrote the second and third, he wished he'd have done differently. He didn't go on to reveal what those things were.

influential in Britain. In 2003, the **BBC** adapted the trilogy for Radio 4, and **Nicholas Hytner** staged a six-hour adaptation of the trilogy that sold out the **National Theatre** for months and was heralded by **Dr Rowan Williams**, the archbishop of Canterbury, as a "near miraculous triumph".

The controversy hasn't harmed sales of the books. At the last count, they had been translated into 39 languages and sold in excess of ten million copies. Pullman has, typically, attributed this success to luck. "Had I been classed as an adult fantasy writer the books would never have flown off the shelves. Nothing succeeds like a book recommended by your children."

That might sound unduly modest, but he has a point. There are so many turgid adult fantasy novels – me-too sagas inspired more by the profits made by *Lord Of The Rings* than the work itself – that *His Dark Materials*, great as it is, might have struggled to stand out.

Though Pullman fans have grown tired of the comparisons with J.K. Rowling's **Harry Potter** series, the buzz created by her first novel *Harry Potter And The Philosopher's Stone*, published the same year – 1997 – as *The Subtle Knife*, didn't do his sales any harm and, paradoxically, probably helped his critical standing. The trilogy was embraced by many critics who found the Potter novels too populist and too scarily successful.

For the record, Pullman has read *Harry Potter And The Chamber Of Secrets* and says he's glad Rowling invented Harry but, as he hasn't admitted to reading any other title in the series, he can't have been unduly impressed. Soon, Potter movies were competing at the world's multiplexes with Peter Jackson's adaptation of *Lord Of The Rings* and Hollywood suits began scouring the bookshelves for any other fantasies that might deliver box-office gold. Fantasy was suddenly so big that it was in danger of being given the ultimate pop culture kiss of death: becoming the umpteenth thing to be described as "the new rock and roll".

"I MAY RETURN TO JESUS, BUT IF I TELL PEOPLE WHAT I'M GOING TO DO SOMETHING PREVENTS IT, SO I DON'T ANTICIPATE."

For Pullman, a man who prizes the enforced solitude of the writer's life, fame must have its discomforts. In 2004, in search of more space and privacy, he sold the modest family home in Oxford and bought a modernized 16th-century farmhouse in the village of **Cumnor**, a ten-minute drive from Oxford station. The shed he wrote his novels in was sadly jettisoned – donated to his friend Ted Dewan, the illustrator.

Apart from being drawn into an intermittent, often profitless, argument with the Christian right, Pullman has used his celebrity to air his impassioned views on education (especially its increasing marginalization of the imagination and the British government's mania for testing), literature and global warming, fire a few critical salvoes at the Narnia books and make the odd, unpublicized, donation to help victims of torture.

He has written other fiction – his modern fairytale *I Was A Rat* (1999) is a delight, as is *The Scarecrow And His Servant* (2004) – but he has not written a full length novel since *The Amber Spyglass* was published, though he has occasionally talked longingly of returning to the Sally Lockhart series.

Pullman admitted, in an interview with the *Sunday Times* in 2004, that he was finding it hard to avoid the "travel and distractions" that plague successful authors. One of those distractions has been the rather stately progress of his trilogy, optioned by New Line Cinema as long ago as 2002, to the big screen.

He has also had to handle the devotion of fans who don't want the trilogy to have ended. For some "sraffies"– many devoted fans have adapted the mulefa word for Dust to describe themselves – it is still hard to accept that the logic of the story in *His Dark Materials* does, as Pullman insists, dictate that Will and Lyra must be separated in different worlds.

In late 2003, he published **Lyra's Oxford,** a slim volume containing a short story set in Oxford featuring Lyra and set two years after the trilogy has ended. There were already quite a few loose ends left after *The Amber Spyglass*, but the tale of Lyra, the witch and the alchemist **Sebastian Makepeace** gave Pullman even more room for manoeuvre in the years – and books – to come.

Good as the story was, its very compactness meant it was doomed to disappoint many fans enthralled by the epic sweep and intellectual ambition of *His Dark Materials*. The readers' reviews on Amazon, for example, run from one star to five.

The book had a crossword puzzle cryptic quality. Accompanying the story were, as Pullman put it, "some other things" – notably a postcard from **Mary Malone,** a former nun featured in *The Subtle Knife,* a card for the cruise liner **SS Zenobia** and an odd map of Oxford – which Pullman noted enigmatically in his brief introduction "might be connected to stories that haven't happened yet."

The book that hasn't happened yet – to the increasing frustration of many fans and the consternation of the world's squirrels – is *The Book Of Dust*. This is described not as a sequel to the trilogy but an illustrated companion volume of stories that may feature some secondary characters from *His Dark Materials*, explaining how the Texan adventurer **Lee Scoresby** first met **Iorek Byrnison,** the witch **Serafina Pekkala** fell in love with **Farder Coram** and how **Asriel** and **Mrs Coulter** came to know each other. It will not, he indicated once, feature Will and Lyra in the same story, but it may continue the story started in *Lyra's Oxford*, which introduced the intriguing Makepeace, a mad alchemist who may well not be mad or, indeed, an alchemist.

Other elements the book might include are histories of **Dust**, the alethiometer (presumably building on the one he wrote for his American publisher's website), the subtle knife and the first angelic rebellion.

In March 2004, in a debate at the National Theatre with the **Archbishop of Canterbury,** Pullman was asked by Dr Williams why it was that **Jesus** hardly figured in *His Dark Materials*. He replied: "There's a sort of reference to the teaching of Jesus which I may return to in the next book – but I don't want to anticipate too much because I've found that if I tell people what I'm going to write about, I don't write it, something happens to prevent it, so I'd better not anticipate that too much." This caused a ripple of surprise in the audience. Nobody was quite sure how serious he was. Pullman says he regards Jesus as

Divine inspiration: Jesus may, Pullman says, star in his fiction, possibly in *The Book Of Dust*

a "moral genius", but was he really going to weave the Son of God into his fiction? Asked that very question for this book, Pullman replied succinctly and enigmatically: "Oh yes."

In an email to author Tony Watkins, Pullman said: "To hear the church, you'd think that Jesus was completely obsessed by the question of homosexuality and what a threat it was to the family. But he never mentions homosexuality and his view of the family is that you should leave them behind entirely. My view would say that he's not a God at all, but a man – a man of genius, a great moral leader and storyteller – who died. The resurrection was made up to bolster the shaky church and to bolster Paul's fantasies about the imminent of end of the world." That certainly suggests *The Book Of Dust* will prove at least as controversial as its predecessors.

Pullman admits, on his website, that he started making notes for *The Book Of Dust* in the summer of 2005 – and has often referred to it in subsequent entries – but no firm publication date has been set. In the spring of 2007, in a Q&A with *The Guardian* newspaper, he said he was working on "a sequel to *His Dark Materials*. It's going to be a long book and I'm only part way through it." This does sound like *The Book Of Dust* but, less encouragingly, also sounds as if completion of the "long book" is some way away.

The other challenge he faces, as he develops the story in whatever way he chooses, is that the terrain – and the characters – will soon no longer be his own. He will, like **Ian Fleming**, have to compete with the celluloid depictions of his inventions. And that will, for an author like Pullman, be an uncomfortable experience. **Nicole Kidman** may be a brilliant actress, but her screen portrayal in Chris Weitz's movie *The Golden Compass* might simplify the marvellous complexity and ambiguity that is Mrs Coulter.

THE FANTASTIC FOUR

With the trilogy only completed in 2000 – and, rumours suggest, many fictional avenues still to be explored – it is too early to make a definitive assessment of *His Dark Materials'* place in the canon of English literature. But the novels are far too significant to be pigeonholed by constant comparisons with the competing volumes by Rowling, Tolkien and Lewis.

Pullman has damned the Narnia stories as racist, misogynist, afflicted by an "ugly vision" and, for all their religious allegory, surprisingly un-Christian. This demolition job is a bit over the top – it might even be seen as a bid for supremacy in a certain fictional terrain – because some of Lewis's motifs draw, like Pullman, on pagan folklore. But Lewis's series doesn't have a great deal more than nostalgia to offer the adult reader. Though Pullman credits Lewis with asking the right questions, the Narnia books have a theological certainty about them which makes it easy to see why they have been so firmly embraced by the Christian right in America.

Rowling is an entertaining writer – apart from her interminable account of the quidditch world cup in *Harry Potter And The Goblet Of Fire* – and her novels are driven by verve, character and a thrilling sense of narrative inevitability. But they are so hugely popular partly because, whatever Rowling's intentions, they can be read as rattling good yarns that don't force readers to confront difficult philosophical, intellectual or religious issues.

Tolkien's *Lord Of The Rings* is a powerful story, a tale told with the authority of myth. Yet Pullman has dismissed Tolkien's epic as "fundamentally infantile", more interested in "maps, plans, language and codes" than human beings.

He might simply be jaundiced by the incessant, slightly misleading, comparisons between his work and Tolkien's. The two trilogies are of similar length (1100–1200 pages), both play with language, introduce fictional species, contain many exotically named characters, draw heavily on myths, are driven by a titanic struggle between good and evil and take place, largely or completely, in their own fictional universes.

Although they are both written by **Exeter College** graduates, the trilogies reflect completely contradictory world views. Tolkien is a Christian who embeds religious messages in his trilogy, Pullman is an atheist who demonizes the Church in his. Tolkien, as Pullman suggests, didn't create a single believably complex character in *Lord Of The Rings* (though this isn't to say his creations aren't memorable). Pullman gives us four: Will, Lyra, Asriel and Mrs Coulter – more than some authors of fantasy novels create in a career.

The trilogies are not mutually exclusive. Some *Lord Of The Rings* fans have hailed Pullman's masterpiece as the best work of its kind since Tolkien stopped writing. The *Rings* saga's mythic qualities have allowed others – environmentalists, computer hackers, dissidents in Communist Eastern Europe and rock musicians – to find their own subtexts. *His Dark Materials* is just as epic in its sweep but is, especially in *The Amber Spyglass*, more didactic. There's less scope for outsiders to reinvent the work and give it their own slant.

It is hard to imagine *His Dark Materials* without the precedent set by Tolkien and Pullman understands the inevitability of the comparison. "Because Tolkien is such a huge presence in the landscape of fantasy fiction, people feel they have to refer to him. It's like Mount Everest. When you're talking about a mountain, you say, 'It's not quite as high as Mount Everest' or 'It's less than half as high as Everest.' Tolkien is the reference point." With *His Dark Materials*, Pullman has created a new reference point.

··†··

His Dark Materials
The Trilogy

Instrumental break: once you start looking, you find timepieces that resemble the alethiometer everywhere — like this one in St Mark's Square, Venice

MATERIAL EVIDENCE

The remarkable tale of *His Dark Materials*: from the lunch where the idea was mooted to the story in *Lyra's Oxford*

HOW IT ALL STARTED

In 1993, **Philip Pullman** felt that the time had come to write something big and ambitious. The idea crystallized over a lunch of sausages and mashed potato with his agent, when the two were discussing their shared love for Milton's *Paradise Lost*. Pullman declared that he would like to write his own version of the third chapter of Genesis, and, buoyed by his agent's enthusiasm, he set about finding the links between the "series of unconnected images" that were floating around his mind: Lyra overhearing a private conversation while hiding in a wardrobe; a window to another world; "the bear in armour, and the witches coming up through the clouds".

From pretty early on, he knew that the story would be divided into three sections and that the third part would culminate in an act of renunciation in a garden. Pullman doesn't like to plan his books too closely – "because then you're not surprised by anything" – but the basic outline of the trilogy was clear by the time he sat down to write Chapter 1. He got stuck at first, but once he discovered that **Lyra** had something called a **dæmon**, the story began to flow and *His Dark Materials* really began. As he explained to scholars Wendy Parsons and Catriona Nicholson, "I wrote the words 'Lyra and her dæmon' and I realized I didn't know why she'd have a dæmon or what her dæmon was but thought it sounded intriguing, so I wrote the rest of the chapter. And in the first draft, as I wrote it down, everybody's dæmon changed, even the adults'." Then, as he began to consider the theme of innocence and experience, he had the liberating idea that only children's dæmons would change.

He wrote roughly three A4 pages – about 1100 words – a day with a ballpoint pen, powering through the difficult bits known in the trade as writer's block ("Plumbers don't get plumber's block, why should writers be the only profession that gives a special name to the difficulty of working, and then expects sympathy for it?") until he had a draft he wanted to type into a computer. Finally, when he felt that it was "sort of all right", he sent it off to the publisher.

The title is from *Paradise Lost*: "Unless the Almighty maker them ordain/His dark materials to create more worlds", though Pullman had thought of calling it *The Golden Compass*, which is what the first novel would be called in America.

Michael Chabon, in an entertaining, perceptive review in the *New York Review Of Books*, sets Pullman's trilogy firmly in the context of **epic fantasy**, which, for him, is not a term of disparagement or condescension.

"Epic fantasy is haunted: by a sense of lost purity and grandeur, deep wisdom that has been forgotten, Arcadia spoilt, the debased or diminished stature of modern humankind; by a sense that the world, to borrow a term from John Clute, the Canadian-born British critic of fantasy and science fiction, has 'thinned'", he argues. "This sense of thinning – of there having passed a Golden Age, a Dreamtime, when animals spoke, magic worked, children honoured their parents, and fish leapt filleted into the skillet – has haunted the telling of stories from the beginning. The words 'Once upon a time' are in part a kind of magic formula for invoking the ache of this primordial nostalgia."

The first great British work of epic fantasy, Chabon argued, was *Paradise Lost,* which, "with its dark lord, cursed tree, invented cosmology and ringing battle scenes, its armoured angelic cavalries shattered by demonic engines of war", has been the starting point for many novelists. Some of Milton's heirs – especially Tolkien and Lewis – have taken the mood, the aching loss of innocence, from Milton but not the central story. But Pullman was different. He wanted his story to be about people – "not beings that don't exist, like elves or hobbits" – and about a universal human experience: growing up. For Pullman, the point

WORDS AND PICTURES

Publisher **David Fickling** suggested having "little symbolic illustrations" at the start of each chapter, and Pullman soon took to the idea and, although not an illustrator, insisted on doing them himself. As it turned out, their naïve style fitted the tone of the books perfectly. Pullman first drew the pine twigs, which he later used for Chapter 17, *The Witches*, and then the head of a polar bear, which he used for Chapter 10, *The Consul And The Bear*. He worked on pieces of white Bristol board, six centimetres square, keeping the images as simple as possible. In *Northern Lights*, he framed each one in black until Chapter 23, *The Bridge To The Stars*, when Lyra confronts the reality of other worlds and the frame disappears. The pictures of *The Subtle Knife* have a greater confidence and a new purpose – indicating the world in which the chapters' events are taking place – but, under pressure to finish *The Amber Spyglass*, Pullman chose quotes from the likes of John Milton and William Blake, as "a way of acknowledging their influence". He has since drawn pictures for this third book, too. They are in the tenth anniversary edition.

was never to write fantasy. The point was to use fantasy to say something he thought was true about the way we live, hence his often-quoted remark that his novels are "stark reality". The narrative of innocence, experience and the **Fall**, surely one of the primal human stories, takes centre stage in his novels and in the bodies and souls of his heroic twosome: Lyra and Will.

The story started, he says, with them growing up, and he found himself writing a novel about different worlds because that seemed the "most vivid and exciting" way of telling the story.

ΠORTHERΠ LiGHTS

The novel – *The Golden Compass* in the US – starts with an orphan girl, **Lyra Belacqua**, who lives in Jordan College, Oxford, with her dæmon, **Pantalaimon**. One evening she and her dæmon sneak into the College's Retiring Room. Hidden in a wardrobe, she sees the Master poisoning the Tokay wine intended for her uncle, **Lord Asriel**, and successfully manages to warn him. She then overhears Asriel's lecture to the scholars, in

THE MASTERPIECE BEHIND LYRA AND HER DÆMON

Philip Pullman has often talked about being inspired by art, but it's hard sometimes to specify just how that has affected *His Dark Materials*. The simplest route from art to his fiction probably starts with a neglected masterpiece by **Leonardo da Vinci** and ends with **Lyra** and Pantalaimon.

Lady with an Ermine, right, is the painting that made the idea of a girl and her dæmon vivid to Pullman.

"There's a real connection between the girl and the animal," he said in David Colbert's book on the novels. "That is her dæmon. And though she is dressed more elegantly than Lyra, if you made a few alterations, she could be Lyra."

In the painting, Leonardo emphasizes the connection between the lady and her ermine by making the elegant curve of her hand correspond to the animal's movement. Her bent wrist echoes the creature's raised paw.

The painting is regarded as one of Leonardo's masterpieces – although a minority of critics still maintain that it is not by him at all – but, because of its tortuous history, it is not as globally famous as such works as *Mona Lisa* or *The Last Supper*.

The lady with the ermine is probably **Cecilia Gallerani** a mistress of the **Duke Ludovico Sforza** of Milan, one of Leonardo's most generous patrons. The ermine is the symbol of her lover but it could also be a pun on her name: the Greek for ermine is **Galee**.

Sforza would probably normally have kept the painting, but he and Gallerani, who later achieved some fame as a poet, split up, after she had borne the Duke a child.

The painting then effectively vanished for a few centuries, turning up in Italy around 1800 when it was bought, by **Prince Adam Jerzy Czartoryski** of Poland. It has never – apart from the odd tour – strayed too far from Poland since. During World War II, it was hung on the wall of the office of **Hans Frank**, the Nazi Governor-General of Poland. Frank claimed to be an art lover, but, as he displayed the painting directly above a steam radiator, he could hardly be called a real connoisseur.

There is a rumour that the ermine is actually a ferret. The novelist **Terry Pratchett** in his famous *Discworld* series refers to this suggestion parodying the painting as **Woman Holding Ferret** by Leonard of Quirm.

The partnership of people and animals fascinated Leonardo. We know from sketches and notes that he planned to paint Jesus and a lamb, Leda and the swan, even Madonna and the Christ child holding a cat.

Like Pullman's dæmons, the animals all had some significance, which the artist, in his usual cryptic way, invited us to figure out. The ermine, for example, was a symbol of chastity, an ironic jest if Gallerani had already given birth to the Duke's illegitimate child.

The Da Vinci code: in Leonardo's *Lady With An Ermine*, the animal is a symbol of the lady's lover, the Duke of Milan. For Pullman, the painting had dæmonic significance

VOCABULARY WORKSHOP

aërodock airport
anbaric electric
Anglia England
atomcraft nuclear powered
bene elim angels
brantwijn brandy
Brytain Lyra's Britain
cauchuc rubber
chocolatl chocolate
chthonic underground
coal-silk nylon/polyester
Corea Korea
dæmon soul
Fra Father
genniver/ jenniver juniper
ghast person without dæmon
gyptians waterfaring gypsies
gyropter helicopter
marchipane marzipan
nalkainens headless ghosts
naphtha oil
night-ghast ghosts that haunt dreams
Nipponese Japanese
Norroway Norway
oratory a church
panserbjørne armoured bears
Peaceable Ocean Pacific Ocean
philosophical scientific
photogram photograph
photo-mill radiometer
projecting lantern slide projector
Roman Latin
sky metal meteorite iron
smokeleaf tobacco
Skræling Native American
Tartar Siberian

which he shows photograms of golden particles named **Dust** and of the image of a city behind the **Aurora Borealis**.

Lyra's world is like ours yet different. The technology is 19th century, the theology 16th century. We gradually discover that science does not really exist; it is referred to as **experimental theology** and is firmly under the thumb of a powerful Church. The subtlety and consistency with which Pullman underpins the unreal sets the novel apart. This is not a Disneyfied fantasyland of elves, dwarves and goblins – there are too many ominous echoes of the real world.

In many ways, Lyra's childhood is idyllic, a series of adventures and minor street wars made more pleasurable by the general absence of parental restraint and her secret conviction that she is no ordinary urchin, that the grandeur and intrigue of Jordan College and **Asriel** is mysteriously connected to her. This idyll is brilliantly disturbed by the omniscient narrator's matter-of-fact observation that "For no reason that anyone could imagine, people were beginning to disappear".

The games of Lyra and her Oxford friends revolve around the **Gobblers**, a near-legendary group of child-kidnappers who, it is revealed, include a beautiful young woman with a golden monkey dæmon. One day, this woman – **Mrs Coulter**, a high-ranking figure in the Church – arrives at Jordan and

DÆMON GEEZERS

Having trouble remembering who has which dæmon? Worry no more.

Character	Dæmon
Lyra	Pantalaimon, finally becomes a pine marten
Will	a cat called Kirjava
Asriel	Stelmaria, a snow leopard
Mrs Coulter	a golden monkey, never named in the books
Roger Parslow	a terrier called Salcilia
Mary Malone	an alpine chough, one of the crow family
John Faa	a crow
Farder Coram	Sophonax, a cat
Serafina Pekkala	Kaisa, a snow goose
Lee Scoresby	a hare called Hester
Master of Jordan College	a raven
John Parry/Stanislaus Grumman	Sayan Kötör, an osprey
Lord Boreal	an emerald-eyed serpent
Sir Charles Latrom	a snake with "gold-rimmed black eyes"
King Ogunwe	a cheetah
Father Gomez	a green-backed beetle
Father Hugh MacPhail	a lizard
Father Heyst	a lizard
Father Borisovitch	a crow
Dr Cooper	a rabbit
Ma Costa/Tony Costa	a hawk
Ruta Skadi	Sergi, a bluethroat
Lena Feldt	a snow bunting
Jacob Huismans	a ferret
Juta Kamainen	a robin
Dr Martin Lanselius	a green serpent
Jotham Santelia	a snake
Fra Pavel	a frog
Brother Louis	a rabbit
Cardinal Sturrock	a macaw
Umaq	an arctic fox
Swiss Guardsmen	wolf-dogs

The Jordan College Enquirer is the only adult with a changeable dæmon. In the books, his dæmon, we are told, "at the time was coiled in the form of a snake".

shows a great interest in Lyra, charming her and persuading her to come and live with her in London. As she is preparing to leave, the Master kindly gives Lyra a rare and archaic device called an **alethiometer**, an instrument that can discern the truth.

"LYRA'S IDYLLIC CHILDHOOD IS DISTURBED BY THE OBSERVATION THAT, FOR NO APPARENT REASON, PEOPLE ARE BEGINNING TO DISAPPEAR."

In London, Mrs Coulter's allure palls. The golden monkey persecutes Pantalaimon mercilessly, and, at a cocktail party, Lyra learns that Mrs Coulter is no less than head of the **General Oblation Board** and must be one of the chief **Gobblers**. In terror, Lyra runs away and, after a nightmarish progress through the grubbier parts of London, finds refuge among the **gyptians**, a good-hearted waterfaring people from Eastern Anglia. Here, she becomes friends with **Farder Coram** and the gyptian king **John Faa**, who reveals that her real parents are none other than Asriel and Mrs Coulter.

The gyptians have lost many of their children to the Oblation Board and are mounting a mission to Norroway to rescue them. The expedition comes to Trollesund, where Farder and Lyra visit Dr Lanselius, the Witch-Consul, to ask for the support of the witch-clans. Lanselius confirms the rumours that Lyra is the subject of a great prophecy. Their next encounter is with the aëronaut **Lee Scoresby** and the exiled king of the panserbjørne, **Iorek Byrnison**, who has had his armour stolen. By now, Lyra has become adept at using the alethiometer, and she is able to find the missing armour – securing Iorek's help and friendship. The group sets off for the Oblation Board's Station at Bolvangar.

They have not gone far when they come under attack, and Lyra is captured by Samoyed hunters who take her directly to Bolvangar.

It is now clear that the Oblation Board are severing children from their dæmons here, and, although Lyra finds Roger and plots a mass break-out, only the intervention of Mrs Coulter saves her from the operation.

Mrs Coulter explains that the metaphysical vivisection called **intercision** is intended to keep children innocent and free of **Dust**, but Lyra now knows better than to trust her, frees the children and escapes.

Together with Roger, Lee Scoresby and the witch-queen **Serafina Pekkala**, she departs for Svalbard to find Asriel, who is being held prisoner by **Iofur Raknison**, the usurper-king of the panserbjørne. She tricks Iofur into facing Iorek in a duel, which restores Iorek to his throne.

The odd couple: Lyra (Elaine Symons) has "creative differences" with her dæmon Pan

THEY SAID IT...

"Worthy of the bonfire – truly the stuff of nightmares"
Leonie Caldecott, *Catholic Herald*

"As well as giving his readers stories that tick with the precision, accuracy and grace of an 18th century clock, he also writes like an angel"
Robert McCrum, *The Observer*

"I must say, I don't feel he's about to invoke dark forces and make off with a cup of my blood"
Deborah Ross, *The Independent*

"I hate Will, he is an immense bore"
A reviewer on Amazon.com

"His sales in America are more than just a phenomenon, they are a counter-cultural force"
Ed Vulliamy, *The Observer*

"My eight-year-old daughter expressed what I imagine is a near-universal response of readers, young and old, to *His Dark Materials* (and probably the ultimate secret of the series' success): 'I wonder what kind of dæmon I would have!'"
Michael Chabon

"Will does really cool stuff for one book and then spends the next book being completely boring"
Abigail Nussbaum on the *Asking The Wrong Questions* blog

"By the end of the series, Lyra and Will have to overthrow the Authority, rescue the dead (did I mention they make a trip to the realm of the dead *à la* Dante?), save the mulefa, heal the breach between the worlds, prevent the Gobblers from intercising children's dæmons, and establish the Republic of Heaven, all the while remaining in a state of innocence so that they can either relive or renounce Eve's choice in the Garden of Eden"
Daniel Moloney, *First Things*

"*Northern Lights* and the sequels are a celebration of the richness of life, a fantastic illumination on prejudice that is the heart of every religion, a harsh judgment on humanity and the most uplifting, harrowing, inspiring literature that has been written in decades"
Sam North, Hackwriters.com

"The book [*Northern Lights*] is very well written but could do with better punctuation. The sentences are sometimes overly long and do not lend themselves to being read aloud."
Iestyn's online book reviews

"The character of Roger is a bit underdeveloped. Lyra's attachment to him is apparently very important, but I really don't feel it because they don't do that much together before he is taken by the Gobblers"
Marrije, *Duck For Cover* website

"If *Northern Lights* and *The Subtle Knife* were books for adults disguised as children's books, *The Amber Spyglass* is a book for children disguised as an adult's book"
Sean Harnett, *Spike* magazine

"In several places, Pullman employs long expository lumps. These usually come in the form of an adult explaining something (for several pages) to Lyra. In most cases, the adults would never have bothered explaining such detail to a young child, who couldn't care less about such details, and Pullman often explains that Lyra didn't even understand the discussion anyway. These lumps get in the way of an otherwise clean writing style that quickly engages the reader and creates a vivid picture of Lyra's familiar, yet strange, world"
Terry Jeffress, *Interrogation Reports* blog

"After all the complexities and complications that Lyra and the cast go through, to be told that love will save the world just doesn't cut it. Somehow Pullman has run out of steam"
The Open Critic website

"This is classified as children's fiction but it is as uncompromising and passionate as writing gets"
Francine Stock, novelist, presenter of BBC Radio 4's *The Film Programme*

"Ultimately, to save the world and re-establish the Republic of Heaven, Lyra and Will must make the ultimate sacrifice. That's where I felt a bit of disappointment sneak in. To make all the equations work out, Pullman has to introduce sexuality into characters that I felt were still too childlike for it to be convincing. He shuts doors and ties up loose ends in a way that feels, for the first time, slightly artificial. But that's a minor flaw in what stands with *Lord Of The Rings* as one of the most resonant fantasies of all time"
Polly Shulman, Salon.com

"Lyra is completely enamoured of aristocratic, ruthless and superior people, particularly as personified by her father Lord Asriel, Iorek the unstoppable killer giant bear-king, and the grandly inscrutable Northern witches. Lyra is a proud little aristocrat who barely seems surprised at all the hints and portents that she is the most special little girl in the whole universe. She spends most of the book surrounded by various hangers-on who feed her narcissism (and prove their worthiness) by recognizing how special she is"
J.T. Whelan, Amazon.com

"What distinguishes Pullman's work is its toughness, its unwillingness to accept the easy answers or deliver the expected effects"
Michael Berry, *San Francisco Chronicle*

"Philip Pullman ultimately fails as a writer in *His Dark Materials*, not because of his views on religion, but because he simply can't resist the temptation to preach about them, putting art to the service of manipulating his young readers' opinions"
Amy Welborn on amy.welborn.com

Asriel has established his own laboratory here, where he can study other worlds, and he has his own ideas for intercision. When Lyra is asleep, he abducts Roger and vanishes into the wilderness. She and Iorek give chase, passing through a battle between the witches and Mrs Coulter's Tartar soldiers, but the two have to part when they come to a weak snow bridge.

Lyra reaches Asriel alone. He has connected Roger and his dæmon to a machine beneath the Aurora Borealis, and although Lyra manages to free him his dæmon remains trapped and Asriel severs them – releasing enough energy to make a bridge to another world. With the arrival of Mrs Coulter, he vows to destroy the source of Dust (it is a lie, we later realize, something he says because he wants to keep Mrs Coulter with him). He sets out into the sky, while Lyra, who has come to the conclusion that anything her parents dislike is probably "a good thing", follows to try to stop him.

The novel closes with Lyra and Pantalaimon turning away from the world they are in, looking towards the sun and walking into the sky – an epic, optimistic finale that sets things up beautifully for the next novel.

In around 400 pages, **Northern Lights** (aka *The Golden Compass*) tells a compelling story in which each crisis seems to blossom naturally from the one before and introduces us to an intriguing cast of characters. We don't know quite what to make of Asriel and Mrs Coulter, but we'd like to know more about them, Lyra and Iorek Byrnison are, for a child of destiny and an armoured polar bear, surprisingly complex and believable.

Pullman also gives us a convincingly drawn alternative reality. One reason it works so effectively is that he has a sure sense of knowing just what to leave to our imagination and what to spell out.

In the UK, the novel won a couple of literary prizes and was lauded by most reviewers of children's books. In the US, the novel crossed over into the adult fiction market, with many critics insisting that the age of the reader was irrelevant. The novel, in their eyes, was good enough to stand as a classic work of fiction. In a review in the *Washington Post*, Michael Dirda said that Pullman

PRONOUNCING THOSE TRICKY NAMES

Just to be sure you're not caught out.

Iorek YOR-ick

Iofur YO-fur

Kirjava KEER-yah-vuh

Lyra LIE-ruh

Pantalaimon pan-tuh-LIE-mon

Salmakia sal-MACK-ee-uh

Serafina Pekkala SEH-ra-fee-nuh PEK-ka-luh

Tialys tee-AH-lis

Xaphania za-FA-nee-uh

had, by inventing Lyra, created a great character, in the tradition of Alice, Dorothy and Bilbo Baggins, who would appeal to adults and children alike.

THE INTRICACIES OF THE ALETHIOMETER

Pullman's American publishers got it wrong when they renamed the first book *The Golden Compass* ("at the time", Pullman has said, "I didn't have the clout to resist"), because a compass is not the best visual reference for the alethiometer. True, the alethiometer is referred to by that term a number of times, but this pivotal device is actually described as more like "a large watch or a small clock", made of a "thick disc of brass and crystal" with three winding wheels and three shorter hands that can be set to point to any of 36 tiny painted pictures instead of numbers (see p.179 for more details on the symbols).

The compass reference makes more sense when you consider how the alethiometer performs. Once the three short hands are set in position, a longer hand swings "like a compass needle", floating across the images. Only with grace and training can the user understand the message it is giving – which is always the truth. As Farder Coram notes, in the original Greek, *alethia* means truth, and *meter* means measure. There are conflicting opinions on how many of these devices still exist.

Lyra's alethiometer, also referred to as a symbol-reader, is the key to her decision-making throughout the books, but the readings are not always straightforward. She sees the instrument as having moods. She comes to "sort of know when it's going to be cross or when there's things it doesn't want me to know", and her state of mind affects her ability to understand what it is telling her.

She realizes, ultimately, that she read the alethiometer by grace but must, as she grows up, regain that ability through hard work. The Master of Jordan College advises her to make the study of the instrument her life's work. She can start this by studying at St Sophia College under **Dame Hannah Relf**. There is no St Sophia

Alchemy lessons: Khunrath's *Amphitheatrum Sapientiae Aeternae* inspired the alethiometer

College in Oxford in our world, and in Lyra's world, the name must signify the wisdom she may acquire from the ancient goddess of that name who, in some myths and in the books, led the first rebellion against God.

Fascinating as the alethiometer is, would Lyra really want to study it for life? Possibly. As Pullman has made clear in his fictional back story for the instrument, many famous men have devoted their lives to the alethiometer – some were even martyred for it. Her lifelong course of study will take her into the arcane realms of mysticism and magic, on a strange intellectual journey that starts with the activities of an alchemist called **Heinrich Khunrath** in Prague (see p.206), whose best-known book, *Amphitheatrum Sapientiae Aeternae*, is full of engraved illustrations packed with symbolic and textual information displayed in concentric circles.

> "LYRA'S ALETHIOMETER HAS BEEN LINKED TO THE MORMON BRASS BALL THAT TOLD THE FAITHFUL WHERE TO TRAVEL."

Pullman admitted in one Q&A: "My source for the alethiometer was partly the emblem books of the Renaissance and the memory theatre as described in a wonderful book by Frances Yates called *The Art Of Memory*."

The memory theatre, as described by the Renaissance scholar **Giulio Camillo**, was a way of using symbols to organize human knowledge into a system. But the real visual stimulus for Pullman's stroke of genius was the **emblem books**, illustrated tomes which used pictures or symbols to express a moral.

Pullman has been intrigued by the idea of using images to convey information ever since he read *Superman*, *Batman* and *Eagle* comics when he was a boy. He was fascinated by the emblem books – the most famous is Andrea Alciati's *Emblemata Liber* (Book of Emblems) – and found one in a library in Oxford with a spinning wheel. It looked, he said later, "as though someone had actually drawn the alethiometer".

In our world, the alethiometer has been likened to the **liahona**, a round brass ball of "curious workmanship" with "two spindles" used by the Mormon prophet Lehi. One of the spindles would point in the direction Lehi and his party had to travel but only if the people consulting it had "faith and diligence". If they weren't consulting it properly, or doubted their faith, the liahona would simply stop working. Like the alethiometer, the liahona was likened to a compass. The parallels are certainly intriguing, but there's no evidence Pullman knew of the Mormons' brass ball when he invented the alethiometer.

THE SUBTLE KNIFE

The second novel opens with a gamble. Having thrilled
us with Lyra, Iorek, Asriel and Mrs Coulter in *Northern
Lights*, Pullman puts them all on the shelf for a while,
opening *The Subtle Knife* with a quietly heartbreaking
scene, set in our world, in which a twelve-year-old boy
called **Will Parry** is trying to palm his mentally ill mother
off on his bewildered piano teacher. What makes the
scene all the more harrowing is that we already know that
Will dearly loves his mother and is abandoning her only
out of pure desperation and fear.

Will is an intriguing character. He is blessed with his own kind of invisibility
spell, a Harriet-the-spy ability to be unnoticed by other people, and possessed of
a kind of stubborn courage and strength of will that, as the story unfolds, makes
him a natural leader and unsettles allies and enemies.

Mother and son are being harassed by a group of men, probably employed
by one of the many security agencies, secular and religious, that exist in the
books, who are looking for a folder that belonged to Will's missing father,
John. One day, Will finds one of the men in their house and accidentally kills
him. ("Everything was going to plan really. Except that he'd killed someone,"
Pullman notes, a conjunction worthy of Orwell's *1984*.) On the run, looking for
somewhere to sleep in the suburbs of Oxford, he sees a cat vanish in mid-air
on **Sunderland Avenue** and decides to follow, bitterly convinced that "whatever
this new world was, it had to be better than what he'd just left". He finds
himself in the alien, abandoned city of **Cittàgazze**, where he bumps into **Lyra**.

At first, the pair are suspicious of one another, but Lyra consults her
alethiometer. She asks whether he is friend or foe and is told: "He is a
murderer." Pullman then tells us: "When she saw the answer, she relaxed at
once." It's a small, telling scene. Lyra does the exact opposite of what most
conventional heroines would do in this situation: she relaxes because she senses
that his strength may come in useful. Such moments add immeasurably to the
power of the novels. The alethiometer also tells Lyra to help Will find his father,
who vanished in June 1985.

Asriel's hole in the sky has thrown Lyra's world into chaos. Mrs Coulter and
the Church are desperate to know why Lyra is considered so special, and, having
interrupted one of their torture sessions, Serafina Pekkala persuades her clan

DYSFUNCTIONAL FAMILIES

Normal families are rare in *His Dark Materials*, as rare as they may have been in Pullman's childhood (see p.18).

Lyra starts the novels assuming she is an orphan and by the end, having lost both Mrs Coulter and Asriel (who she discovers are her real mother and father) she is orphaned for good. Will sets off in search of his father, finds him briefly but loses him, permanently, to death. The usurper king **Iofur Raknison** orphaned himself by unwittingly killing his father. And there's **Tony Makarios**, who has no father and whose neglectful mother is a drunk.

The orphans are matched by a less persistent motif: bereaved parents. Grief from the loss of their son is still so sharp that **Serafina Pekkala** cannot bear to see **Farder Coram**. **Ma Costa's** anxiety for her abducted son Billy alerts Lyra to the strange disappearances plaguing Oxford. **Roger Parslow's** father, who works on the walls and roofs of Jordan College, must be in mourning for his vanished son. Parental grief and anger drives the **gyptians'** expedition to

Norroway. **John Parry** is haunted by the guilt of being separated from his wife and son. And poor abandoned **Elaine Parry** must, in her lucid moments, be tortured by agonising speculation about her son's whereabouts. The motif carries on in *Lyra's Oxford* as **Yelena**, the witch, tries to kill Lyra, blaming her for the war that killed her son.

What do all this heartache and dysfunction add up to? **Michael Chabon** argues that the real subject of *His Dark Materials* is not "the eternal battle between the forces of idealist fundamentalism and materialist humanism, it is a story about how adults betray children; how children are forced to pay the price of adult neglect, cynicism, ambition, and greed, and how they are subjected to the programs of adults, to the General Oblation Board".

Given the losses and separations that marked Pullman's childhood, it seems more than coincidental that the most sympathetic parents in the books are often surrogates like **Iorek Byrnison**, Serafina Pekkala and **Lee Scoresby**.

to support the girl. Lee Scoresby, too, wants to help her, and he begins his own expedition to find a man named **Stanislaus Grumman**, who he believes can help to find an "object that gives protection to whoever holds it".

It also transpires that other witches are rallying to support Asriel, who has built himself a fortress in an empty world and is launching a cosmic rebellion against the tyrannical Authority, or "God".

The basalt fortress is huge – it takes 15 minutes by anbaric locomotive just to journey into the heart of the mountain to find the armoury. It feels like the kind of grandiose, secluded lair in which a Bond villain could happily entertain absurd pipedreams of world domination.

From this point on, the book leaps between worlds and characters. To learn more about Dust, and about the disappearance of John Parry, Will and Lyra return to Will's Oxford, where Lyra visits the **Dark Matter Research Unit** and meets **Mary Malone**, a lapsed nun who understands that Dust is conscious. Lyra then makes the mistake of accepting a lift from the overly friendly **Sir Charles Latrom**, who steals her alethiometer. She and Will go to Sir Charles's house, but he refuses to return the device unless they fetch him a particular knife from Cittàgazze.

The world of Cittàgazze is overrun with **Spectres**, translucent beings that eat the dæmons of adults. Only children are safe there. Spectres are afraid of only one thing, **the subtle knife**, and when Will loses two fingers in an attempt to gain possession of it, he is identified as the rightful knife-bearer. The knife has the power to cut windows between worlds, and the children successfully cut their way into Sir Charles's house and steal back the alethiometer.

"ASRIEL'S FORTRESS IS SO HUGE, IT TAKES 15 MINUTES BY ANBARIC TRAIN TO REACH THE ARMOURY."

In the **Siberia** of Lyra's world, meanwhile, Lee Scoresby's quest has brought him to Stanislaus Grumman, who turns out to be none other than **John Parry**, who left his own world by accident in an Arctic blizzard and is himself searching for the knife-bearer. At the same time, in Will's Oxford, Mary Malone finds a way of using her computer to communicate with Dust, which instructs her to "play the serpent" and to pass through the window on Sunderland Avenue into Cittàgazze.

The book builds towards its climax as Serafina Pekkala's witch-clan save Will and Lyra from a mob of children in Cittàgazze. Together they flee to a mountain, but others are close behind. Lee and John Parry have arrived from Lyra's world – pursued by the Muscovite soldiers of the Church, who manage to kill Lee in the battle of the gorge. **Mrs Coulter** is also in the world, torturing another witch, who discloses that Lyra is destined to become a second Eve.

When Mrs Coulter tells her victim: "We have a thousand years of experience in this Church of ours, we can draw out your suffering endlessly," she does sound a bit like a suave Nazi interrogator in a potboiler war movie.

One night, in the witches' camp, Will finds he cannot sleep and walks up the mountain, where he meets his father. He fights him before he recognizes his

THE ANGELIC HOST

There are countless billions of angels in the books, and they are a quarrelsome bunch. The conflict between Asriel and the **Authority** can, in some ways, be seen as part of a continuing civil war between angels. The first rebel angels, led by **Sophia**, failed, but this time around, though they don't conquer the Church, they do get rid of the Authority and his regent **Metatron**.

Angels come in various shapes and guises, though they can all move between worlds without relying on windows. The **shadow-particles** talking to Mary Malone through her computer present themselves as angels, and Metatron is too dazzling to look at, has feathered wings and is blessed with something like the ability to read people's thoughts. Even people can, rarely, become angels.

Made up of Dust, angels suffer from body envy possibly because their physical status is so changeable. When Mrs Coulter reaches for Metatron's hand near the abyss, there is nothing to grasp. Yet the dusty regent is soon delivering a few skull-crushing blows and cries out in pain when Mrs Coulter stabs his eyes with her fingers. The love between **Baruch** and **Balthamos** suggests angels can be united by deep emotional bonds, but this may not be the norm. They are supposed to live for thousands of years but they are not, if the pathetic excuse for a deity known as the Authority is anything to go by,

long-lost dad. John Parry is just able to tell him to take the knife to Lord Asriel – it is the only weapon that can kill the Authority – before a witch whose love he once spurned shoots him dead with an arrow. Angry and desolate, Will picks up his father's cloak. The scene ends on a note of quiet pathos as Will looks back "at the dim shapes of his father, the witch, of his father again" before heading back down the mountain. On his return to camp, Will finds that Mrs Coulter has taken Lyra and that two angels, Balthamos and Baruch, have arrived and want him to accompany them to Lord Asriel without delay because "the enemy's power is growing every minute".

Angelic delight: Pullman's angels are not placid prayers, they are quarrelsome egotists

Asriel and Iorek don't appear at all in *The Subtle Knife*, a major risk on Pullman's part. But the book is so inventive, chilling, and persuasive that we don't really notice. The middle novel in a trilogy is often held to be as hard to pull off as the "difficult second album" in rock, but this is the exception to that rule. Pullman is an unashamed fan of genre fiction, spending much of his time when he was supposed to be studying at Exeter College reading American thrillers. He paces this novel with the precision of a high-class thriller. *The Subtle Knife* is a very different kind of novel to *Northern Lights*, distinguished by an intriguing juxtaposition of imaginary worlds and contemporary Oxford, and was so well received that it set up massive expectations for the next instalment.

Peter Hitchens, no fan of Pullman's religious views, chuckled over the scene in which Mary Malone is ordered, by angels through a computer, to go on a long journey and told: "You must play the serpent." It is a curious scene, a risky flight of the imagination, but it still works. Though most readers warmed to Will's courage, strength and astonishing ability to pass by unseen, a minority of critics and readers regretted the shift, preferring the story when it seemed to spring out of Lyra's consciousness, as it did in *Northern Lights*.

THE ÆSAHÆTTR, A LEGENDARY WEAPON

Before the subtle knife even existed, there were legends about it. The cliff-ghasts called it "æsahættr" – "god destroyer" – and seemed to believe it had special powers. The knife was invented three centuries ago by a group of men, philosophers, who were too smart for their own good and cut windows into worlds as gleefully as a child with a new pair of scissors chops into curtains and coloured paper. Such an inauspicious start may explain why this one-of-a-kind, beautifully subtle and immensely powerful knife can now only be used properly by its bearer, a person chosen by the knife itself. In this respect, it is rather like the Arthurian sword-in-the-stone myth, which has been traced back as far as **Merlin**, a 12th-century poem written by French poet Robert de Boron.

The knife looks like a double-bladed dagger. The blades are roughly eight inches long, and the rosewood handle is covered with illustrations of angels. One edge can cut through any material for anyone who happens to hold it, but it is the other edge that makes it subtle and burdensome for its bearer. Only with training from the knife's former bearer can the new owner use it to cut into other worlds. For Will, the learning curve is steep. He doesn't know he's to be the new bearer until his predecessor **Giacomo Paradisi** recognizes him as such because the knife has

Is this a subtle knife I see before me? Will (Michael Legge) waves the knife at the National

MOMMIE DEAREST

When you've spent two novels having a seriously good time loathing **Mrs Coulter**, it is a tad disconcerting when the ball-breaking ice maiden's *froideur* is finally melted by the irresistible power of maternal love.

One of the great villains of recent popular literature, vicious, smart, seductive and inexorable, her belated acquisition of a heart in *The Amber Spyglass* was regarded as "unfortunate" by Michael Chabon.

Earlier in the trilogy, Mrs Coulter is simply callous, inventing intercision and using her beauty – and the odd chocolatl – to lure children to a fate

worse than death. But even for Pullman, Mrs Coulter remains a real iceberg of a character. "I like writing about her," he has admitted, "because there is absolutely nothing she wouldn't do."

Her motivation is submerged. We are not quite sure why she's such a keen cutter, just as we are a bit perplexed when she comes good in the end. Some would call that a failure in characterization, but in books – as in life – there are many personalities we never truly know. And the more we puzzle over **Marisa** – not, let's face it, the best first name she could have – the more intriguing we find her.

marked them both in the same way – by slicing off two fingers from their left hand. Bearing the knife is a burden and a duty ("You haven't any choice: you're the bearer, it's picked you out", Will's father tells him) but it does have some privileges, protecting the bearer from enemies. Besides, which boy of Will's age wouldn't want a knife that could cut a window into another world?

Fashioned by the **Guild of Torre degli Angeli**, the knife comes with four instructions: all windows opened with it must be closed (a diktat sadly ignored by the Guild themselves), the bearer alone should use it and keep his own identity as bearer secret (a rule Will quietly ignores), and it must only be used for good. To use the knife, the bearer does not need great physical force but must channel their mental strength and concentrate hard. Similarly, when he has to repair the weapon, it isn't simply Iorek's skills as a metalsmith that put it back together. Will has to be in the right frame of mind.

> "BEARING THE KNIFE HAS ITS PRIVILEGES. WHICH BOY WOULDN'T WANT TO CUT INTO NEW WORLDS?"

The mending of weapons – usually swords, sometimes knives – is a recurring motif that goes right back to the Holy Grail sagas of **Chrétien de Troyes** and **Norse myth**. It appears in Wagner's *Ring Of The Nibelungs* and Tolkien's **Lord of the Rings**, in which Elrond reforges the broken sword Narsil, symbolizing the resurrection of a lost line of kings. Iorek's mending is more pragmatic, devoid of such mythic resonance.

Although Stanislaus Grumman recognizes that the knife is the "one weapon in all the universes that could defeat the tyrant the Authority" – living up to the name æsahættr – there is one thing stronger: love. When Will's consciousness strays from the cutting of a window with the knife to Lyra and he touches her tear on his cheek at the end of *The Amber Spyglass*, the knife finally shatters. When it breaks the second time we are led to conclude that it will never be whole again.

The truly subtle thing about the knife is the fact that it both meets – and fails to meet – the prophecies made about it. The weapon isn't, as Grumman insisted, needed to destroy the Authority, but Asriel, not having the knife, does fail, just as the cliff-ghasts had so gleefully predicted.

The idea of a knife with special powers recurs in ancient mythology, though many of these weapons weren't especially subtle. The Egyptian god **Thoth** used a knife – sometimes depicted as a crescent-shaped moon – to slay evildoers. A special knife – referred to as "athame" – still has a ceremonial role in **Wicca** and other forms of modern witchcraft. One popular superstition about knives is that if you give someone a knife it will sever your relationship with that person, much as it does between Giacomo Paradisi and Will.

THE AMBER SPYGLASS

The longest and easily the most complex of the three books, *The Amber Spyglass* opens with some of Pullman's finest descriptive writing as he takes us to a cave in the Himalayas where **Mrs Coulter** is keeping **Lyra** in a drugged sleep – full of dreams of Roger in the land of the dead. Resisting the demands of the angels, **Will** determines to rescue her, and so, with the forces of Metatron, Regent of the Authority, closing in, he agrees to let Baruch fly to the basalt fortress, to ask for **Lord Asriel**'s help. Baruch is, however, injured on the way, and is barely able to speak before he dies.

On the other side of the conflict, the Church's **Consistorial Court of Discipline** has decided Lyra must die. They know Mary Malone is destined to find her, so they send an assassin, Father Gomez, to follow her. Other Church forces are also on Lyra's trail. A fleet of Church zeppelins is heading for the Himalayan cave, as is a fleet of Lord Asriel's gyropters and Will and Balthamos – with Iorek Byrnison – and it is they who arrive first. Will plans to escape through a window, and wakes Lyra, but his knife breaks as Mrs Coulter returns. Two of Asriel's Gallivespian spies take Mrs Coulter captive, but she soon escapes Asriel's basalt fortress in Asriel's Intention Craft and heads for the Consistorial Court.

SOURCE MATERIALS

The chapters in *The Amber Spyglass* all start with a quote that has influenced the novels. But there are many nods to other texts. Apart from the obvious sources (Milton, Blake et al), the last novel acknowledges Dante, the myth of the wounded fisher king, Peter Pan, Wordsworth's *Ode To Immortality*, *Star Wars*, *Perelandra* (the space novel by C.S. Lewis), Frank L. Baum's Oz books, Pullman's sci-fi novel *Galatea*, superhero comics and the Kabbalah. This is intertextuality – a term coined in 1966 to describe the way in which authors shape the meaning of their work by alluding to other texts – taken to the nth degree.

Another Fall: Lyra (Elaine Symons) tempts Will (Michael Legge) with a fruit and more besides

As this flurry of events is underway, Mary Malone travels through Cittàgazze and from there to the land of the mulefa, where she begins to learn about the origins of consciousness. She devises a spyglass with lacquer lenses through which she can see Dust, and realizes that it is flooding from the air.

Despite his reservations, Iorek agrees to help Will repair the knife. Like the angels, the Gallivespians insist the two children come with them to Asriel, but Lyra has other ideas. Plagued by guilt at her unwitting role in Roger's murder, she decides she must travel to the **land of the dead** to apologize.

Accordingly, she, Will and the two reluctant Gallivespians cut a window to the world of the dead, where they are forced to leave their dæmons behind to proceed – a temporary, necessary betrayal prophesied by the Master of Jordan College. Once in the land of the dead, they find the ghosts of Roger, Lee Scoresby and John Parry, and narrowly avoid a bomb intended by the Consistorial Court to blow up Lyra. By exploiting the harpy guards' weakness for true stories, they manage to cut a window into another world and release the ghosts into the outside air.

> "THE THIRD NOVEL WAS THE HARDEST TO WRITE. IT WAS THE LONGEST AND PEOPLE WERE NAGGING ME ALL THE TIME."

The bomb might have missed Lyra, but it created a hole leading to the abyss beneath the worlds, and the all-important Dust is haemorrhaging into nothingness. The stage is set for the last cosmic battle. Mrs Coulter has now joined forces with Asriel, and sets out for the **Clouded Mountain**: the fortress of Metatron, the de facto ruler of the multiverse. She manages to charm him, and to trick him to the edge of the abyss, where she and Asriel attack him. Together they plummet into eternity.

Arriving in the world of the mulefa, Will and Lyra meet Mary Malone, who tells them the story of how she fell in love, a tale that encourages them to do the same. To underline the point about Mary playing the **serpent** – it can't be coincidence that Pullman has named his tempter after the mother of Jesus, can it? – she gives them some fruit, which Lyra then lifts to Will's mouth, knowing what will follow.

This is the prophesied second Fall, and, despite the frantic efforts of the assassin Father Gomez, it secures the future of existence. For the first time, Will is able to see his dæmon, a cat called **Kirjava**, and he and Lyra are blissfully happy. But they have work to do.

IT'S IN THEIR KISS

As love scenes go, **Will** and **Lyra**'s liberating clinch at the end of *The Amber Spyglass* isn't quite up there with **Burt Lancaster** and **Deborah Kerr**'s legendary, often-spoofed, kiss on the beach in *From Here To Eternity*, but it's much more mysterious.

"Like two moths clumsily bumping together, with no more weight than that, their lips touched." That's how Pullman begins the kiss.

But it isn't long before Will, his body thrilling to the word "love" is kissing Lyra's face "over and over again, drinking in with adoration the scent of her body and her warm honey-fragrant hair and her sweet moist mouth".

Their parting moment is described with great delicacy: "Everything about her was soft; and that was one of his favourite memories later on." The line is worthy of **F. Scott Fitzgerald**.

Literal-minded readers have complained that they would like to know, definitively, once and for all, if Will and Lyra physically consummated their love.

Pullman is normally willing to discuss the books at length. On this matter he

has been no help whatsoever. Asked once to be more specific, he replied: "My imagination withdrew at that point. I don't know what they did. I wrote about the kiss – that's what I knew happened. I don't know what else they did. Maybe they did, maybe they didn't. I think they were rather young to but still…" (For the record, Lyra is thirteen and Will is probably twelve or thirteen.)

Their youth has shocked a few critics, while others have been puzzled by the cosmic significance of their embrace, one complaining that there is absolutely nothing in the trilogy to explain why this kiss is so important. That's not quite true. The kiss is a symbol of Will and Lyra's journey from innocence to experience, which, for Pullman, is no bad thing. Now they can get on with the rest of their lives, the Republic of Heaven and so forth.

The idea of Will and Lyra having *al fresco* sex in the Botanic Garden has left some readers feeling a bit queasy. But the easiest way to get around that is to hold the thought that they only kissed. A lot.

It becomes clear that all of the windows between worlds must be closed in order to stop the spread of Spectres, and the children must part. The book concludes with Lyra back at Jordan College, where she decides to study the alethiometer and build the "Republic of Heaven" where she is.

Pullman admitted, in an email, that **The Amber Spyglass** was the hardest book of the three to write "because it was the longest and the one people were nagging me for all the time and because I had to tie up as many loose ends as

I could." It took him three years to finish. And, although it got, if anything, a better critical reception than the first two novels (becoming the first "children's novel" to win the *Guardian* fiction prize), it has not worn as well.

Some didactic passages slow the pace, dismaying many critics especially Michael Chabon who complained: "My heart sank as it began to dawn on me, around the time that the first angels begin to show up in *The Subtle Knife*, that there was some devil in Pullman, pitchfork-prodding him into adjusting his story to suit both the shape of his anti-Church argument and the mounting sense of self-importance evident in the swollen (yet withal sketchy) bulk of the third volume and in the decreasing roundedness of its characters."

Chabon might have been able to skip these passages if it were not for the way, he felt, they deadened the character that had always intrigued him most, **Lyra**, who, he says, "lost nearly all the tragic, savage grace that makes her so endearing in *The Golden Compass*". His lament was echoed by the critic for *The Complete Review*, who griped: "Lyra is dangled tantalisingly in front of the reader but she does nothing (and not that much is done to her).

> "THERE WAS SOME DEVIL IN PULLMAN PRODDING HIM INTO ADJUSTING HIS STORY TO SUIT HIS ANTI-CHURCH ARGUMENT."

It's a disappointment." *Spike* magazine went further, arguing that Lyra and Will, "the characters that had so signally set apart the first two volumes", had been "completely lobotomized", the power of love having deprived Lyra of her spunk and Will of his anger. Some readers felt that other main characters – especially Asriel, Iorek and Serafina – had been just as diminished by the demands of plot. The mulefa polarized opinion: their appearance prompted a small band of readers to give up on the trilogy altogether.

The need to tie up so many loose ends does choke some of the fun out of proceedings, and, for the first time in the trilogy, Pullman seems to have more characters and themes than he quite knows what to do with. The final battle with the Authority, to which the books seemed to be building for pages and pages, disappointed some readers, although eschewing the usual all-powerful God for a completely knackered deity was a clever twist. As an omniscient narrator, Pullman could have shown us more of this colossal conflict, but chose not to. Perhaps he was opting not to compete with the last battle in Narnia or the epic conflicts in Tolkien's *The Two Towers*. He would probably argue that this is just how the story came to him.

The credibility of Mrs Coulter's redemption is still hotly debated, although this controversy may just reflect the fact that many critics regretted the loss of such a wonderfully drawn villainess. Being a torturer and a proud parent are hardly, history suggests, mutually exclusive traits.

The trilogy's tragic denouement felt inevitable to Pullman. Asked by a reader why the ending had to be so sad, he replied: "There was nothing I could do about it, that was implicit in it from the very beginning and if you look at the book carefully you will see a lot of little patterns throughout that you might not have noticed, all of which have to do with two things or two people or a person and a place that were very close to each other and are split apart.

"Now that happens a great deal in the book and if you notice that pattern you will see it turning up all the way through and I had to be true to that pattern because that is the basic pattern of the whole story."

The denouement does suit the arc of the story, but it is not without irony. After chastising **C.S. Lewis** for kicking Susan out of **Narnia** because she was too concerned about lipstick and boys, he curiously felt obliged to impose a far sterner ethic on his hero and heroine than Lewis ever did.

A few readers have grumbled in various forms that if all these windows had been left open for hundreds of years and still not brought the world to an end, surely one could be left open for sixty or seventy years so that Lyra and Will could see each other?

All these are flaws, not fatal weaknesses. It is hard, as Pullman has said, to achieve artistic perfection in a novel of this magnitude. The sojourn in the land of the dead, one of the most memorable episodes in the entire trilogy, more than compensates for some of the parts that don't quite click.

The Amber Spyglass is grander and less intimate than its predecessors, but it is still a good novel, though it does not stand on its own as successfully as *Northern Lights* or *The Subtle Knife*.

A SUBTLE MACGUFFIN?

The subtle knife is so important to *His Dark Materials* that the second novel is named after it and it is, we are told, the only weapon that can destroy the Authority. Yet in the final battle, we realize that a strategically applied teaspoon could have ended the decrepit deity's miserable existence. By the end of *The Amber Spyglass*, the knife is shattered, for good. Ultimately, the subtle knife becomes a kind of **MacGuffin** – a device that advances the plot or motivates characters – but has little other relevance. Another example of this is the mysterious briefcase in *Pulp Fiction*. Does this make Tarantino's movie or *His Dark Materials* any less enjoyable? Not a bit.

THE POWER OF THE SPYGLASS

The amber spyglass is different from the alethiometer and the subtle knife in two crucial ways: it is the only major piece of technology to be invented during the books, and it is the only one of these instruments that anyone can use – as long as they know how to look through two lenses.

Mary's wish to see **Dust** (or sraf) prompts her, with the help of the mulefa, to make this telescope-like device. While Dust is invisible to her naked eye, the "comparison of sraf to the sparkles on water" suggests a way in which she might see it, because "it might be that the Shadow-particles, when they behaved like waves of light did, were capable of being polarized too."

Mary wonders if an instrument made from sap-lacquer might do the trick, so she finds a flattish piece of wood which she planes then covers with more than forty coats of the lacquer until the surface is "at least five millimetres thick".

After a whole day of polishing the mirror-like structure and failing to see Dust, Mary realizes the wood must be cut away so that the lacquer can be used as a sheet through which she can search for the sraf. When she has split the sheet in two and used the two halves one in front of the other "like a

Solar flair: with the spyglass, Galileo changed the way we see the solar system

photographic filter" and a hand-span apart, she notices that the "doubleness" of vision the lacquer causes has disappeared and she can see "everything in its normal colour, but brighter and more vivid". She still can't see sraf. Only by a chance touching of the lacquer sheet with seedpod oil does she come to see the golden sparkles of **Dust**. To keep the lacquer sheets a hand-span apart, the mulefa use a bamboo tube to create a spyglass that keeps two discs of the material in the right positions.

The amber spyglass created by this cooperative venture is also handily compact, small enough to fit nicely into Mary Malone's pocket.

In our world, the most influential spyglass ever produced probably belonged to the Italian scientist **Galilei Galileo** (1564–1642). The first eyeglass appeared in the 13th century, but in 1608, someone in Europe – there is no consensus as to exactly who – found that if you placed a lens for the farsighted about 13 inches away from a lens for the nearsighted, and peered through the nearsighted lens, distant objects would miraculously appear as if they were close by. If you put those lenses in a tube, you had a spyglass.

Galileo refined this principle, experimenting with different lenses and working out the mathematical equation that identified the instrument's ability to magnify. By 1609, he had a spyglass that could magnify objects twenty-fold. Not as clever as seeing Dust but good enough for Galileo to peer deep enough into the heavens and conclude that everything in the solar system did not, as the Roman Catholic Church insisted, revolve around the sun. His book suggesting as much led to him being found guilty of "grave suspicion of heresy" by the Inquisition, and he spent the rest of his life under house arrest. The Catholic Church finally admitted, in 1992, that its treatment of Galileo was an error.

One unlikely side-effect of Mary Malone's laudable efforts is the existence of a self-proclaimed "ethereal alternative Gothic" rock band in Massachusetts called **Amber Spyglass**.

THE NAMING GAME

Pullman chooses his names with care. Some have obvious significance, others contain cryptic hints like crossword clues, a handful are probably private jokes (there's one in *Lyra's Oxford*) and a few seem remarkably coincidental.

The famous experimental theologian **Boris Rusakov**, for example, shares his name with a Russian physicist who lectured at Oxford University briefly in the 1990s. **Stanislaus Grumman**, as John Parry becomes in the books, shares his surname with **Leroy Grumman**, the American aeronauticist whose aviation company designed the module for the **Apollo 11** moon landing.

The origin of the outlandish surname **Belacqua** is more problematic. One of **Samuel Beckett**'s fictional alter egos is **Belacqua Shuah**, the anti-hero of the Irishman's first novel *Dream Of Fair To Middling Women*. **Mrs Cooper**, Will's put-upon piano teacher, may be a nod to **Susan Cooper**, one of Pullman's favourite novelists. **Mary Malone** – surely coincidentally – is the name of a British theatre actress who played Juliet in a screen version of Shakespeare's *Romeo And Juliet* back in 1908. Similarly, **Jotham Santelia** almost shares his surname with the Italian Futurist designer **Antonio Sant'Elia**.

LYRA'S OXFORD

A short book published by Pullman in 2003, *Lyra's Oxford* contains a fold-out map of *Oxford By Train, River And Zeppelin*, a map of the Oxford in Lyra's world and, centrally, a short story named *Lyra And The Birds* – featuring some wonderful illustrations by John Lawrence.

The book opens with a fictitious quote from a Baedeker-style travel guide to the coasts of Bohemia (Pullman tells us it is fictional by spelling the writer's name Baedecker) about the mysteries of Oxford "where the real and the unreal jostle each other in the streets" and "windows open into other worlds". And, although the short story is the most significant part of the book, Pullman has revealed that it only emerged after he started doing a bit of research. "I thought it would be fun to put together some documents and bits and pieces from Lyra's world, such as a map of the Oxford she knows, and as I did, I found a story beginning to take shape," he says on his website.

The story is set two years after the end of *The Amber Spyglass*, when Lyra is fifteen but still wounded by the recent past: "Since she and Will had parted... the slightest thing had the power to move her to pity and distress; it felt as if her heart was bruised for ever."

She and Pantalaimon are sitting on the roof of Jordan College when they spot a storm petrel being mobbed by starlings. The bird turns out to be a witch's dæmon, which is trying to find an alchemist, Sebastian Makepeace, who may be able to cure his witch of a mysterious illness. Lyra agrees to visit the alchemist, but, as she arrives, she realizes that she has walked into a trap. She is attacked by the witch but saved at the last minute by a diving swan. It transpires that the witch and Makepeace were once lovers, and that their son was killed during the war in *The Amber Spyglass* – a conflict the witch blames on Lyra.

Though some fans complained about the story's brevity – one estimating that it took him 20 minutes to read – there was general relief that Lyra, although still pining for Will, was back to her old self, sparring nicely with Pantalaimon. Her story had a simple, unforced charm, and there was a sense, which had been slightly lacking in the frantic finale to *The Amber Spyglass*, that Pullman was having fun with the characters again. The highlight of the short story was, as John Ezard in *The Guardian* noted, the image of "all of the animate creatures of the city striving clumsily to protect this obdurate girl, in gratitude for what she has done for their universe".

WHO WAS ZENOBIA?

SS Zenobia, advertised as "the most up-to-date and comfortable cruise liner afloat" in a brochure in *Lyra's Oxford*, is aptly named. The liner cruises around the Levant and the Middle East and must be named after the real-life 3rd-century queen of **Palmyra** who is referred to in the book.

A beautiful, well educated, Syrian woman, **Zenobia** married Odaenathus, the king of Palmyra, in 258 but he was assassinated, along with her stepson, in 267. Zenobia then ruled Palmyra on her son's behalf. She expanded the empire in battle, becoming known as the "warrior queen" and the "new Cleopatra" after conquering Egypt in 269. Her success did not last long. In 272–273, **Aurelius**, determined to reunite the Roman empire, thrashed the Palmyrans in battle. Zenobia and her son were taken as hostages. Her son died on the journey to Rome and there are conflicting traditions about Zenobia's demise. She is said to have starved herself to avoid captivity or been exhibited as one of the spoils of war by Aurelius and given a nice villa.

The facts don't really do Zenobia justice. The **Historia Augusta**, the collection of unreliable biographies of Roman emperors, praises her beauty ("So white were her teeth many thought she had pearls in place of her teeth"), her capacity for drinking with generals and notes: "She hunted with the eagerness of a Spaniard".

CRUISE
BY
S.S. ZENOBIA
to
THE
LEVANT

Card games: this card in Lyra's Oxford suggests Lyra might be heading east to the Levant

Pullman has said *Lyra's Oxford* is "a sort of bridge between the trilogy and a longer book coming later, to be called *The Book Of Dust*". It seems likely that Makepeace will become a major new character, while Dr Polstead, who quizzes Lyra, looks like a promising, possibly villainous, addition to the cast.

The rest of *Lyra's Oxford* consists of various documents and artefacts, collected, as it were, by some chance cosmic event. There are advertisements for fictional books – including, bizarrely, one by **Mrs Coulter** named *The Bronze Clocks Of Benin* – as well as a postcard from Mary Malone and information about the cruise ship **SS Zenobia**.

There is a strange discrepancy in the arrival and departure times for the liner.

The ship is due to leave Famagusta at 7pm on Wednesday 30 April and arrive in Lakatia at 7am on Friday 1 May. In other words, the Thursday would have fallen on a date that doesn't exist: 31 April. That is just one of the mysteries in *Lyra's Oxford*, but, as the heroine tells her dæmon: "Everything means something, we just have to find out how to read it."

So we are left trying to read meaning into fragments. Who is **Angela Gorman** and why is she getting a postcard from Mary Malone? Who was meeting at a café in **Smyrna** at 11am on Monday 11 May? The date is circled on the SS Zenobia's itinerary. The surprising conclusion seems to be that *The Book Of Dust* may be set partly in the **Levant**, a typically old-fashioned – for Pullman's fictional world – geographical entity that roughly corresponds to the part of the Middle East bounded by the Mediterranean Sea on the west and the northern Arabian Desert and Upper Mesopotamia to the east and includes Israel, Syria, the Lebanon and part of Iraq. Even the name of the cruise liner, SS Zenobia, refers, through the historical queen of the same name, to this part of the world. Does this mean that Lyra is heading there next?

··✝··

HIS DARK MATERIALS
The Adaptations

The riddle of Oz: Australian star Nicole Kidman's enigmatic persona made her Pullman's choice to play Mrs Coulter, whose icy heart is melted by maternal love

ADAPTING PULLMAN

Writing *His Dark Materials* was tough enough, but adapting it for stage and screen has been a Herculean labour

Today's savvy, commercially ruthless entertainment industry increasingly regards fiction, drama, Broadway musicals and movies not as separate works of art but as content to be repackaged and sold to the masses in as many different ways as possible. You've read the book, so why not see the film, buy the soundtrack CD, collect the action figures and play *His Dark Materials* Top Trumps cards with your friends? If a film or a book proves especially popular and durable, it becomes a franchise.

This process may sound crass, but it has brought some truly epic and original works to the big screen. It's hard to imagine either *Lord Of The Rings* or *His Dark Materials* being filmed if they had started out as a screenplay. The single-sentence pitch for Pullman's masterpiece might have been: "It's *Paradise Lost* meets quantum physics, but with armed polar bears." Luckily, the trilogy's massive global sales – and **New Line Cinema**'s blockbuster success with *Lord Of The Rings* – provided the kind of hard evidence Hollywood understands best. The novels also have, to the delight of the studio marketing departments, brand recognition and that makes promoting the films of the books so much easier.

So when **New Line Cinema** announced, in 2002, that it had bought the screen rights to *His Dark Materials*, the only surprise was that it had taken so long. The first novel, *Northern Lights*, had been published seven years before. But, as a studio, New Line had been preoccupied by Peter Jackson's *Lord Of The Rings* movies, released between 2001 and 2003, which generated a cumulative global box office take of $3 billion. The spectacular, if less consistent, grosses for the Harry Potter series showed movie financiers that those figures were no fluke.

Searching for similar fantastic sagas, there were only two obvious candidates: C.S. Lewis's **Narnia** novels (which were snapped up by Disney, piqued by its own stupidity in passing up the chance to film Tolkien's novels) and *His Dark Materials*. The deal was done, but the journey from signing contracts to completing the movies has proved far longer and more troublesome than New Line, Philip Pullman or publishers Scholastic Books could ever have imagined. The delays have proved trying for those of us who can't wait to see all good toyshops full of battery-powered plastic mulefa. Luckily for Pullman's British readers, the **BBC** proved rather quicker off the mark.

THE SOUND OF THE TRILOGY

In September 2002, BBC Audiobooks released the trilogy on **cassette**, entirely unabridged, with Pullman himself narrating and a full cast playing the various roles. As Pullman used to teach and lecture, it's no great shock that he reads his own words so well. The cast did almost as well, though one reviewer on Amazon noted that Pantalaimon becomes increasingly Welsh from Chapter 6 and that the gyptians occasionally sound like relatives of the Grundy family in the BBC Radio 4 soap *The Archers*. The BBC Audiobook is still available on cassette and CD.

The first dramatic adaptation of *His Dark Materials* was broadcast on **BBC Radio 4** in January 2003. The three 150-minute radio plays, adapted from the novels by **Lavinia Murray**, were lavishly cast. Actor **Terence Stamp** was Lord Asriel, Bill Paterson brought his idiosyncratic brand of gravitas to the Master's role, while ubiquitous character actors Kenneth Cranham and Peter Marinker played Farder Coram and Lee Scoresby respectively. **Emma Fielding** judged Mrs Coulter beautifully, while **Tracy-Ann Obermann**, later to achieve infamy as a murderess in the BBC soap *East Enders*, shone as Serafina Pekkala. The hardest roles to cast were always going to be Lyra and Will. **Lulu Popplewell** (who has since had a small part in Richard Curtis's sweet, if self-satisfied, rom-

The waiting game: seven years after *Northern Lights* was published, New Line talked to Pullman

com *Love Actually*) was magnificent as Lyra. Daniel Anthony's Will was, some said, the weakest part of the plays. Billy Cowie's atmospheric music is, alas, no longer available on his website (*www.billycowie.com*).

Turning such a blockbuster work of fiction into seven and a half hours of radio drama could, at worst, have felt more like a process of data compression than adaptation, but Murray did a remarkable job. She made some changes to the stories, notably turning the angel **Balthamos** (Ray Fearon) into the narrator of the story and naming Mrs Coulter's anonymous dæmon **Ozymandias**, after the famous sonnet by **Percy Bysshe Shelley**. Pullman didn't sound too delighted by the decision, telling one fan: "I didn't choose that name, and to be frank I don't think I would have done."

Good as the plays are, they do, as the **Bridge To The Stars** website noted, contain a few odd, funny or awkward lines. There's a quip about gridlock on the M40 near Oxford, an especially unfortunate moment when Mrs Coulter is asked "Are you a Gobbler?" (and replies, "Yes I am") and a strange allusion to *Star Trek*.

Some of the magic was inevitably lost in the journey from printed page to broadcast, but the plays work as standalone radio drama and as companions to the books. A box set of the plays – available on CD and cassette – is available from the BBC and on Amazon.

EXIT PURSUED BY A CLIFF-GHAST

When **Nicholas Hytner** took over as artistic director of the **National Theatre** in London in April 2003, he knew he wanted to produce something epic. Ideally, he wanted to stage a work of sufficient magnitude to make it clear that, under his leadership, Britain's most famous theatre had entered a dynamic new age. This epic wouldn't just be big, it would be long – an experience in which adults and children could immerse themselves. Better still, this landmark production would help Hytner attract a completely different audience to the National, another part of his remit.

Adapting *His Dark Materials* for the stage seemed, in this context, a wonderfully appropriate idea to Hytner. There was one small problem. The novels were widely held to be impossible to stage.

The Guardian's Kate Kellaway raised just some of the most glaring questions when she visited the National before the play had opened: "How do you stage animal mutability? How do you cut through one world to another with a knife? How do you present harpies, angels, armoured bears? Or show the audience mythological Dust?" And then there's those dragonflies with spies on their backs, the scary cliff-ghasts and the mulefa with their seed pods.

> "THE APPARENT IMPOSSIBILITY OF PUTTING THE BOOKS ON STAGE MEANT THEY HAD TO BE DONE AT THE NATIONAL."

The National was aware of these – and many more obstacles – right from the start. **Nicholas Wright**, who adapted the play, recalled that the project started when "Nicholas Hytner asked me whether I had read *His Dark Materials*. I told him I had and went on to say that the audacity of the books, their immediacy, and the apparent impossibility of putting them on stage at all meant that they simply had to be done at the National."

Hytner, Wright, Michael Curry, the puppetmaster hired after his fine work on *The Lion King*, and costume designer Jon Morrell (who struggled to costume fit the dæmon-puppets) had few illusions about the scale of the task before them. But the biggest challenge was surely Wright's. It would take a very subtle knife indeed to cut the epic trilogy so it became a compelling two-part drama without alienating the hundreds of thousands who cherished the books.

Fated lovers: Mrs Coulter (Lesley Manville) consoles Asriel (David Harewood) at the National Theatre

He explained the rationale behind his adaptation to *The Guardian*: "I didn't compress: the last thing anybody wanted was a squashed-book show. I had to select, cut and then rearrange. Then came the much longer job of letting it breathe until it felt natural and organic. What I dreaded was the books' seriousness about the big questions: God, loyalty, the environment, death."

So how well did Wright and Hytner succeed? Many critics felt there could be no middle way. The two three-hour plays would either be a triumph or a disaster.

"YOU'VE GOT A COW ON YOUR BACK, A BEAR-HEAD ON YOUR ARM AND A CRUTCH."

The reviews said otherwise. *The Guardian* reviewed it twice, first by theatre critic **Michael Billington**, who gave it three stars (out of five) and later by **Dr Rowan Williams**, the Archbishop of Canterbury, who hailed it as "a near-miraculous triumph". Pullman fans, as shown by the reviews posted online generally agreed with the archbishop, though often they had small – and different – reservations about the dramatization.

Yet the praise was far from unanimous. The *Daily Telegraph* reviewer, a Pullman fan, complained: "There were long stretches when I was bored."

The problem – if there was a problem – wasn't the acting. Most reviewers agreed that **Patricia Hodge** was a fine Mrs Coulter, ambivalent enough to suggest the struggle between her maternal instincts and her desire for power. Hodge did later suggest that the role had more to do with moving the plot forward than getting inside the character. "It doesn't sustain your soul, but it was a jolly nice thing to be part of," she said.

Timothy Dalton's Lord Asriel, owing more to an explorer like Sir Ranulph Fiennes than the actor's sojourn as 007, was something of a triumph. **Anna Maxwell Martin**, a twentysomething playing the child heroine Lyra, carried the show with an assured performance. **Dominic Cooper**, as Will, was less universally acclaimed although, as this happened with the radio play too, this may say as much about the character as Cooper's ability. His dedication certainly can't be faulted. He also played a Tartar guard and a panserbjørne. "They're real nightmare parts: the costumes are made from off-cuts of leather, so you've basically got a cow on your back, a bear-head on your arm and a crutch," he said later. Maybe the discomfort got to him when he finally took to the stage as Will. Among the supporting actors, **Tim McMullan** impressed as Lee Scoresby, a Machiavellian cleric and the operator of a diminutive Gallivespian spy.

Bear necessities: the panserbjørne square up for action at the National Theatre

Nor was the staging to blame. The technical brilliance of the puppet-dæmons, the quality of the production values, the versatility of the revolving stage (which, at different times, was an Oxford college, Himalayan peaks and the bowels of a ship) and the attention to detail was almost faultless. Sometimes the journey between universes became hard to follow for playgoers who hadn't closely read the books. The most moving sequence was Will and Lyra's heart-rending descent into the land of the dead. The scene where the dead are released from captivity caught Pullman's vision beautifully when the untethered dead merged with the wind and trees. The gyptians didn't fare so well, with some aficionados of the books feeling they had been reduced to providing comic relief.

Some critics took issue with Wright's adaptation. His decision to restructure the story so the play starts with Will and Lyra looking back on their adventures did seem to eliminate much of the dramatic tension. The decision to axe certain characters – notably **Mary Malone** – upset some fans, though others could see the point of the pruning. One reviewer wished Wright had pruned a bit more, saying the first play felt as if it was trying to cram in too much. Billington felt the play highlighted the way Pullman's "didactic anti-clericalism demonizes religion to the point of absurdity" and doubted whether *His Dark Materials* could be adapted at all, saying that the trilogy, more than any other recent novel, depended on the reader's relationship with the words and the writers and sources who inspired those words. Seeing his work performed left Pullman shaken and stirred. Later, on his website, he enthused: "Everything about it, from the programme to the music to the amazing staging to the dæmon-puppets to the brilliant cast, was superb."

Commercially, *His Dark Materials* was such a smash that it came back to the National for a second run with a completely different set of actors. **Elaine Symons** (Lyra), **Michael Legge** (Will), **David Harewood** (Asriel) and **Lesley Manville** (Mrs Coulter) were every bit as impressive as their forerunners. Pullman singled out Symons and Legge, saying they had, like Martin and Cooper, left him deeply moved by the way they had got under the skin of Lyra and Will. In March 2006, Warwick's Playbox Theatre staged an impressive low-budget version of Wright's play, disproving claims that it could only work on the bigger stages of London and New York.

Even those who liked Wright's play often admitted that it was easier to see the books working as a movie. Hytner, though, wasn't convinced: "By its very nature, film will be obliged to fill in all of the gaps and leave nothing to the imagination." Pullman shared Hytner's caution. Erica Wagner, interviewing the author for *The Times*, said she didn't like the idea of a movie, because she felt that "the film is, in a sense, in my own head – I don't want another". Pullman understood her reservations, saying: "Cinema is a totalitarian experience. You are dominated by the cinema: by the director's timing, the cuts he chooses, where the camera moves. Then there's the disappointment you almost always feel when you see the film of the book: you know she doesn't look like that, or he wouldn't wear those clothes and, oh, they've gone and changed the ending."

THE MOVIE DEAL

In the mid-1990s, Deborah Forte, a producer hitherto best known as the woman in charge of the animated children's series *Clifford The Big Red Dog*, read the manuscript of *Northern Lights* and decided she wanted to make a movie out of it right away. She started talking with Pullman about her idea and has recalled: "When Philip and I sat down to talk about the film [in 1997], we both said that our first choice as Mrs Coulter would be Nicole Kidman."

If every decision had been that simple, the movie of *His Dark Materials* might already have been released. But the trilogy's journey through what moviefolk call **development hell** has been so protracted and painful that, until the winter of 2006, the very fate of the film of the books seemed to hang in the balance.

New Line acquired the rights – from Forte's company Scholastic Entertainment – in the spring of 2002. As part of the deal, Forte was confirmed as the movie's producer. In essence, New Line bought the rights to the whole trilogy but will only film the last two novels if the first movie is a commercial smash. In May 2002, New Line approached **Tom Stoppard**, the award-winning playwright who had scripted Terry Gilliam's dark fantasy *Brazil*, to write the screenplay for the first movie *The Golden Compass* (the US title for *Northern Lights*).

Stoppard admitted later: "I was attracted to Philip's wide reference to everything from particle physics to *Paradise Lost* – too attracted in my first draft. I was asked, quite rightly, to make the script more 'Lyra-centric'. The job became harder the further one got into the trilogy because Philip makes time and space elastic. This doesn't trouble the reader, but it is harder to deal with in a film. I wrote a screenplay that took the story a little way into the second novel, and a treatment of what would be the second and third films."

"WHEN PHILIP AND I SAT DOWN WE BOTH SAID OUR CHOICE FOR MRS COULTER WAS NICOLE KIDMAN."

His script was read by New Line and Pullman and gathered dust waiting for a director. In May 2004, New Line announced that **Chris Weitz** would direct. This alarmed many Pullman fans. Weitz's biggest smash had been the gross-out comedy **American Pie**. Only a month later, word was leaked that Stoppard's script had been junked. In a statement, New Line said they felt it was important that Weitz, as a writer/director, should bring his vision to the project. They added, in an attempt to placate fans of the books, that Pullman, who had met Weitz, agreed with this approach.

In September 2004, after reading a few bulletin boards and realizing just how worried fans were, Weitz took the unusual step of contacting the Bridge To The Stars fansite, requesting an interview to put the record straight. The full text of the talk is on *www.bridgetothestars.net*. It was clear he was a Pullman enthusiast and that his detailed treatment of the first novel, written to convince New Line he was the man to direct the movie, might leave Stoppard's script hanging in the wind. Pullman's verdict on the treatment was reassuring: "It was model of how to condense a story of four hundred pages into a script of 110 or so. His vision of the way it should be told on screen matched my own."

Child of destiny: Dakota Blue Richards felt she could play Lyra when she read the novels

KILLING GOD OR SELLING OUT?

Weitz did make one remark in this interview that suggested, to some, that he, New Line and Pullman were selling out the novels. Critics had been wondering how the trilogy's views on religion would play on the big screen in an era when the religious right was so hugely influential that, in 2004, it was credited with saving **George W. Bush** in the presidential election. In this interview, Weitz said, after a talk with Pullman, that the Authority could "represent any arbitrary establishment that curtails the freedom of the individual, whether it be religious, political, totalitarian, fundamentalist, communist, what have you".

Surely, some fans insisted, this was a sell-out, just the kind of crass commercial decision they had feared. Not so, said Pullman, insisting his real quarrel was not with religion but with "those who pervert and abuse religion, or any other doctrine, to dominate and suppress human freedom". The cries of betrayal seemed overblown, but Pullman's response didn't sound quite right either. Despite the example set by his beloved grandfather, he couldn't seem to imagine any churchman in the books who didn't pervert and abuse religion.

The media simplified, amplified and distorted the debate to such an extent that New Line soon found itself under fire and – so the official version goes

– Weitz resigned as director in December 2004, blaming unspecified "technical challenges". By now, *The Golden Compass* had started to look doomed, and it wasn't until August 2005 that a new director, **Anand Tucker** (best known for the dark biopic *Hilary And Jackie*), was appointed. He quit eight months later, blaming "creative differences", amid rumours of rows over budget constraints. The game of musical directors' chairs finally ended when Weitz took over again in May 2006 and galvanized the production of the movie.

CASTING LYRA

After open public auditions that attracted 10,000 English schoolgirls, twelve-year-old **Dakota Blue Richards** was cast as Lyra. Pullman, who had watched a DVD of the audition, championed her, saying her bone structure and the way she carried herself just seemed to suit his vision of Lyra. The decision to hold an open casting call was unusual for a movie of this magnitude – it's more often used as a cheap publicity ploy – but Forte felt it paid off, saying: "Dakota is an uncommonly good actress and personifies a lot of the characteristics of Lyra."

Richards already knew the books. "My mother read them to me when I was about nine, and I saw the plays at the National Theatre," she told reporters at Cannes. "I thought if I could play any role, it would be Lyra. I have treated the experience as if I am in two different worlds: the normal life of being who I was before, and all this. I try not to let the film affect going to school, and being me."

CASTING MRS COULTER

The easiest decision New Line had to make was casting **Nicole Kidman** as Mrs Coulter. Pullman had agreed with Forte that she would be ideal and even spoke of the character resembling the Australian actress. But Kidman's casting wasn't settled until July 2006, with some reports claiming the star and New Line had trouble agreeing a fee. Kidman was also a friend of **Paul Bettany** and may have been disappointed to hear that he wouldn't, after all, play Asriel. **Harry Knowles**, the grossly influential online movie buff who launched *www.aintitcool.com*, saw some of Kidman's scenes during his on-set visit. "I like Kidman because she sometimes makes horribly embarrassing choices as an actor," said Knowles. "She throws herself at roles in strange ways, and when it pays off it can be riveting.

In the big scene I saw, she was in fine eccentric form." Alluring and mysterious, giving cinemagoers a sense that nine-tenths of her personality is still hidden from the viewer, Kidman seems perfect casting for the captivating villainess.

Casting Asriel

Pullman's left-field suggestion was that **Jason Isaacs** (Lucius Malfoy in the *Harry Potter* films) should play Asriel. New Line and Weitz – perhaps fearing that might blur the boundaries between two movie franchises – ignored him. **Eric Bana** (*The Incredible Hulk*) and **Paul Bettany** (the deranged albino monk in *The Da Vinci Code*) were approached, but eventually **Daniel Craig**, the new 007, became the second Bond actor to be cast in this role. To grow into the part, Craig soon grew a fetching beard that made him look a bit like D.H. Lawrence. One of the problems was that Asriel doesn't do much in the first novel and may only appear in two sequences in the movie. Craig will have a much bigger role in the third instalment if New Line adapt the entire trilogy.

Casting Serafina Pekkala

Eva Green, who shot to fame as Vesper Lynd opposite Craig in *Casino Royale*, was quietly cast as Serafina Pekkala. She was attracted to the role after reading the trilogy and worked with her voice coach Roisin Carty to achieve what she calls "a medieval Scandinavian drawl" designed to make the witch seem other worldly and from a different age. Even more than Kidman's choice, the much lusted after Green might be New Line's shrewdest piece of casting. Harry Knowles, after watching the shooting of some footage in which she learns to fly, quipped: "I am prepared to go on record as saying she is hot."

Casting Lee Scoresby

It's hard to know what to make of Pullman's suggestion that **Samuel L. Jackson** should play Lee Scoresby. The star who is still most associated in the public mind with Quentin Tarantino's *Pulp Fiction* certainly has Scoresby's laconic swagger, so maybe his casting would have proved a masterstroke. Instead, New Line cast this

The name's... Asriel, Lord Asriel: Daniel Craig looks more like D.H. Lawrence than 007 in the film

one straighter. As **Lee Van Cleef**, the actor Pullman said had partly inspired the character, had ridden off into the sunset for good, New Line cast the next best thing: wiry, lanky **Sam Elliott** who has spent thirty years in the saddle in various movies since he made his blink-and-you-miss-it debut in *Butch Cassidy And The Sundance Kid*. Pullman met Elliott on a set visit in October 2006 and concluded: "Sam's resemblance to Lee Scoresby in my mind is just astonishing. His Lee has all the presence, the experience, the battered integrity, the humour, and the courage of the aëronaut who first walked into my story thirteen years ago."

SUPPORTING PLAYERS

Adam Godley, the fortysomething English actor who has played a string of supporting parts in many children's movies (from *Thunderpants* to *Nanny McPhee*) one of the toughest jobs as the voice of **Pantalaimon.** The black English actor **Nonso Anozie**, a graduate of the Royal Shakespeare Company, should bring rare gravitas to the voice of Iorek Byrnison and provide a fascinating foil to the grizzly tones of **Ian McShane** as Iofur Raknison.

The cast is rounded out with a corps of experienced, actors, largely Britons. **Jim Carter** (superb as the father in Dennis Potter's *The Singing Detective*) plays

John Faa, **Tom Courtenay** (Oscar-nominated for his turn as the hammy actor in *The Dresser* and a fiery revolutionary in *Dr Zhivago*) is Farder Coram, **Claire Higgins** (most famous as the evil Julia in two *Hellraiser* movies) plays Ma Costa and **Jack Shepherd** (known to British audiences as dull, dour, decent Cornish TV cop Wycliffe) is the Master. The multi-talented **Simon McBurney**, whose resumé includes helping to write and produce *Mr Bean's Holiday* and the award-winning play *Mnemonic*, is an intriguing choice as Fra Pavel, the priest who can read the alethiometer but behaves with all the urgency of a heavily sedated sloth.

In the director's chair

New Line can't be accused of playing it safe by choosing Weitz to direct *The Golden Compass*. A producer/writer/filmmaker/actor, Weitz has plenty of hits to his name (*American Pie* as producer; *About A Boy* as director; *Antz* as writer), but he has only been the credited director of two films: an okay remake of *Heaven Can Wait* called *Down To Earth* (2001), starring Chris Rock, and *About A Boy* (2002), a surprisingly edgy – for a Hugh Grant romantic comedy – adaptation of the Nick Hornby novel. Weitz penned the Oscar-nominated screenplay.

> "Weitz read His Dark Materials on the set of About A Boy. He felt the books left Tolkien 'in the dust' for depth."

Weitz showed a good eye – and ear – for the nuances of British culture in *About A Boy*. Although a native New Yorker, he studied at sixth form in London and read English literature at Trinity College, Cambridge. His instinctive feel for the textures of English school and university life convinced Pullman that he understood Lyra.

Besides, as Weitz told the Bridge To The Stars website, he had studied 17th century literature, knew Milton and Blake quite well and was "a lapsed-Catholic crypto-Buddhist, which I feel is appropriate for the piece". His passion must have shone through in his detailed proposal to adapt the novels.

Weitz started in movies sharing a screenwriting credit on *Antz* (1998), the animated insect flick that was sharper and funnier than its Disneyfied rival *A Bug's Life*. In 1999, he topped that with *American Pie*, which he produced and his brother Paul directed. It was such a smash it spawned *American Pie 2* (2001).

THE MAIN CREW

Director Chris Weitz
Novel Philip Pullman
Screenplay Chris Weitz
Producers Bill Carraro, Deborah Forte
Original music Alexandre Desplat
Cinematography Henry Braham
Film editing Anna V. Coates

THE CAST

Nicole Kidman **Mrs Coulter**
Daniel Craig **Lord Asriel**
Eva Green **Serafina Pekkala**
Dakota Blue Richards **Lyra**
Adam Godley **Pantalaimon (voice)**
Nonso Anozie **Iorek Byrnison (voice)**
Jim Carter **John Faa**
Tom Courtenay **Farder Coram**
Charlie Rowe **Billy Costa**
Clare Higgins **Ma Costa**
Sam Elliott **Lee Scoresby**
Simon McBurney **Fra Pavel**
Jack Shepherd **Master**
John Franklyn-Robbins **Librarian**
Magda Szubanski **Mrs Lonsdale**
Paul Anthony-Barber **Bolvangar doctor**
Jason Watkins **Bolvangar official**
Hattie Morahan **Clara**
Ian McShane **Iofur Raknison (voice)**
James Rawlings **Passing scholar**
Bill Hurst **Trollesund captain**
John Bett **Thobold**

He then helped write and co-directed (with Paul) *About A Boy*, a critical and commercial success helped by an affecting, less mannered than usual, performance from Grant.

During filming, Chris began reading *His Dark Materials* because so many people had recommended it. "I was absolutely stunned by the imagination, daring and intelligence of the books," he said later, feeling that it left Tolkien "in the dust" for ambition and depth. By 2005, he had become embroiled in the saga of *The Golden Compass*. When the film is released, will be his first new movie as a director for five years.

His appointment was greeted with dismay by fans led to believe that the likes of Sam Mendes, Terry Jones or Ridley Scott might direct. But Weitz, in his Bridge To The Stars interview, tried to reassure fans, saying his film will be inspired as much by the work of **Akira Kurosawa** and **David Lean** as by the more obvious reference point, Peter Jackson's *Lord Of The Rings*.

He has talked of balancing human relationships and spectacle, preferring the wonder of the early *Star Wars* to the later stultifying technical extravaganzas. He has also cited as reference points for his film Stanley Kubrick's attention to detail (notably in *Barry Lyndon*) and the way Francois Truffaut portrayed children as significant people.

Although Stoppard felt that Pullman's "imaginative inventiveness is

Great expectations: can Weitz make *The Golden Compass* a critical and commercial smash?

a gift to cinema", that imagination, ranging across time and space, poses obvious problems for any director. In an era when almost any effect can be computer generated, the crux may not be what the dæmons look like but whether any movie can really handle Pullman's rich tapestry of themes and whether cinema audiences will commute between parallel universes as happily as readers have.

With a budget of $150 million, *The Golden Compass* is New Line's most expensive movie since the *Rings* films. It might be easier for Lord Asriel to tear a rift in the fabric of space than for Weitz to meet everyone's expectations.

MAKING THE MOVIE

The Golden Compass, says Weitz, "offers everything a filmmaker would want – a compelling story, fascinating characters, psychological and philosophical depth." But Pullman's vision would, he knew, be the sternest test yet of his credentials as a filmmaker. There were obvious generic issues – how would the film balance the novel's many moods? – and some very particular ones. How, for example, would Oscar-nominated costume designer Ruth Myers dress a parallel universe?

In part, the answer lay in the quality of the crew. In the light of Weitz's admiration for Lean, it can be no coincidence that the movie is edited by **Anna V. Coates**, who worked on *Lawrence Of Arabia*, Lean's last undisputed masterpiece. The look of the film is partly in the hands of **Denis Glassner**, the production designer who won an Oscar for *Bugsy* and who does similar chores on many Coen brothers movies. The crucial responsibility of realising dæmons, Spectres and gyptians fell to supervisor **Mike Fink** (*X-Men*, *The Road To Perdition*) and producer Susan MacLeod (*Die Hard: With A Vengeance*). Peter Jackson had his own special effects studio for the *Rings* movies, but Weitz and New Line turned to **Rhythm & Hue**, the company most famous for making Marlon Brando speak from beyond the grave in *Superman Returns*.

Cast, crew and budget didn't finally come together until spring 2006, and shooting started in earnest in June with Weitz back in the chair. The movie, which only finished shooting in the summer of 2007, was filmed largely in Oxford, Shepperton and Norway, with occasional excursions to the much-filmed Bourne Wood, near Farnham in Surrey and the Old Royal Naval College in Greenwich, London.

Though footage was shot in Bergen and Svalbard, the village of **Trollesund** was created at Shepperton Studios. After his set visit in October 2006, Pullman marvelled: "The Trollesund set is unbelievably real. You'd swear those grimy battered houses had stood there for a hundred years or more; and then you walk around the back and see the raw new unpainted wood behind, the props holding it up, the weights holding it down."

> "YOU'D SWEAR THE GRIMY BATTERED HOUSES OF TROLLESUND HAVE BEEN THERE FOR A HUNDRED YEARS, UNTIL YOU SEE THE PROPS HOLDING THEM."

Many fans are curious to know just how heavily involved Pullman is in the film. He doesn't have final scripting or casting approval, but New Line haven't sidelined him. The novelist has been consulted about Weitz's appointment and the casting of Lyra and Mrs Coulter. Online critic Harry Knowles, on his set visit, felt Pullman's spirit was everywhere. "The people who love Pullman's books tend to be a little evangelical about them, and I can say for sure that fans are involved at every level of this film."

New Line has spared no effort to make *The Golden Compass* a smash. But the most difficult question they face was raised by Knowles after his set visit.

"What's the thirty-second version of *The Golden Compass*? Or even the sixty second version?" If New Line can't find a succinct slogan that sums up the movie, Knowles worries, they won't attract a big enough audience to make the next two films worthwhile.

New Line will not want to pull out after one film. A script for *The Subtle Knife* has already been commissioned but no green light will be given until all the box-office receipts have been counted. As a movie these days is generally not considered profitable unless it rakes in twice its budget at the box office, *The Golden Compass* will need to gross nearly $300 million to make the decision to proceed a foregone conclusion.

"WHAT'S THE THIRTY-SECOND VERSION OF *THE GOLDEN COMPASS*? OR EVEN THE SIXTY-SECOND VERSION?"

The worst case scenario was that Weitz would make a film with the pace of *Barry Lyndon*, the length of *Lawrence Of Arabia* and the deadpan seriousness of Akira Kurosawa. But the footage shown to selected film journalists and previewed at Cannes suggests that Weitz has done a remarkable job. The added bonus – for all concerned – is that the December 2007 release date means they won't be competing with the boy wizard. *Harry Potter And The Half-Blood Prince* isn't due until December 2008.

Fantastic adventures

If you ever wonder why Hollywood is flooding the world's cinemas with fantasy movies, just check out the list of the ten highest-grossing movies on the Internet Movie Database. The only film in the top ten that doesn't have a strong fantasy element is the biggest ever blockbuster, James Cameron's *Titanic*. The other nine movies have starred boy wizards, Jedi knights, comical ghostly pirates, and rejuvenated dinosaurs. The second highest grossing movie ever is the third *Lord Of The Rings* movie: *The Fellowship Of The Ring* (which took in $1.13 billion at the global box office), followed by *Pirates Of The Caribbean: Dead Man's Chest* ($1.06 billion), *Harry Potter And The Sorcerer's Stone* ($968 million) and *Star Wars: Episode 1 – The Phantom Menace* ($922 million).

So there are billions of very good reasons why Hollywood is so keen to intrigue us with superheroes, giant apes, cuddly aliens, children hiding in wardrobes, cyborgs, mummies (the Egyptian bandaged variety), museum security guards, dragon's eggs and tomb raiders.

In part, Hollywood sees the fantasy genre as its secret weapon in the battle with television for audiences. Epics such as the Harry Potter and *Lord Of The Rings* series have a scale that TV finds hard to match and require a budget, for computer-driven special effects, that even the biggest TV co-production deal will struggle to fund. Spiralling budgets (Peter Jackson's *King Kong* cost $207 million) have worried some studios, but once you start playing the expectations game it's hard to stop. The need, as Nicholas Hytner put it, to leave nothing to our imaginations has never seemed more urgent.

Because many fantasy novels are part of a trilogy, a quartet or an even longer series, Hollywood executives know that if the first movie works, they have a franchise on their hands. Though critics groan about sequelitis, the studios know that, on average, a sequel will attract at least two-thirds of the audience who watched the first movie. If a studio is really lucky, as New Line discovered with its Tolkien movies, the audience doesn't shrink, it builds.

Without that sustained track record of commercial success, *His Dark Materials* wouldn't have been filmed at all. And, no matter how well or badly Weitz's adaptation does at the box office, fantasy movies will continue to be produced on an industrialized basis.

Fox is already shooting the first movie of Susan Cooper's series *The Dark Is Rising* (which Pullman admires) and Deborah Forte has already lined up her next property: Philip Reeve's quartet of post-apocalyptic novels called *The Hungry City Chronicles*. Disney own half the rights to adapt the **Artemis Fowl** series. *Eragon*, the biggest grossing movie to star a dragon, may yet spawn a sequel based on the other books in Christopher Paolini's *Inheritance* trilogy (once again Pullman is a fan).

Tolkien will return to the cinema in 2009 with MGM's version of *The Hobbit*, Disney's Narnia series will continue to be rolled out (*The Chronicles Of Narnia: Prince Caspian* is due in the summer of 2008) unless the box-office returns dictate otherwise, and there are at least two more movies in the Harry Potter series still to come.

But Hollywood only seems interested in certain kinds of fantasy novels. The works of some masters – notably **Michael Moorcock** and **Ursula K. Le Guin** – have been largely ignored. Le Guin's Earthsea novels have, though, been taken up by Goro Miyazaki, son of the famous Japanese director, who filmed them as *Tales From Earthsea* (2006). The movie isn't that well known, but Goro did a much better job than the Sci-Fi Channel with its horrendously bland adaptation, which LeGuin angrily disowned.

Thirty years ago, before the *Star Wars* phenomenon changed all the rules, Pullman's novel would have been lucky just to catch the eye of a talented maverick such as the animator **Ralph Bakshi** or the stop-motion special effects genius **Ray Harryhausen**, a Hollywood veteran whose animated statues were one of the highlights of *Jason And The Argonauts* (1963) and were, indeed, probably more animated than most of the cast.

It was Bakshi, not Peter Jackson, who made the first movie of *Lord Of The Rings* back in 1978. But his animated version of the first two books effectively ran out of money. Bakshi was pioneering a technique called rotoscoping, in which animators trace over live-action film movement. He had already made the acclaimed animated post-apocalyptic fantasy *Wizard* (1977). This bombed commercially but became such a cult favourite that, in 2004, it was finally released on DVD after an online petition.

The wizardry of Oz: Baum's creation, superbly captured by MGM, influenced Pullman. Dorothy's unmasking of the omnipotent wizard parallels Will's realization that the Authority is feeble

Deprived of the budgets and the tools that became available to Jackson and to George Lucas, whose first science fantasy *Star Wars: A New Hope* (1977) was one of the biggest hits of the 1970s, pioneering filmmakers like Bakshi and Harryhausen were doomed to struggle. They did most of their work in an era when, as far as Hollywood was concerned, the typical fantasy movie was characterized by big ideas, small budgets and laughable special effects.

Star Wars set the new trend, and in the last quarter of a century, blockbuster fantasy movies – be they sword-and-sorcery epics like *Conan The Barbarian* or more imaginative one-offs like Gilliam's *Brazil* – have seldom been off our screens. The return of the **Caped Crusader**, one of Pullman's favourite superheroes, in Tim Burton's *Batman* (1989) might have cheered the novelist, although the self-consciously dark, postmodern take on the tale probably struck him as yet another case of "artistic capers" spoiling a good story.

Pullman likes movies as a form of entertainment and as a source of ideas – camera angles, plot twists, themes, even soundtrack effects – that he can steal for use in his fiction. There is no compelling evidence in *His Dark Materials* that the fantasy movie genre has had a massive influence on him.

He is a master allusionist, but relatively few of the works he alludes to in the books are movies, with the exception of a nod, in the character of Balthamos, to *The Magnificent Seven* (see p.97) and to the world of spaghetti westerns with the naming of Lee Scoresby.

> "FANTASY MOVIES WERE CHARACTERIZED BY BIG IDEAS, SMALL BUDGETS AND LAUGHABLE SPECIAL EFFECTS."

Very occasionally in the books, Pullman uses a certain phrase that seems to pay deliberate homage to the movies. Our first glimpse of Mrs Coulter is of a beautiful lady in a "fox fur coat", an image which seems to place her in the pantheon of great film noir heroines. Like the seductive but malevolent heroines played by such actresses as Jane Greer in such noirish classics as *Out Of The Past*, Mrs Coulter spends most of the books manipulating the men around her, rather than being manipulated by them.

There are some intriguing parallels with one classic work of Hollywood fantasy, Frank L. Baum's *The Wizard Of Oz*, brilliantly adapted by MGM with Judy Garland as the Lyra-like Dorothy, and with the films of Hayao Miyazaki. The Japanese animator and the novelist have even been studied, in David R. Loy and Linda Goodhew's *The Dharma Of Dragons And Demons* (Wisdom), for the Buddhist lessons allegedly imparted in their work.

The story of Oz – in celluloid and literary form – has had a significant influence on Pullman's imagination. As the fantasy writer **J.L. Bell** has shown, Pullman's *The Scarecrow And The Servant* is directly influenced by Oz, paying homage to specific scenes and character names.

The resonances between *His Dark Materials* and Oz are less exact, but they are significant. Dorothy leaves her home, embarks on a series of fantastic adventures, supported by a motley crew of friends (instead of armoured bears, Dorothy has a cowardly lion), and discovers that the supreme being, the wizard worshipped in Oz, is a fraud. A benevolent, well-meaning fraud, far nicer than the Authority who has gone awry in *The Amber Spyglass*, but still a fraud. The fact that Mrs Coulter has a golden monkey for a dæmon may, in part, reflect Pullman's enthusiasm for the magical land of Oz, where the **Wicked Witch of the West** has a crack squadron of flying monkeys to do her evil bidding.

The parallels with the works of Miyazaki are even more striking. The Japanese animator/director has explored many of the themes and motifs that define *His Dark Materials* in *Kiki's Delivery Service*, *Howl's Moving Castle*, *My Neighbour Totoro*, *Princess Mononoke*, *Castle In The Sky* and *Spirited Away*. Both filmmaker and novelist are intrigued by feisty heroines, the 19th century as a setting, strange and elaborate flying machines (especially zeppelins), doom laden environmental scenarios, imaginary creatures, alternate universes and virtuous witches. Miyazaki's latest film, *Howl's Moving Castle*, was an adaptation of the novel of the same name by **Dianna Wynne Jones**, like Pullman an Oxford graduate and the first children's novelist, Pullman has acknowledged, to explore the ramifications of the theory of multiple universes.

··†··

PART II
THE KEYS TO
HIS DARK MATERIALS

HIS DARK MATERIALS
The Characters

The angelic host: rebel angels in *Paradise Lost*, as envisaged by Gustave Doré.
Without that first rebellion, Asriel could not have challenged the Authority.

LEADING PLAYERS

The greatest figments of Pullman's imagination: from the
Authority to Xaphania, with a few dæmons in between

THE AUTHORITY

Demented, powerless, indescribably aged, terrified and crying like a baby,
the Authority is a feeble fake God who was merely the first of the angels and
has, since the time of Moses, had about as high a public profile as **Howard
Hughes** in his later years. Asked just how the Authority got into such a sorry
state, Pullman replied in an email: "Age. Time. He is subject to change just like
everything else." Even his grandiose title is ironic. Just as the enfeebled Hughes
was ultimately at the mercy of his phalanx of security guards, the Authority has
been sidelined in his own kingdom.

BALTHAMOS

The older and more passive of the two angels who try to bring Will to Lord
Asriel, **Balthamos** is haughty and cowardly – although his love for his partner,
Baruch, is so great that he feels his death, even at a distance. In honour of

Baruch's memory, Balthamos pledges to help Will in any way he can, reluctantly pretending to be his dæmon. When threatened, Balthamos runs away, reappearing at the end, ravaged by grief and guilt, to kill the assassin **Father Gomez**.

Pullman has said that Balthamos was inspired by Lee, the character played by **Robert Vaughn** in *The Magnificent Seven* (1960), also a faint-heart among heroes, who redeems himself dramatically at the end of the movie by saving several prisoners and killing three villains. The inspiration may have been unconscious. "*The Magnificent Seven* has been with me for a very long time, since my boyhood," he said in an interview soon after the books were published. "When I think about it, Balthamos is playing the Robert Vaughn part. When the fight comes, he runs away, but he comes back right at the end and plays an important part."

> "BALTHAMOS IS REALLY PLAYING THE ROBERT VAUGHN PART IN THE MAGNIFICENT SEVEN."

BARUCH

Together with Balthamos, Baruch is one of two **low-ranking angels** who escape Metatron to fight in **Asriel**'s army alongside many of their angelic peers. The younger, stronger, faster and kinder of the pair, he was once a human – the brother of Enoch, who became **Metatron**. He was saved from the land of the dead by Balthamos, "the fount of all knowledge and joy," as he calls him. Although angels are technically asexual, it is strongly suggested Baruch is gay.

Baruch enters the story in *The Subtle Knife*, when he tries to take Will to Asriel. Baruch usefully locates the missing Lyra and tries to bring crucial information to Asriel concerning the girl, the Regent and the subtle knife, but on his approach to the fortress he is injured by enemy scouts and dies, whispering Balthamos's name.

Like Enoch, Baruch is an apocryphal figure in Christian teaching, although the **Book of Baruch** is included in the Greek and Vulgate Bibles. His name comes from the Hebrew Barûkh, meaning blessed.

LORD ASRIEL BELACQUA

As Lyra plays Eve within this reworking of the Biblical story, so **Lord Asriel**, her father, plays **Satan**. Asriel is a tall, dark, powerful man with an animal

THREE REBELS, TWO LORDS, ONE DEVIL

Arrogant, rebellious, always dark and often with a complex sexual history, the heroes of Lord Byron's poetry have a great deal in common with **Asriel** and all have their roots in the proud, passionate, terrifying **Satan** of Milton's *Paradise Lost*.

The protagonist of Byron's *Manfred*, for example, is "an alien, mysterious and gloomy spirit, superior in his passions and powers to the common run of humanity, whom he regards with disdain."

Asriel's goals may be virtuous, but he belongs to a long tradition of Satan-inspired characters, who run throughout Romantic and Gothic literature – from **Schedoni** in Ann Radcliffe's *The Italian* to **Heathcliff** in Emily Brontë's *Wuthering Heights*.

Wild one: Byron is a role model for Asriel

magnetism – about 60 years old – and he impresses and terrifies his daughter (who initially believes him to be her uncle) in roughly equal measure.

A member of the Brytish aristocracy, Asriel lost his fortune in court after killing Edward Coulter, the husband of his lover, **Marisa Coulter**, in a duel. The rest of his history suggests a similarly wild disregard for convention. From John Faa, Lyra discovers that Asriel fought for the **gyptians** in Parliament, and even saved the lives of two gyptian children during the floods of 1953. Elsewhere we learn that he was the lover of the witch queen **Ruta Skadi**, that he is a noted chemist, and that he has "been nursing a rebellion" against the Authority for decades.

If Asriel were to be reduced to a single characteristic, it would have to be resolution. Nothing sways him from his purpose. Imprisoned in Svalbard, he manages to persuade King Iofur Raknison to build him a house more luxurious than his own palace – complete with a laboratory, to continue his work – and he thinks nothing of sacrificing Roger, manipulating his daughter, abandoning Mrs Coulter or triggering climatic chaos (which affects his allies, the bears) as he forges his bridge to the stars.

In this regard, Asriel is again like Milton's **Satan**. His goal may be pure, but such is his ambition that he becomes proud, amoral and even hypocritical. He may be planning to establish a Republic of Heaven, but he remains staunchly aristocratic. At the start of the first novel, he can be found reminding the Butler in Jordan College of his "place", and his appeal to Mrs Coulter – "You and I could take the universe to pieces, and put it together, Marisa!" – hints at the very megalomania he is supposed to be so heroically opposing.

To Lyra at Jordan, Asriel, like his snow leopard dæmon **Stelmaria**, is a cold, glamorous figure who appears only occasionally. In this respect, he is very much like Pullman's own father.

Asriel is not entirely without paternal feeling. He is furious when Lyra appears in Svalbard because she is the only child in the world he would hesitate to "cut". And when Lyra releases the ghosts from the land of the dead, he cannot conceal his delight: "Isn't it something to bring a child like that into the world?"

In the notes by John Parry/Stanislaus Grumman that accompany the tenth anniversary edition of *The Subtle Knife*, we learn that Asriel carried a picture of his daughter ("of whom he was very proud") with him on his travels.

His feelings for **Mrs Coulter** (who, at 35, is young enough to be his daughter) are complex but unquestionably include love – albeit of a competitive, fractious variety. His last words, as he plunges into the abyss, are "Marisa! Marisa!".

PANTALAIMON, LYRA'S DÆMON

Pantalaimon, Lyra's dæmon, appears first in *Northern Lights* as a moth and, when touched by Will at the end of *The Amber Spyglass*, settles as a red-gold pine marten.

Pan is an aspect of Lyra – part-soul and part-conscience – but he is also a separate character, more cautious than the girl and a better judge of character.

It is Pan who recognizes **Mrs Coulter**'s true nature, long before Lyra, and he grasps **Will**'s importance in the Torre degli Angeli almost at once – breaking the taboo to lick his injured hand, which leaves Lyra "breathtaken".

As Lyra grows up, so does Pan. When they part in the world of the dead, they acquire a witch-like ability to travel far from one another, although they remain entirely devoted.

The name Pantalaimon means "all-forgiving" in Greek – and there is a **St Panteleimon** – although its usual abbreviation to Pan also evokes the pagan Greek god. Pullman says the name "just sounded right."

One of Pantalaimon's favourite forms is an ermine, a nod to the painting *Lady With An Ermine*, by **Leonardo da Vinci**, which Pullman loves. In the painting, a young woman believed to be **Cecilia Gallerani** holds an ermine, the symbol of her lover, the Duke of Milan, who commissioned the painting (see p.40).

Pullman has recently revealed that he envisaged **Laurence Olivier** circa 1945 as Asriel. In Hebrew tradition, **Azrael** is the angel of death. In some legends, he provided the handfuls of dirt needed to create Adam and was empowered to separate body and soul – a rather spooky echo of Asriel's role in fatally separating Roger from his dæmon.

Asriel's charismatic ambiguity is such that, even though he doesn't appear at all in *The Subtle Knife*, he is still one of the most intriguing characters in modern fiction. His first name is, weirdly, also an anagram of Israel.

LYRA BELACQUA

As an eleven-year-old orphan living in the labyrinth of Jordan College, in many ways Lyra is the classic children's book hero, untroubled by parental discipline. She is bold, mischievous and intelligent – a "greedy little savage" with dark blonde hair and blue eyes, whose appearance was based on the illustration of "a tough-looking" girl in **Paul Berna**'s *A Hundred Million Francs*. As it turns out, Lyra's parents, Lord Asriel and Mrs Coulter, are very much alive but both are questionable characters, and the girl's loyalties remain firmly her own.

Lyra's loyalties explain much in *His Dark Materials*. Since her *de facto* family are the Scholars of Jordan College and the children of Oxford, when Roger, the Jordan College kitchen boy, is abducted by the General Oblation Board, Lyra has no hesitancy in going to the Arctic to rescue him. He is effectively her brother. Later, when Asriel sacrifices Roger, Lyra is so distraught that she travels to the land of the dead to apologize for her unwitting involvement. She even rids herself of Asriel's surname and becomes **Lyra Silvertongue** – the name given to her by Iorek Byrnison when she tricks the vain, greedy Iofur Raknison into thinking that she is his dæmon.

> "LYRA IS A TRICKSTER, A LIAR, AS HER NAME SUGGESTS, BUT SHE IS ALSO INNOCENT AND UNCALCULATING, AND THIS IS THE KEY TO HER ROLE."

Lyra is a trickster – a liar, as her name suggests if you say it out loud – but she is also innocent and uncalculating, and this, more than anything, is the key to her role in the books. Lyra is the child of destiny, fated to become a "second Eve" and to succumb to the temptation of "the serpent" (Mary Malone) and restore the multiverse to harmony by falling in love. For this to happen, her innocence is essential. As Dr Lanselius puts it, "she must fulfil this destiny in ignorance of what she is doing." In her adventures, Lyra brings "an end to death" by opening the world of the dead, makes "a great betrayal" by leaving **Pantalaimon**, falls in love with **Will Parry** and stops the flood of **Dust** into the abyss.

But, right to the end, she remains unaware of the significance of her actions. She follows her own feelings as much as she does the alethiometer, although she learns to become more perceptive about others' feelings after meeting Will.

The difference, of course, between *His Dark Materials* and the Biblical story is that when Lyra loses her innocence and becomes an adolescent, it is an entirely good thing. On her return to Jordan College, she may be "awkward in her growing body", but she is also on her way to becoming a "beautiful adult".

Pullman started *His Dark Materials* with the aim of telling Lyra's story. Everything else – her parents, Will, even her dæmon – came later. Her name – the term for a small harp and the name of a constellation – came to him the instant he envisaged her. As it sounds like the Latin word for wolf, some have said the name shows he intended to suggest she was a wild child. But there is a less oblique link. **William Blake**, a huge influence on the books, wrote a poem called "The Little Girl Lost" in which a girl called Lyca is conveyed, sleeping, to a cave. A line from the poem opens the first chapter of *The Amber Spyglass*. Lyra is even described as a "little girl lost" when she can't read the alethiometer in *The Subtle Knife*.

"Sir Charles Latrom is poisoned, a fitting end for a fixer who uses too much cologne and whose surname spells 'mortal' backwards."

Lord Boreal

Smooth, sly, powerful, rich, elderly and fatally attracted to Mrs Coulter, **Lord Boreal** – or **Sir Charles Latrom**, as he is known in Will's world – is the only character to have established identities in both Lyra's and Will's world, and, unlike John Parry/Stanislaus Grumman, can travel at will between both to maintain his health. A classic Machiavellian fixer, Boreal/Latrom seems to have strolled into the multiverse from the kind of paranoid political thriller penned by Richard Condon. If it weren't for Latrom, Will would never have realized he was the bearer of the subtle knife. But the randy old goat is seduced by Mrs Coulter, who poisons him after quizzing him about the subtle knife. A fitting end for a man who sweats a lot, wears too much cologne and whose surname Latrom is "**mortal**" spelt backwards.

His name has many meanings. **Boreal** is a species of owl; **Boreas**, in Greek mythology, is the god of the north wind whose arrival signals winter; and **Boreal** is part of Borealis, the word never used to describe the Aurora in the books.

Iorek Byrnison

The rightful king of the panserbjørne, **Iorek Byrnison** first appears in the town of Trollesund, where he is living as a drunkard and a blacksmith, having had his armour stolen by the local people. Lyra's initial impression is of an enormous bear – ten feet tall with small black eyes, yellow-white fur, opposable thumbs and claws the "length of daggers" – but her sympathy for him is immediate. Once she has used the alethiometer to help Iorek recover his armour, he almost becomes a surrogate parent.

As it turns out, Iorek's throne was stolen from him by **Iofur Raknison**, who, in a battle over a female, drugged Iorek's opponent so that he failed to signal surrender. As a result, the opponent died, and Iorek was exiled and became a mercenary – fighting in the **Tunguska** campaign alongside Lee Scoresby. In this capacity, he joins the gyptian attack on the **Bolvangar Experiment Station**. But he is instinctively moral – "pure and certain and absolute" – and he leads the charge to rescue Lyra. Iorek's affection for her becomes all the greater when she tricks Iofur into facing a challenge, allowing Iorek to recover his kingdom. It is he who dubs her Lyra Silvertongue.

Iorek is proudly, defiantly an animal. He has no dæmon and cannot be tricked, but his involvement with humans has its cost. When he agrees to help Will restore the subtle knife, he has doubts for the first time – "Doubt is a human thing, not a bear thing" – and his failure to reach Asriel at the end of *Northern Lights* leads to cataclysmic climate change. In *The Amber Spyglass*, he is seen leading his panserbjørne across Siberia towards the colder climes of the Himalayas, but he soon returns to join the cosmic rebellion.

Like Balthamos and Lee Scoresby, the bear king may owe something to **Westerns**, one of Pullman's favourite movie genres. He is an ursine variation on that most common of Western archetypes: the disgraced hero, drinking to forget, who regains his self-belief to triumphantly vindicate himself, a part the likes of Lee Marvin, Dean Martin and Robert Mitchum have all played many times. For many critics, Iorek is one of the greatest characters in the books. His relationship with Lyra is subtly drawn and there is a sense that he could have so many more stories to tell. After the dæmons, armoured bears may have been Pullman's happiest invention.

THE CHAPLAIN

A very minor character, the Chaplain deserves a mention as the only **virtuous priest** anywhere in *His Dark Materials*. One of the Scholars at Jordan College responsible for Lyra's education, he is described by the Librarian as supporting Asriel and takes a keen interest in Dust. His physical appearance is mentioned only by Lyra, who says his fingernails are even dirtier than hers.

FARDER CORAM

Farder Coram is **gyptian** seer. He is old and crippled, with a "skull-like" face, but warm and good-humoured, as his dæmon, a golden cat named Sophonax, reflects. As a young man, Farder saved **Serafina Pekkala** from a huge, red bird – possibly another witch's **dæmon** – and the two fell in love. They had a son who died in childhood. The books' chronology means, the writer Laurie Frost speculates, the son could have been a victim of the largely forgotten **flu epidemic** of 1957, which directly killed 6,716 people in England and Wales. His death left them heartbroken, and they parted. Serafina sent medicinal herbs when Farder was wounded by a poisoned arrow during the war with the Skrælings, but she can no longer bear to see him in person.

> "FARDER CORAM AND SERAFINA PEKKALA'S SON COULD HAVE DIED IN THE FORGOTTEN FLU EPIDEMIC OF 1957, WHICH TOOK OVER 6,000 LIVES."

Farder's main role is as a tutor and mentor for **Lyra** on their journey to Trollesund. Old, wise and adept in the science of Rusakov Particles (Dust), he can explain how to read an alethiometer and its symbols.

Pullman has hinted that Coram's tragic, youthful romance with Pekkala may yet feature in *The Book Of Dust*.

SPY, DÆMON, MONKEY, AND BAT PERSECUTOR

Mrs Coulter's dæmon, the **golden monkey**, has long, lustrous hair, a black face and claw-like hands, characteristic of a golden lion tamarin.

He is unable to conceal his true nature as effectively as Mrs Coulter and reveals their cruelty to **Pantalaimon**, Lyra's dæmon, almost from their first meeting.

Just like a witch's dæmon, the monkey can travel some distance from Mrs Coulter, which allows him to operate as a spy and, on his first appearance, to snatch Tony Makarios's dæmon, Ratter, while the boy is being distracted by Mrs Coulter.

For a time, Mrs Coulter's growing love for **Lyra** does not seem to affect him quite so acutely. In the Himalayan cave, he expresses his general displeasure by pulling the wings off live bats. But when **Father MacPhail** almost severs him from Mrs Coulter in the silver guillotine, he ultimately falls into line, and by the end he too fights **Metatron** with dæmonic fury.

Unlike many more minor dæmons, the monkey remains nameless throughout the books. Pullman has said that he "doesn't have a name because every time I tried to think of one he snarled and frightened me." Pullman has admitted this dæmon is inspired by a sinister simian in Sheridan Le Fanu's ghost story *Green Tea*.

MARISA COULTER

Mrs Coulter is Lyra's mother and the cruel, intoxicating force who sets the events of *His Dark Materials* in motion. She is about 35, but younger in appearance, with black hair, dark eyes, pale skin and a graceful physique whose power over men she exploits to the limit. "She is completely free of moral restraint," says Pullman. "There is nothing she wouldn't do."

Having failed to win influence through her late husband, the politician **Edward Coulter**, she has turned her attention to the Church and become head of the **General Oblation Board** – abducting and "cutting" children for no better reason it seems than, as Metatron alleges, "lust for power".

When Mrs Coulter arrives at Jordan College, **Lyra** considers her the "most wonderful person I've ever met" and is enchanted by the "kind and wise" lady's stories. The illusion does not last long.

By the time the two are living together in a chic flat in London, Mrs Coulter's golden monkey dæmon is making Lyra "ill with fear". Soon she is desperate to escape.

Various influences have been ascribed to the character of Mrs Coulter. Some have drawn a link with **Ann Coulter**, the American conservative polemicist, but she didn't achieve her peculiar brand of fame until after Pullman had written the first two novels. Adapting the books for the National Theatre, playwright Nicholas Wright and costume designer Jon Morrell thought she should, ideally, be played by **Marlene Dietrich**. The German star being unavailable through death, British actress Patricia Hodge was cast. Hodge has also played the public figure Mrs Coulter is most often likened to in the UK: the steely, resourceful, if unglamorous, **Margaret Thatcher**.

The novelist and literary editor Robert McCrum first made the comparison in his review in *The Observer*. Pullman has publicly accused the former prime minister of creating a kind of "moral anarchy" in Britain, which does rather tally with his remarks about Mrs Coulter's lack of scruple.

Pullman's superb anti-heroine snootily tells Lyra the **Chthonic railway** is "not really for people of their class", a striking parallel to Mrs Thatcher's suggestion that anybody over 30 who travelled on a bus should consider themselves a failure. And, like Thatcher, Mrs Coulter is surrounded by – and usually outwits – a coterie of powerful men.

Mrs Coulter's London life, with its fashionable people and parties, comes straight from Pullman's childhood. For a year after his father's death, he and his brother Francis stayed with their grandparents in Norwich while their mother, **Audrey**, lived in "another dimension of glamour"

> "LYRA NOTICES THAT WHEN HER MOTHER IS ANGRY HER SKIN HAS A 'METALLIC SMELL'. COULTER COMES FROM THE LATIN *CULTER*, MEANING KNIFE."

in Chelsea. Mrs Coulter's polar coldness may reflect the family's view of Audrey as "difficult". Pullman has said she would often "suddenly shut off affection".

This is where the comparison ends. Mrs Coulter is not just distant, she's actively sadistic. Even the researchers at Bolvangar consider her enthusiasm for intercision "**almost ghoulish**". She approaches her goals with rare intelligence and such "force in her soul" that the witch Lena Feldt is struck by it.

Her weakness is her affection for Lyra. From the start, she is trying to come to terms with her maternal feelings, which assert themselves with ever-greater ferocity until, by *The Amber Spyglass*, she has drugged and imprisoned Lyra in a cave in the Himalayas – aware that she would never stay with her voluntarily. Instead of shutting off affection for her daughter, Mrs Coulter slowly turns it on, although her maternal love does have a peculiar narcissistic quality.

Ultimately, this twisted love makes and destroys Mrs Coulter. In her passion for Lyra, she both forgets herself and discovers new depths to her skills – lying

Prime suspect: Mrs Thatcher and Mrs Coulter share a lot, such as a distaste for public transport

"with her whole life" to deceive the mighty **Metatron**. Though she learns the importance of telling the truth in *The Amber Spyglass* before Lyra does, her redemption comes late and at a terrible cost. By luring Metatron into the abyss with Lord Asriel, she saves Lyra's life and the future of existence but commits herself to falling forever.

Mrs Coulter might excuse her obsession with cutting by claiming she is a victim of **nominative determinism**, a term coined by *New Scientist* magazine to describe the amusing tendency for certain people to have names that reflect their jobs. A coulter is a blade, from the Latin word **culter** meaning knife. The point is reinforced when Lyra notices that her mother's skin gives off a "**metallic smell**" when she is angry and an odour of "heated metal". It's hard to know how to take this. This could simply be an amusing pun, Pullman's way of telling us that she is a second subtle knife or a metallic nod to Thatcher, the Iron Lady.

JOHN FAA

Enormously powerful, even in his seventies, John Faa – **Lord Faa**, as he is known – is the King of the Eastern Anglia gyptians. As Lyra notices at once, Faa has the same strength and presence as Lord Asriel, and he shows an Asriel-like resolution as he leads 170 of his men to Bolvangar to free the children being held by the **Oblation Board**. John Faa's close friend is Farder Coram, and, to Lyra at least, Faa is contrastingly huge, scary and dismissive of her as a child. Yet he does show great sensitivity when explaining her true parentage to her. As Will recognizes in the land of the mulefa, he is "a shelter and a strong refuge".

In our world, the name John Faa is shared by several famous gypsies in history – the most prominent of all being Johnny Faa, **King of the Gypsies**, who is said to have run off with the Countess of Cassillis in the 16th century and to have been hanged by her furious husband. Some legends conflate his story with the ballad **Johnnie Faa**, which was sung before this gypsy monarch was born.

FATHER GOMEZ

Yet another nasty priest, Father Luis Gomez – "**trembling with zealotry**" – is the youngest member of the twelve-strong Consistorial Court of Discipline, and the assassin sent by **Father MacPhail** to follow **Mary Malone** and kill **Lyra**. On his mission, he travels through our world to Cittàgazze, and ultimately to the world of the mulefa, where – just as he is aiming his rifle – he is attacked by Balthamos and drowns in the struggle. His body is then eaten by a family of large blue lizards. Although Father Gomez has his own morality, and a horror of hurting anyone he considers innocent, thanks to the doctrine of pre-emptive absolution he has no qualms about murdering those he considers guilty.

> "FATHER GOMEZ HAS HIS OWN MORALITY. HE HAS A HORROR OF HURTING THE INNOCENT BUT NO QUALMS, IF ABSOLVED, ABOUT MURDER."

Juta Kamainen

Juta Kamainen is a red-faced, black-haired witch – young, at a hundred years old, and with a passionate temper. One of twenty **Latvian witches** to join forces with Serafina Pekkala, she is the sentry at the Cittàgazze campsite who follows Will on his walk up the mountain, to ensure his safety. But the appearance of **Stanislaus Grumman** (John Parry), who once spurned her love, fills her with ungovernable hatred. Having killed him with an arrow, she then kills herself.

Hugh MacPhail

Father Hugh MacPhail is a tall, dark Scot made haggard by a strict diet of bread, fruit, water and exercise. As the **President** of the Consistorial Court of Discipline, he can dispense **pre-emptive absolution**, with which he absolves Father Gomez. The most vicious cleric in the books, MacPhail is zealous, manipulative and so fanatically anti-Dust that he kills himself in a final attempt to assassinate Lyra, looking "like some gloomy Spanish painting of a saint in the ecstasy of martyrdom". Fittingly, his dæmon is a lizard.

Dr Mary Malone

The only good nun is a lapsed nun, and **Mary Malone** has gone one better and become principal researcher at a **Dark Matter Research Unit**. Stocky, red-cheeked and close to middle age, Mary lives in the Oxford of our world, where she works in a cash-strapped laboratory containing the *I Ching* and a computer dubbed "the Cave", which, like the amber spyglass, can detect Dust. Mary is the serpent to Lyra's Eve – a force that will bring her to temptation and knowledge

– and, from the moment she smashes her computer, lies to the police and enters Cittàgazze, she is enacting her destiny.

Most of Mary's story takes place in the world of the mulefa. Here, she constructs the amber spyglass and is able to see and understand Dust. Her discoveries lead her to spiritual peace, and, with the help of Serafina Pekkala, she is even able to perceive her dæmon, an **alpine chough**. Here, too, Mary looks after Will and Lyra and tells them her story of lost love – allowing the two to fall in love themselves. Coming from the same world, her relationship with **Will** is crucial. In the appendix to the tenth-anniversary edition, she considers becoming his legal guardian.

The appendix includes some other fragmentary writings by Mary – one as basic as a note to her landlady to let the plumber in – from the Magisterium archives. A postcard she has sent appears in **Lyra's Oxford**, but the scrawled message is so generic it's hard to judge Pullman's future intention. But she is one of his favourite characters. In *The Amber Spyglass*, she even gets to deliver his dismissal of Christianity as "a very powerful and convincing mistake".

Metatron

Officially Regent to the Authority, **Metatron** is, in fact, the principal force of repression in the multiverse. Vain and cruel, he appears to Mrs Coulter as a "tall, powerful" man "in early middle age", but such is his light and his captivating gaze that she can't tell whether, like other angels, he is naked and winged. Metatron has transformed the **Clouded Mountain** into a fortress. He has the strength of a horse, a brilliant intellect honed over four millennia as an angel and two great flaws.

As a man, Metatron was called **Enoch**. He was the great-great-great-great-grandson of Adam and enjoyed the attentions of numerous wives – a weakness that still affects him. His

THE NAMING OF METATRON

There are over a hundred potential origins of the word **Metatron**. Some scholars say it is made up. For others, it springs from the Latin word "Metator" meaning "guide" or "messenger". But its root could be Greek. Some say it stems from two words which, taken together, mean "behind the throne". But it could be derived from two other Greek words that mean "change" and "pass away" – a reference to the way Enoch is taken by God and changed into an angel. Other scholars see parallels with the name **Mithras**, the Persian god. Whatever he is called, in whatever myth, this uppity individual thinks he is God. Truly a legend in his own mind.

other weakness – a blind desire to destroy Lyra – plays him into the hands of Mrs Coulter, whose charms lead him, fatally, to the edge of the abyss.

Although Metatron is not mentioned in the Bible, in the Book of Genesis Enoch is a patriarch. In the apocryphal Books of Enoch, he becomes Metatron and is placed by God on a throne beside his own. In some tales, Enoch and his fellow giant sons of God took human wives but, unable to control their appetites, turned to violence and cannibalism.

Giacomo Paradisi

Will's white-haired predecessor as holder of the subtle knife, **Giacomo Paradisi** is described by Stanislaus Grumman as a "good man, but limited" who is crushed by the burden of bearing the knife. Yet, like an ageing gunslinger passing on trade secrets, he has enough authority to teach Will how to use the knife. Job done, he hands it to Will knowing it means his own certain death. He plans to poison himself before the Spectres torment him.

Colonel John Parry

John Parry (aka **Jopari** and **Dr Stanislaus Grumman**) is a former Royal Marine, the father of **Will** and a legendary explorer in two worlds. In 1985, he left Oxford on an expedition to investigate an "anomaly" in the Arctic, accidentally passed into Lyra's world and was unable to get back. He then became a shaman in a **Siberian Tartar** tribe (where his head was trepanned) and a scholar at Jordan College, but the difference between the worlds has reduced him from the blue-eyed, strong-jawed man remembered by Will's mother to the gaunt, grey-haired, mortally ill figure whom Will encounters in Cittàgazze.

Part-mystic and part-boy scout, John is an ideal figure who bears some relation to Pullman's own missing father. In the books, his most important role is his absence. Will is obsessed with finding him, and when the pair meet, John is barely able to tend his son's wounded hand and to explain his importance as the bearer of the subtle knife before **Juta Kamainen**, a witch whose love he has spurned, shoots him dead with an arrow.

John has a second chance to help Will in the land of the dead, when he shows Will and Lyra how to avoid Father MacPhail's bomb and, with Lee Scoresby, takes on the Spectres, allowing the children to escape. For Will, his words "Well done, my boy" are of overwhelming importance.

The pain of separation from his wife Elaine and son is revealed in the tenth anniversary edition when his handwritten notes break down as he tries to discuss the issue. After several false starts that begin "As for Elaine", he concludes simply: "I cannot speak".

As Grumman, Will's father is obscured by a fog of legends, misapprehension and obfuscation. At various times, people can't decide if he is dead or alive (his supposedly shrunken head is presented by Asriel at the start of the trilogy), English or German, a geologist or an archaeologist. He is also one of the few characters to express much enthusiasm for the idea of a "Republic of Heaven".

There was a famous Arctic explorer called **Sir William Edward Parry** (1790–1855) but John – and Will – could be named to honour **Idris Parry**, the University of Manchester professor whose translation of **Kleist**'s essay *On The Marionette Theatre* introduced Pullman to a writer who became a major influence.

WILL PARRY

Moral and resolute, with brown eyes so fierce that Serafina Pekkala doesn't dare look into them, **Will Parry** is Lyra's dedicated companion. Will is 12 years old and comes from **Winchester** in "our" England, where he lives with his mother **Elaine**. His father, John, had disappeared on an Arctic expedition when he was a baby. On good days Elaine is "full of love and sweetness". More often she is plagued by "enemies" – apparently paranoia and obsessive-compulsive disorder – and, since the age of 7, Will has been forced to look after her at home and to defend her reputation and honour against bullies in the playground.

> "WILL MAY BECOME A DOCTOR, WILL LIVE UNTIL AT LEAST HIS MID-SEVENTIES AND NEVER FORGET LYRA."

As with Lyra, much of Will's character derives from his upbringing. His witch-like ability "not to attract attention" comes directly from school, as does his bravery and his skill at fighting – even though violence does fill him with "a mortal horror". He has also learned the importance of loyalty. When he has to choose between his promise to his father to go to Asriel and his need to find Lyra he feels himself "pulled apart".

As the bearer of the subtle knife, Will loses two fingers, sees his father die, rescues Lyra from a Himalayan cave, frees the ghosts from the land of the dead and finds a world where Lyra can re-enact the fall of Eve. And yet he remains as "implacable" as ever. As Ruta Skadi says, he is "the same kind as **Lord Asriel**".

In the end, Will's discovery of **Lyra** is his discovery of himself. For much of the trilogy, he cannot escape his childhood. When he returns from Cittàgazze to his own world, it is out of a need to find his father, while his most "pressing reason" to repair the subtle knife is to get back to his mother. In Lyra, however, he finds a love of his own, and even though the two must part, it is through her that he becomes able to see his dæmon, a black-and-grey cat named **Kirjava**.

Asked once what he thought would become of Will, Pullman replied: "I think he will go home and find that his mother is already in hospital, being looked after. I think Mary will help him make everything straight about the man he killed. Later I think he'll go to medical school and become a doctor." We do know, from the phrase "sixty years and more would go by" in *The Amber Spyglass*, that he lives until at least his mid-seventies and never forgets Lyra.

ROGER PARSLOW

The kitchen boy at Jordan College, **Roger Parslow** is Lyra's close friend and a crucial voice of caution in her early adventures – although he mostly plays the books' great victim. Having been kidnapped by the **General Oblation Board**, Roger is taken to the Experiment Station at **Bolvangar**, where he is rescued by Lyra. He helps to release the other children but is soon kidnapped again – this time by **Lord Asriel**, who severs him from his dæmon, **Salcilia**, to blast a hole to Cittàgazze. Even in death Roger remains woefully passive. In Lyra's dreams, he calls to her pitifully. Because of her unwitting part in his murder – sometimes, Pullman seems to be telling us, good people can make bad things happen – she decides to go to the land of the dead and apologize. When Lyra and Roger's ghost are finally reunited, Roger becomes the first ghost to pass through the window cut by Will and evaporate outside.

SERAFINA PEKKALA

Pale, blue-eyed and beautiful – with a wreath of scarlet flowers in her fair hair – **Serafina Pekkala** is the queen of a clan of witches from Lake Enara. Like all witches, she is able to travel far from her dæmon **Kaisa**, a snow goose, and she can live to a great age – already, she is three hundred years old – but her bravery, compassion and devotion to Lyra are all her own.

Forty years before the events of the books, Serafina was saved from drowning by **Farder Coram**, and as the gyptians travel north towards Bolvangar, he decides to call in the debt. The two have a long and tragic history, but Serafina responds immediately, and her obligation to Farder becomes genuine commitment to their cause when Kaisa explains the horrors being perpetrated by the **General Oblation Board**. From this point, Serafina is one of Lyra's staunchest allies. In Bolvangar, she saves Lyra and Roger from the clutches of Mrs Coulter, and in Cittàgazze, she saves Lyra and Will from the children orphaned by the Spectres. Her ruthlessness is the equal of her kindness. In *The Subtle Knife*, she enters the torture chamber on the Church's ship, puts one of her clan out of her misery and fights her way out again, dispensing death and dodging bullets.

Pullman has revealed that Serafina's name came from a **Helsinki telephone directory**. Pekkala certainly sounds Finnish, but there are plenty of Italian restaurants around the world called Serafina.

IOFUR RAKNISON

The usurper-king of the panserbjørne, **Iofur Raknison** is vain, greedy and treacherous. In contrast with Iorek Byrnison, he has a strong desire to be human and has built a human-style civilization in Svalbard – complete with art, trade, universities, a stone palace and armour so ornamented it is almost camp. The gold leaf that sheaths his six-inch claws is either a precursor of **bling** or a sign that he needs a new personal stylist. He has even formed an alliance with the Oblation Board, and it is thanks to **Mrs Coulter** that he acquired the herb with which he drugged Hjalmur Hjalmurson – forcing Iorek Byrnison into exile. These human affectations have diluted Iofur's integrity as a panserbjørn and damaged his immunity to tricks. Lyra exploits this weakness when she persuades him that she is Iorek's dæmon and that he should face Iorek in a duel – giving the real king his chance to recover the throne.

LEE SCORESBY

A cool, laconic Texan in Svalbard, **Lee Scoresby** is as much a combination of the actor **Lee van Cleef** and the 19th century Arctic explorer **William Scoresby** as his name suggests. In appearance, he is all Van Cleef. Tall and "whiplash-lean", with his narrow black moustache and blue eyes, he is the rugged adventurer of *The Good, The Bad, And The Ugly* – although, unlike the character **Angel Eyes**, he

Split personality: laconic, iconic Lee van Cleef was half the inspiration for Lee Scoresby

is kind, polite and averse to violence. Lee is an "aëronaut" balloonist, prospector and mercenary, who saved Iorek Byrnison's life in the Tunguska campaign, but his dream is to retire to Texas with a cigar, a glass of bourbon, a few head of cattle and, just possibly, Serafina Pekkala – who he not so secretly hankers after (though he never reveals his feelings to her).

Even his aphorisms sound fresh off the range. Arguing with Grumman about the need to defend the Spectre orphans, he says: "Seems to me the place where you fight cruelty is the place where you find it, and the place you give help is where you see it needed." Or, as **Randolph Scott** once put it, "There are some things a man can't ride around."

In Trollesund, Lee is hired by the gyptians to help the children at Bolvangar, and while he remains in Lyra's company for only a few days, he becomes one of her most useful and devoted friends. During the battle with Mrs Coulter and the Tartars, he saves Lyra, Roger and Iorek with his balloon. He loses the girl when they are attacked by cliff-ghasts but remains fiercely loyal – setting out to find both her and the subtle knife, which he believes will protect her.

When he and Grumman are trapped in a narrow gorge, Lee allows Grumman to escape before staging his own recreation of the battle of the **Alamo**, shooting eighteen Muscovites and blowing up a zeppelin before he and Hester, his hare dæmon, die at high noon. Even death cannot kill his heroism. As a ghost, he holds back the Spectres so Lyra and Will can escape to the world of the mulefa.

CHEVALIER TIALYS

Human in appearance but small enough to ride a red-and-yellow dragonfly, Chevalier Tialys is a **Gallivespian** who compensates for his size by being arrogant and self-involved. But he is honourable and – working for Asriel – a fine spy. He and his companion, Lady Salmakia, arrive in the Himalayas in *The Amber Spyglass* to protect Will and Lyra and bring them safely to Asriel. They stun Mrs Coulter and kill the Swiss guards with their poisonous spurs, and they even accompany the children to the land of the dead, where Tialys discovers the **harpies'** weakness for true stories. He and Salmakia are 8 years old and nearing the end of their lives, but his death, fighting cliff-ghasts, grieves Will.

XAPHANIA

The most heroic of all angels, **Xaphania** is one of Lord Asriel's high commanders and, it is suggested, the angel who led the first angelic rebellion – having discovered that the **Authority** was not the creator, as he had claimed.

Like other angels, Xaphania is winged, naked and luminous – although she appears "not shining, but shone on", and such is her rank and enormous age ("her lined face was older than that of any living creature Mrs Coulter had ever seen") that she is clearly visible to the human eye. It is she who finds the entrance to the abyss, into which Asriel, Metatron and Mrs Coulter will finally plunge. And she has the unenviable task of tidying up afterwards. With her characteristic blend of firmness and kindness (echoing Michael in *Paradise Lost*), she explains to Will and Lyra the importance of **Dust**, the fact that only one window can remain open and that the subtle knife must be destroyed.

HIS DARK MATERIALS
The Inspirations

THE
HOLY
BIBLE,

Conteyning the Old Testament,
AND THE NEW:

Newly Translated out of the Originall
tongues: & with the former Translations
diligently compared and reuised, by his
Maiesties speciall Comandement.

Appointed to be read in Churches.

Imprinted at London by Robert
Barker, Printer to the Kings
most Excellent Maiestie.

ANNO DOM. 1611.

◀ It all starts here: without The Bible, Milton wouldn't have written *Paradise Lost*, which would have made it impossible for Pullman to imagine *His Dark Materials*

SOURCE MATERIALS

Your guide to the grumpy poets, mistrusted visionaries and suicidal essayists behind Pullman's masterpiece

o novel is written in a literary vacuum. And Philip Pullman has been more open about this than most authors. "I have stolen from every book I have ever read," he flatly admits in the acknowledgements to *The Amber Spyglass*. And he hasn't just stolen from books. Asked to name a **movie** that had influenced him – apart from *The Magnificent Seven* – he said in an email: "Too many to list. Every time I see a well-turned bit of plot or a surprising (and truly expressive – most are not) camera angle, or hear a soundtrack that deepens and clarifies the story (*Eraserhead*) I steal it at once." Any chapter tracing his inspirations faces an obvious problem: where to stop?

It's easier to know where to start: **The Bible**, without which the novels would not exist, and the "three debts" that he acknowledges above all the rest at the end of *The Amber Spyglass*: to John Milton's *Paradise Lost*, the works of William Blake and Heinrich von Kleist's essay *On The Marionette Theatre*. Some novels and novelists – Mikhail Bulgakov's *The Master And Margarita* and the works of **Michael Moorcock** and **Ursula K. Le Guin** – he has deliberately tried to stay away from because, he said in an email, "I tend to avoid people I might be too easily tempted to steal from. We all steal all the time, of course, but I like to steal from unexpected places." Many of those unexpected places are acknowledged in the epigraphs that start each chapter in *The Amber Spyglass* (see p.126).

THE BIBLE

The fundamental influence on *His Dark Materials* is, of course, **The Bible**, and particularly the first three chapters of Genesis, which describe God's creation of Adam and Eve, who live in innocent contentment in the Garden of Eden until the serpent (only later identified with Satan) tempts Eve to eat from the Tree of Knowledge, and they are cast out into the world. As **Lord Asriel** puts it, Adam and Eve are "like the square root of minus one: you can never see any concrete proof that it exists, but if you include it in your equations, you can calculate all manner of things that couldn't be imagined without it." In *His Dark Materials*, Lyra re-enacts **the Fall** – reversing the Biblical message, with knowledge leading to fulfilment, not evil – but the essential story also illuminates all three books and the thematic movement from innocence to experience.

> "I LOVE THE LANGUAGE AND THE ATMOSPHERE OF THE KING JAMES BIBLE AND THE BOOK OF COMMON PRAYER"

As well as the events of the Fall, the books are littered with Biblical references. The first angelic rebellion is drawn in part from the Book of Revelation and many other allusions lurk in the text. When Lee Scoresby asks the dying Magisterium's censor why he was trying to kill him, the censor replies "By their fruits shall ye know them" (Matthew 7:16). Mrs Coulter describes her love for Lyra as "a mustard seed", an allusion to Jesus' parable of the mustard seed and later tells the Regent, "Keep behind me Metatron", an obvious reference to Jesus' phrase "Get thee behind me, Satan" which appears twice in the Gospels.

The Bible of Lyra's world is quoted at length. In style, it is the same as the **1611 King James** version, except that the Fall is associated with the "settling" of the dæmon – so that, for instance, "And the eyes of them both were opened, and they knew that they were naked" (Genesis 3:7) becomes "And the eyes of them both were opened, and they saw the true forms of their dæmons."

For all his outspoken atheism, Pullman has admitted, "I love the language and the atmosphere of the King James Bible and the 1662 *Book Of Common Prayer*". You can find proof of that love throughout *His Dark Materials*.

THE LIFE OF MILTON

John Milton (1608–74) was an English poet, political radical and civil servant who, among other things, coined the word satanic. He grew up in Cheapside, in London, and studied at Christ's College, Cambridge, where, with his long hair and poetic inclinations, he was known as the "Lady of Christ's".

In 1638, he made a tour of France and Italy – where he met such luminaries as the astronomer Galileo and developed a hatred for confessional, authoritarian Catholicism – but he returned home at the start of the **English Civil War** and began to write tracts on behalf of Oliver Cromwell's Parliamentarians.

He published several pamphlets – including *Areopagitica*, his famous attack on censorship – and in 1649 was appointed Secretary for Foreign Tongues in the Parliamentarian government. But by 1654 he was blind, and he had to dictate his work, including *Paradise Lost*. Even after Cromwell's death in 1658, he clung to his republican principles. With the restoration of **Charles II**, he hid for a time (he had written a famous tract defending the execution of Charles I).

His magnum opus, *Paradise Lost*, was published in 1667 (a second edition, in 1674, explained why the poem didn't rhyme), with *Paradise Regained* following in 1671. Milton died of kidney failure in 1674 and was buried in the church of St Giles, Cripplegate.

PARADISE LOST

Pullman first encountered Milton's epic poem as a sixteen-year-old student, and found it "intensely enthralling" – although he studied only the first two books at the time. Later, the most famous epic poem by an Englishman would provide the spark for Pullman's greatest success, being so influential that he once described the novels as "*Paradise Lost* for teenagers".

The poem retells the first three chapters of Genesis and aims to "justifie the wayes of God to men". It opens (with due drama) with **Satan** and his fellow rebel angels in Hell, chained to a lake of fire. In defiance of God, they decide to corrupt His creation, Earth, so Satan and his children, Death and Sin, escape their bonds and set off. Arriving at the **Garden of Eden** (in book four), Satan, wracked with envy and malice and becoming ever more grotesque, assumes the forms of a cormorant, a toad and a serpent to insinuate his way inside. He tempts **Eve** – which results in her and Adam's expulsion by God.

William Blake, who studied the poem, said Milton was "of the Devil's party without knowing it", a point that is particularly convincing in the first two books, where Satan is depicted as proud, vengeful, liberating and even heroic.

Visions of paradise: one of John Martin's 1823 illustrations for *Paradise Lost*

It is hard to avoid drawing parallels between Satan's predicament and Milton's own life. Milton wrote *Paradise Lost* between 1658 and 1664, amid the last days of Oliver Cromwell's **Protectorate**, the Puritan rebellion that had been his life's cause. Satan is certainly a much more sympathetic and nuanced character than you might have expected from a Puritan, and, in a sense, Pullman follows these trends to their natural conclusion by making the rebellion morally necessary. As he has said repeatedly, "I am of the Devil's party, and I know it."

Aside from these major links between the two works (the Satan role being divided between **Lord Asriel**, **Mary Malone** and, briefly, **Father Gomez**) there are others that are more subtle. One is the title itself, which comes from book two: "Unless the Almighty maker them ordain / His dark materials to create more worlds." Another is the conflict between fate and free will. As Serafina Pekkala says, Lyra must pursue her adventures "as if it were her nature and not her destiny", much the same conflict faced by Eve in *Paradise Lost*.

The tone of the poem, too, is crucial to the books – particularly *The Amber Spyglass*. Lord Asriel, for instance, launches his cosmic rebellion from a fortress

MONARCHS AND MONSTERS IN PARADISE

Milton's masterpiece has proved flexible enough to be interpreted as accusing monarchs, damning Cromwell and bemoaning the alienation of modern man

Paradise Lost was not a bestseller. Published in **1667**, during the reign of Charles II, it sold **3000** copies in eleven years. Milton, a prominent Cromwellian, was in disgrace. Rather than backtrack, he wrote *Paradise Regained* and *Samson Agonistes*, coded accounts of the defeat of the English Commonwealth and prophecies of the fall of the Stuarts and the return of a republican state.

One interpretation of *Paradise Lost* says that Satan is, in part, a portrait of **Charles I**. The house of Stuart did fall – swept away by the **Glorious Revolution** of 1688 – but Milton was not alive to rejoice or to savour the republication of *Paradise Lost* by **Jacob Tonson** who used drawings, mostly by the Belgian artist John Baptiste Medina (1659–1710), to suggest that **James II**, the last Stuart monarch, was a satanic figure.

Tonson and his nephews reprinted *Paradise Lost* again and again – there were sixty separate editions between 1770 and 1825 – and through their efforts the poem was rediscovered and assumed a central place in the English imagination. William Wordsworth, J.M.W. Turner and William Blake would all pay homage to *Paradise Lost*, often reinterpreting it for their own ends.

In Blake's illustrations, for example, Satan looks like a worried idealist. There's still some of Charles I left in him but there's a trace of the worst of **Oliver Cromwell** in his last years as Protector in there too.

To Wordsworth and Blake, Milton was a brave dissident fighting for freedom. But 19th-century illustrations by **John Martin** and **Gustave Doré** eschewed heroism, depicting a modern alienation that seems influenced by Mary Shelley's *Frankenstein*. Martin's illustrations, with their minuscule figures menaced by dark, swirling patterns, suggest that we are all – even Satan – pawns in a universe that is completely out of control.

Satanic majesty: was Charles I Milton's model?

that echoes Satan's "infernal court" Pandaemonium (one of the words the poem introduced to the English language), while Will and Lyra's discovery of love in – and exile from – "their gold-and-silver grove" is Milton's Garden of Eden all over.

Pullman's advocacy – and homage – has helped restore the poem's reputation, which has never quite recovered from being criticized as "withered by book learning" by **T.S. Eliot**. The author of *The Waste Land* said that *Paradise Lost* "could only be an influence for the worse", a contention that Pullman has surely disproved.

WILLIAM BLAKE

Milton's impact on *His Dark Materials* is immense and immediately obvious. **William Blake**'s influence is subtler, although his appearance in nine of the 37 chapter-opening epigraphs in *The Amber Spyglass* is convincing evidence of his importance.

Pullman's attitude towards authority – particularly repressive religion – has clearly been affected by Blake's. In "Garden of Love", for instance, Blake describes a garden of innocent pleasure transformed into a graveyard, and a chapel of priests "binding with briars my joys and desires".

Nor does he restrict his fury to the Church. In "Earth's Answer", he denounces a vain, selfish Old Testament

A VISIONARY LIFE

William Blake (1757–1827) was a visionary English poet, artist and printmaker. He lived most of his life in London, where he was apprenticed at fourteen to an engraver, James Basire, and studied art at the Royal Academy.

From a very young age, Blake was subject to visions. At ten, he claims to have seen a tree full of **angels** in Peckham Rye, and throughout his life felt he was guided by archangels.

In 1773, Blake set up a print shop at 27 Broad Street, London, with his wife, Catherine – an enterprise that failed after the death of his brother in 1787. Blake never achieved success or recognition in his lifetime. Indeed, he was generally regarded as mad, and he illustrated and printed such classic works as *Songs Of Innocence* (1789), *The Marriage Of Heaven And Hell* (1790) and *Songs Of Experience* (1794) himself.

He was a strong believer in free love and racial and sexual equality, and supported the revolutions in America and France, although he abhorred the **Reign of Terror**. Though he died in poverty, Blake persisted in his idiosyncratic views, and his influence on later generations has been immense. As well as Pullman, who, with "a jolt of shocked recognition", first saw Blake's illustrations of **Dante**'s *Inferno* in 1970, his work has influenced **W. B. Yeats**, **James Joyce** and **Aldous Huxley**. His etched *Songs* and prophetic books helped inspire the **graphic novel**.

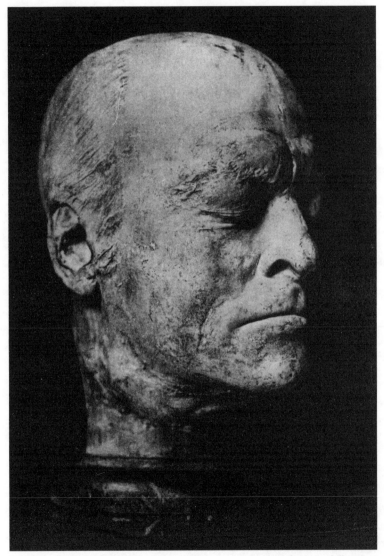

The face of genius: the death mask of William Blake, who was a major influence on Pullman

THE ALLUSIONIST

His Dark Materials is thick with other writers. To start with, there are the epigraphs that start the chapters in *The Amber Spyglass*. As well as The Bible, Milton and Blake, you'll find here lines from Samuel Taylor Coleridge, Emily Dickinson, Edmund Spenser, John Ruskin, John Webster, Lord Byron, John Donne, Andrew Marvell, John Keats, George Herbert, Christina Rossetti and Pindar. The book is prefaced by poems from Rainer Maria Rilke, John Ashbery and a hymn by Robert Grant.

As if all these weren't enough – or enough claim to importance – many other works and writers are alluded to in the text itself.

These include **Dante**, whose plan of the vestibule of Hell in the *Inferno* looks very like the land of the dead; St Augustine, whose thoughts on angels Mary Malone remembers; Plato whose allegory of the cave gives the Cave its name; and various Greek myths about harpies and Hell's boatman, Charon. Keats reappears in *The Subtle Knife* when Mary explains to Lyra how to communicate with the Cave.

The scene in which Siegfried reforges Siegmund's sword in *The Ring Cycle* by **Richard Wagner** appears to have inspired Iorek Byrnison's reforging of the subtle knife (though some Tolkienites cite *Lord Of The Rings* as a model too).

Among many, many other allusions, by retaining the names of pre-Henry VIII Oxford colleges, Pullman recalls *The Alteration* by **Kingsley Amis**, an alternate history novel in which the Reformation never took place.

God that "free love with bondage bound". The Bible and *Paradise Lost* may have provided the structure of *His Dark Materials*, but Blake provided the approach. Pullman reread Blake's work while writing the novels, believing this would help keep him on course.

Like Milton, Blake lived through a time of great political and social upheaval – with revolutions in America and France. His prophetic books turned contemporary politics into a cosmic struggle between **Urizen**, a tyrannical God, and **Orc**, a "Lover of Wild Rebellion, and transgressor of God's Law." Orc is creative and passionate but self-obsessed and full of the seeds of megalomania. There are many parallels between Orc and **Lord Asriel**, and this alternative creation myth – with its roots in early 19th century politics – is a distant prototype of *His Dark Materials*.

Other Blakeian influences are harder to pinpoint. Blake was an artist and printmaker as well as a poet, and some have suggested that his illuminations spurred Pullman to design the woodcuts in *Northern Lights* and *The Subtle Knife*.

Lyca, the protagonist of Blake's poems "The Little Girl Lost" and "Little Girl Found", is an obvious source for Lyra's name. And her growth from innocence to experience spins off some of Blake's most famous poems.

There are many small homages to the poet in the books. To take just two examples: the poem "The Smile" (alluded to when Will sees Mrs Coulter smile) and the painting *Ancient Of Days* (when Mrs Coulter is discussing the Authority's decrepitude with Father MacPhail). Blake was also obsessed by **Spectres**, though to him they were dark forces in the psyche, not monsters that killed others.

"ORC, CREATIVE, PASSIONATE, BUT FULL OF THE SEEDS OF MEGALOMANIA, HAS MANY PARALLELS WITH LORD ASRIEL."

But Blake's most important influence on Pullman remains his interpretation of the Christian message. A poem like "Earth's Answer" may condemn the authoritarian God of the Old Testament, but it also appeals for a return to grace. This paradox lies at the heart of *His Dark Materials*. Blake turns away from an Old Testament God, but turns towards a New Testament God, divorced from dogma and asceticism. This is echoed by Pullman who, with his omniscient, omnipresent, all-good **Dust**, is not so much "killing God", as he so often says, as reclaiming Him from Christianity.

On The Marionette Theatre

Heinrich von Kleist (1777–1811) was a Prussian playwright and essayist whose life was short and tragic. In 1792, he followed family tradition and joined the army – serving in the Rhine campaign in 1796 – but left in 1799 to study law and philosophy at Viadrina University. He was stimulated by the works of **Immanuel Kant**, who argued that reason cannot uncover the true nature of reality, but after a series of failed plays and stories (now considered major works of German literature), in 1811 he entered a **suicide pact** with one Henriette Vogel and shot himself on the shores of the Wansee.

The year before his death, Kleist wrote his philosophical essay, *On The Marionette Theatre*, which Pullman first read in 1978. The essay describes an encounter between the narrator and a dancer friend, who expresses an unfashionable passion for the marionette theatre. His argument goes that physical grace comes either with "no consciousness or an infinite consciousness".

That is to say, a dancer can only be truly graceful without any self-consciousness or affectation, and therefore the greatest dancer must be ultimately innocent or ultimately wise, a puppet or a God.

Kleist illustrates the point by citing the example of a teenage boy who possesses great physical grace until he notices his own similarity to a statue – at which point he becomes self-conscious and awkward.

He also tells of an occasion when he tried to fence a bear, which, having no self-consciousness, rebutted his attacks while ignoring his feints entirely. This inability to be tricked was transferred directly to the panserbjørne in *His Dark Materials*. Pullman pays tribute in *Northern Lights* when Lyra "fences" with Iorek Byrnison.

One connection made by Pullman, but not by Kleist, is in the use of the word **grace**. For Kleist, grace refers to a naturalness of being, whereas Pullman expands this definition into theological territory with its sense of "the unmerited favour of God" (or, in his case, **Dust**). Not that Kleist avoids religion. In a sense, the connection makes itself since the reason humans are not graceful is, Kleist says, because "we've eaten at the tree of knowledge" and the only way that we can return to grace – and paradise – is to "make the journey around the world and see if it is perhaps open somewhere at the back."

This outlook has found its way

THE NARNIA CONTROVERSY

Pullman's loathing for C.S. Lewis's Narnia series – "one of the most ugly and poisonous things I've ever read" – is in a league of its own, though he and Lewis have much in common.

Both taught in Oxford. Both lost a parent in childhood. Both wrote novels in which children enter a cosmic, essentially Christian struggle across magical worlds and ultimately save the day. The killing of Aslan and the bearer of the subtle knife both allude to the sacrificial killing of the king in some pagan myths. At the start of *Northern Lights*, Lyra even hides in a wardrobe. Pullman says this was an accident, even if he enjoys it as "a sort of riposte to the worldview" of the Narnia books.

Among Pullman's many criticisms of Lewis is his **misogyny** and distaste at the onset of sexuality. Famously, Susan doesn't appear in *The Last Battle* because she's "interested in nothing nowadays except nylons and lipstick and invitations" – which does rankle in these politically correct times. In response, **Peter Hitchens** pointed to the various gypsies, African princes and homosexual angels among Pullman's heroic characters and dubbed him "the anti-Lewis". And that is the point. Lewis wrote conservative, Christian novels exalting God. Pullman writes liberal, atheistic novels "about killing God". The two writers' intolerance mirror one another perfectly.

deep into the philosophy of *His Dark Materials*. As she gains knowledge and discovers love with Will, Lyra loses her ability to use the alethiometer and becomes "awkward in her growing body". But she also takes the first steps towards wisdom and a higher form of grace, and, with the alethiometer, sets out "to learn consciously what [she] could once do by intuition". From what Pullman has said, learning won't be easy. "If we work hard and we train ourselves like a dancer, if we undergo all kinds of discipline, pain, suffering, and so forth, we can regain grace." And this grace, he says, is more valuable because it combines grace, beauty and wisdom. Which might make all the discipline, pain, suffering and so forth worthwhile. Or not.

HOMER, THE STORYTELLER

In twelve years of teaching, Pullman reckoned he must have told the stories of Homer's *Iliad* and *Odyssey* 36 times. "The result is that I now have those stories entirely in my head, from beginning to end, and I can call them up whenever I want to." He was lucky, he says, taking a swipe at recent educational reforms, that he had the freedom to decide he would teach his class Greek myths and Homer's stories for a year. "By a lucky chance, it was the best possible training for a writer," he says in his column "I Have a Feeling This All Belongs to Me" on his website. "To tell great stories over and over and over again, testing and refining the language and observing the reactions of the listeners and gradually improving the timing and the rhythm and the pace, was to undergo an apprenticeship that probably wasn't very different from the one Homer underwent three thousand years ago."

But Homer's influence on the books extends beyond a masterclass in timing, rhythm and pace. Pullman sees himself as part of a tradition of **storytelling** that stretches back to Homer.

The jury is still out on whether someone called Homer actually

Mystery man: did Homer look like this?

existed. Most scholars think that such a man, possibly an **aodoi**, an oral poet, was responsible for the *Odyssey* and the *Iliad* , which probably date from the 8th or 7th centuries BC. Tradition says that Homer was blind. Various Ionian cities and the island of Chios claim to be his birthplace. But we have no idea what he looked like, so all illustrations – such as the famous bust on the previous page – are mere suppositions. **Robert Graves**, in his novel *Homer's Daughter*, suggested the poems were written by a Sicilian woman, a theory first expounded by **Samuel Butler**.

> "HOMER MAY HAVE BEEN A BLIND GREEK POET OR, IF YOU BELIEVE ROBERT GRAVES, A SICILIAN WOMAN."

As late as the 14th century, Homer was largely unknown in the West. Knowledge of Greek had declined as Latin spread throughout Europe, and the first 'modern' edition of his works was not published until 1488 in Italy. Today, he is probably the most studied author after Shakespeare.

There are scenes – notably Lyra and Will's visit to the **world of the dead** – where Pullman's debt to Homer is too striking to ignore. Their descent parallels Odysseus's travails with the fleshless spirits in the underworld in **Nekya**, the eleventh book of the *Odyssey*. Homer's hero has to use his sword and a dead sheep to escape. But it is Lyra's ability to tell stories that lead her and Will out of the world of the dead.

The virtual absence of printed books in the trilogy is further testimony to the power of Homeric storytelling. The only two books mentioned by name are the *I Ching* and The Bible. The emphasis elsewhere – not just with Lyra and the harpies but also with the mulefa – is on oral storytelling. Lyra's idea that storytelling is something natural "like running and singing" harks back to the aodoi who, in ancient Greece, were singers as well as poets.

But Homer's biggest gift to *His Dark Materials* is the epic sweep and mythic power of the narrative and the gift of keeping us continually curious. Pullman's trilogy is even more geographically ambitious than Homer's most famous work, aspires to achieve a similar mythic quality and, even after three novels, has left most readers wanting more.

··✝··

HIS DARK MATERIALS
The Science

Scientific Fiction

The quantum physics, superstring theory, WIMPs and psychological truths that infuse *His Dark Materials*

"Do I believe in the multiverse?" Philip Pullman replied in an email for this Rough Guide. "I believe in anything that helps me to write. Fairies, ghosts, whatever. The multiverse is in a different category from those, being the subject of sound scientific theory, as far as I can understand it, but I can't see or feel that either; so it has to be a matter of belief."

Science has fired novelists' imaginations since the days of **Jules Verne** and **Robert Louis Stevenson**. What makes Pullman distinctive, as his remark about science in *His Dark Materials* implies, is that his capacious literary imagination finds room for such cutting-edge scientific concepts as dark matter, parallel universes and entanglement theory alongside such age-old practices as shamanism, alchemy and sympathetic magic.

For a brilliantly written and much longer discussion of the books' scientific dimension, hunt down a copy of *The Science Of His Dark Materials* by John and Mary Gribbin. The aim here is not to duplicate what the Gribbins have done but to explore the main scientific issues raised in the trilogy and shed light on some other aspects of the science in the fiction, like bears, dark energy and why we need a subtle knife to prove there is more than one universe.

"WE'RE ALL SONS OF BITCHES NOW"

At dawn on 16 July 1945, in a place in the American desert called the **Jornada del Muerto** (Journey of Death), a flash of light like the human eye had never seen before signalled the explosion of the world's first **atomic bomb**. The scientists involved knew that nuclear weaponry would change the world, but only a few sensed that it would change science.

The test director **Kenneth Bainbridge** is reputed to have said: "We are all sons of bitches now." If he didn't say it, he ought to have done, because the sentiment was spot on. The invention of a technology that could destroy the world many times over changed the image of science for good. The men in white coats were no longer a secular priesthood, heroes curing diseases, they were shifty, arrogant geeks who might destroy mankind for the sake of an experiment or out of intellectual hubris. As science has become ever more complex, the public, educated to believe in scientific certainty through such fables as **Isaac Newton** and his apple, has become increasingly confused. This is particularly true as scientists – even on an issue as apparently simple as whether eggs are good, bad or indifferent for us – keep changing their mind.

In the scientific dialectic, one scientist proposes something in a learned journal and it is then disproved, amended or qualified by other scientists. This is too nuanced for the media and the public. To make matters worse, scientists have an annoying habit of confronting us with divisive issues – such as stem cell research – that humanity often doesn't fully understand and would rather not face.

How much of this distrust infuses the way science and scientists are portrayed in *His Dark Materials*? The books are full of warnings about

> "I READ AS MUCH SCIENCE AS I COULD UNDERSTAND. THE SUBJECT IS INTOXICATING TO SPECULATE ABOUT."

the perils of intellectual arrogance, most notably when **Lord Asriel** builds a bridge between worlds and doesn't care about the consequences. The "men of learning" whose arrogant prodding broke up particles to release the Spectres in **Cittàgazze** are rebuked, and the heroism of Mary Malone is balanced by the grubby careerism of her colleague Oliver Payne.

Pullman never decisively chooses between the heroic optimism of Verne and the stark pessimistic prophecy of **Mary Shelley**. In the books – as in real life – Pullman is too enthused by scientific possibilities to damn science as thoroughly as he does religion. A gifted amateur like Asriel can change the worlds for the worse with his scientific experiments, but the scientists themselves – even the untrustworthy Payne – are, at worst, pawns in the schemes of such smoothly sinister types as **Sir Charles Latrom**. As the Church, in all its oppressive forms, seems to regard science as a threat or something that must be controlled, it is hard not to conclude that science is, with a few caveats, generally a Good Thing.

Pullman was, he admits, fascinated by the subject at home and bored by it at school. In an email for this book, he said: "I read as much as I could understand. The whole subject is so fascinating and extraordinary that it is intoxicating to speculate about." The uncertainty, the theories and the speculation seemed to inspire, not deter, Pullman. "I did feel obliged to get not so much the science accurate but the stuff going on around the science: scrabbling for funds, being tempted by well-funded but morally questionable projects, that sort of thing." His main concern, he has said elsewhere, was to give the science enough solidity so that it wouldn't look foolish to any science-literate reader. He has certainly done that.

THE SCIENCE OF DUST

The meaning of **Dust**, one of the great riddles in *His Dark Materials*, is yet another reason fans can hardly wait for *The Book Of Dust*. But even that companion volume is hardly likely to settle the debate. These elementary particles are a sparkling puzzle. In an interview on Readerville.com, Pullman waxed lyrical about the stuff: "Dust permeates everything in the universe and existed before we individuals did and will continue after us… we are partners and equals with Dust in the great project of keeping the universe alive." Or, as **Balthamos** puts it: "Matter loves matter. It seeks to know more about itself and Dust is formed." The experimental theologian **Boris Mikhailovitch Rusakov** concluded that these particles don't interact with each other but are attracted to humans and have existed for an indeterminate time.

Dust is inspired by the famous line in Genesis ("for dust thou art, and unto dust shalt thou return") and the poetry of **William Blake**. (The epigraph to Chapter 34 in *The Amber Spyglass*, "Shew you all live / The world, where every particle of dust breathes forth its joy", is from Blake's poem "Europe: A Prophecy".) To the angels, Dust is what they are made out of. Even the **Authority** is made out of

Dust, which makes the Church's view – that this stuff is the root of original sin – a bit odd. To Lyra, eyeing up skulls in the Pitt Rivers museum, Dust is inextricably linked to human consciousness. The mulefa call this stuff "**sraf**". Elsewhere, Dust is the form of thoughts not yet born, shadow-particles and the stuff we become when we die. Yet to Asriel, Dust is a poor substitute for flesh, which makes the angels envy humanity.

> "OUR PARTICLES ARE STRANGE LITTLE DEVILS, MAKE NO MISTAKE. YOU KNOW WHAT? THEY'RE CONSCIOUS."

The suggestion that we are absorbed by nature when we die owes something to the ancient Greek idea that the world – which they called Gaia – is a living organism, an idea adapted by **James Lovelock**, whose views Pullman has cited on his website. To Lovelock, the whole Earth is alive. After monitoring the many ways that rocks, gases and species interact on Earth, he came to the conclusion that to say some things on Earth – like rocks – are dead is as absurd as saying a person is partially dead.

In *Northern Lights*, Jotham Santelia, professor of cosmology, assures Lyra that "The stars are alive, child. Did you know that, child? Everything out there is alive." The idea that matter is sentient is a basic tenet of the obscure philosophical theory known as **hylopathism**. Mary Malone puts the hylopathic view rather well when she says in *The Subtle Knife*: "Our particles are strange little devils, make no mistake. You know what? They're conscious."

All this suggests that the Church's determination to investigate and finally destroy Dust would probably lead to the end of the world. We can infer as much from the mulefa's story. The Church's disapproval of Dust is matched, with much less vehemence, in the **Buddhist** faith in our world. Dust is often used by Buddhists to describe our entanglement with the day-to-day world that clouds our vision and prevents us from becoming truly enlightened.

Dust could, in our world, be **cosmic dust** – the stuff that makes up the very atoms of our body and was present in the early days of the solar system. Around 40,000 tonnes of cosmic dust leaks from space into Earth's atmosphere every year, mainly from meteors. Luckily, most of this tonnage gets burned up, but a few particles – no bigger than the width of a human hair – do fall to earth.

In the books, Dust is widely believed to be somehow linked to the **Aurora Borealis**, which is, in essence, a light show created by charged particles from space. To those who can see it, Dust is as enchanting as the Aurora Borealis. Even **Mrs Coulter**, when she sees it for the first time, exclaims: "Dust is beautiful, I never knew."

It would be simplistic to equate cosmic dust with Pullman's Dust. but he has said that his fictional matter existed before humans, although, with no men and women to be attracted to, these particles must have had a pretty dull life. The **alethiometer** tells us that around 30,000–40,000 years ago, Dust began to

FLIGHTS OF FANCY

The flying machines of *His Dark Materials* span the spectrum of science and then some – from **Lee Scoresby**'s hydrogen balloon and the **Magisterium**'s zeppelins to **Lord Asriel**'s gyropters and experimental Intention Craft.

Put this way, it is easy to see one aspect of their use. Although Royal Mail and passenger zeppelins travel regularly between Oxford and London, zeppelins are used overwhelmingly by the Church: by Mrs Coulter, who arrives in one at Bolvangar, by the Imperial Muscovite Army and the Consistorial Court of Discipline. As the trilogy unfolds, so the zeppelin's Germanic associations begin to inform the Church's sense of repression and danger.

In our world, the military use of balloons was pioneered in the 19th century. Lee Scoresby's balloon is hydrogen-powered. This technology was suggested by the British scientist **Henry Cavendish** as long ago as 1766. He called it "inflammable air" in his drolly named scientific paper *On Factitious Airs*. But hydrogen was not in widespread use until the zeppelin era. Apart from the

hydrogen, Scoresby's balloon seems to belong to a simpler, more innocent age, with its ropes and leather-trimmed basket.

Lord Asriel's flying machines point the way to the future. Powered by the will of the pilot (and moving with the aid of some kind of anti-gravity system), the **Intention Craft** is the perfect vehicle for its ruthlessly single-minded owner, the ultimate private jet. The obvious drawback with the Intention Craft is that it cannot be piloted by the terminally indecisive.

When flying the Intention Craft – rescuing Mrs Coulter, shooting down zeppelins – Asriel is at his most deliberate and glamorous, and it is hard not to see in this image some echo of Pullman's own father Alfred Outram: an RAF pilot, "a warrior, a man of shining glamour", who died in a plane crash in 1953, when his son was just seven. To Pullman the boy, he was a hero who died fighting Mau Mau soldiers in Kenya, and it is surely no coincidence that Asriel – another cold, distant hero – should remain unharmed in the middle of his own air crash.

IS THE AURORA A PATHWAY TO HEAVEN?

It can be no coincidence that **John Parry** disappears while searching for the **Aurora Borealis**. For Parry, the Aurora is a doorway between worlds. In our world, the Inuit of Labrador, Canada, believed the Aurora to be a pathway to heaven. The lights were the torches of spirits leading to heaven souls that had come to a bad end. The whistling or crackling noise said to often accompany the Aurora was, the Inuit thought, the voices of spirits trying to talk to the living.

The Aurora Borealis exists because the sun sends electrically charged particles towards Earth. When this flow of matter, called the solar wind, hits Earth's magnetic field it powers what amounts to a gigantic electrical generator, providing the energy and charged particles to turn on the northern lights. The auroral light is emitted from molecules and atoms of Earth's atmospheric gases.

Solar flares propel the matter within solar winds, helping to shape the colourful aerial displays we see. When a gigantic flare on the sun brought Alaska an awesome red Aurora in 1989, the bursts of geomagnetically induced currents caused transformers to overheat, relays to trip spontaneously and capacitor banks to misbehave, causing havoc for engineers from California to Sweden.

Forecasting auroras would alleviate their effect on communications systems. The Geophysical Institute at the University of Alaska in Fairbanks has been providing online forecasts since 1995, helping such firms as **Alaska Cab** whose office/cab telecoms have gone haywire because of the Aurora. In 1976, for example, a cab driver in Fairbanks somehow received instructions from a controller in New Jersey.

The really controversial mystery about the Aurora is whether you can hear it. The Inuit insist they have heard a sound – a swishing or a crackling – but many scientists say this is impossible. The air where the Aurora dances is probably too thin to carry sound waves. Baffled researchers have suggested the brain might somehow convert the electromagnetic waves to sound or that the electric currents it produces on the ground (which are powerful enough to corrode the trans-Alaska oil pipeline) may create an audible electrical discharge. Either way, the controversy may only be solved when someone actually records the Aurora.

Driving taxis mad: the unpredictable Aurora

surround human artefacts and skulls, being, for some reason, especially attracted to skulls that had been trepanned.

The obvious question is: did anything happen, in our world 30,000–40,000 years ago that Pullman might be alluding to? Not really. The most recent common ancestor, dubbed **Y-chromosomal Adam**, probably lived in Africa 60,000–90,000 years ago. Roughly 31,000 years ago, the species we call **Homo sapiens** crossed from Siberia into North America, and **M343**, a known DNA sequence from Cro-Magnon man carried by most Western Europeans living today, first appears. The last Neanderthals died out 27,000 years ago. The human race would,

> "COSMIC dUSt MAKES UP EVERY AtOM OF OUR BODY AND WAS PRESENt iN tHE EARLY dAYS OF tHE SOLAR SYStEM."

henceforth, consist only of Homo sapiens, all of whom were, of course, made up of cosmic dust. That line from Genesis – "for dust thou art and unto dust shalt thou return" – sounds less like theology and more like a simple statement of fact.

FROM DUSt to WIMPS

Why is it so hard to see Dust? Possibly because Dust is inspired by **superstring theory**, the idea that, at the most microscopic level, everything in the universe is made up of vibrating strings. Actually, as the Gribbins point out, these infinitesimal loops are shaped more like elastic bands but superelastic theory doesn't sound quite so sexy. It would take, the Gribbins estimate, a hundred billion loops of string to stretch across one proton. There are roughly 100,000 protons in an atom. And it would take ten million protons to stretch across two points on the edge of a postage stamp. You would need a very subtle knife to cut these subatomic particles down to these tiny loops and an immensely powerful spyglass to see them. So far, scientists have had to make do with computer simulations.

Superstring theory could explain the **Spectres**. They "whooshed out" of their subatomic particles 300 years ago when **Cittàgazze**'s learned men cut through a loop of vibrating string with the subtle knife, and they have been feeding on human souls ever since. This, Pullman suggests, is what happens when we discover a technology – like the atomic bomb? – too subtle for humanity to handle.

There is another reason we can't see Dust – as suggested by the line from *Paradise Lost* that gave the books their title – this material, or matter, is probably

Galactic puzzle: the odd movements of the Coma cluster led Fritz Zwicky to discover dark matter

dark. The story of dark matter – in essence stuff we can't see but can infer exists from its effects on the matter we can see – really starts in the 1930s when **Fritz Zwicky**, a Swiss astronomer at the California Institute of Technology, began studying the movements of an enormous group of galaxies roughly 300 million light years from Earth called the **Coma** cluster.

Watching the thousands of galaxies circling the centre of the constellation, all held in place by gravity, Zwicky found that a few galaxies were travelling much faster than they ought to be. Clusters of galaxies can hold together for billions of years as long as they have enough mass to generate the gravitational pull to glue them together. Being a patient, methodical sort, Zwicky worked out the combined gravity of all the visible matter and found that it was nothing like enough to glue these galaxies together. There was, he thought, only one explanation: the Coma cluster must contain masses of matter that was not visible, maybe even ten or one hundred times as much matter as he could see.

Few scientists took Zwicky very seriously until the 1970s, when **Vera Rubin**, an astrophysicist at the Carnegie Institute in Washington, discovered a similar problem with **spiral galaxies**. Like Zwicky, she concluded that the only way to explain the strange speed of these galaxies was to assume there was lots of dark matter out there. After Rubin's findings, scientists began to perfect techniques that could help them

WORLD TOUR 1: THE MAJOR WORLDS

Where most of the action takes place.

Cittàgazze

There is the odd mention of Cittàgazze world or the city of Cittàgazze, but it's often up to the reader to decide whether certain references are to Cittàgazze or not. As the only place where you can pass from one world to another (before Asriel opens a hole in the sky above Svalbard), it's here that Will meets Lyra. This must be a strange world because, though the streets are deserted, there are clothes factories and even fridges to store fizzy drinks.

Gallivespians' world

The "little people" or Gallivespians originated and live here alongside the "big people" or humans, doing their best not to get exterminated. Their science is so advanced that the theory of quantum entanglement has practical applications.

Lyra's world

A recognizably Victorian world, although technologically Lyra's universe is an intriguing mish-mash with atomic power, hydrogen and railways but, strangely, as Ceres Wunderkind, the fan fiction writer, has pointed out, no radio. As no specific date is attached to Lyra's world, you wonder if it is supposed to be in the same timespace as Will's.

The mulefa world

Love, peace and harmony finally conquers all in this world where Mary Malone finds an "endless prairie or savanna… most of it covered in short grass" with groups of trees half as big again as redwoods and large flowers facing upward attached to the giant seedpods that are key to the mulefa's survival.

Republic of Heaven

Asriel strives to build his Republic of Heaven in a remote setting. Built on a mountain range emerging from a sulphur lake in a canyon, this basalt fortress is Asriel's command post.

Will's world

Will and Lyra are very uneasy in Will's world. When Will cuts back into it, he sees a place where "machines were turning, chemicals were combining, people were producing goods and earning their living". Not quite dark satanic mills but close enough.

World of the dead

This world's suburbs look like a cross between a refuse dump and a squalid camp, stink of rot and are gradually losing their colour. Lyra then takes the ferry to the island world of the dead, a vast plain scattered with dead trees, dully lit. The land of the dead is basically a prison camp designed by the Authority, and escape is about as easy as strolling out of Colditz. Will can cut a window back out only after following a harpy through tunnels and caves and past an abyss.

map dark matter around the galaxies. On these maps, dark matter often forms a huge, roughly spherical cloud. The latest research suggests that dark matter acts as a kind of cosmic scaffolding around which stars and galaxies gather.

But science hasn't yet answered all our questions about dark matter. We don't, for example, really know what dark matter is. The best guess to date is that this matter is made up of some completely new kind of sub-atomic particle that has mass but doesn't interact with other particles or **WIMPs** (Weakly Interacting Massive Particles) for short. This brings us very close to Dust, as defined in the novels by **Boris Mikhailovitch Rusakov**.

When Pullman wrote the novels in the early to mid-1990s, the existence of a mysterious dark material was, by common consent, the best scientific explanation we had for the way the universe behaved.

But in the late 1990s, some scientists decided that even dark matter didn't completely explain the universe's behaviour – in particular, it offered no clues as to why the universe was expanding at an accelerating rate. They started to focus on something they called **dark energy**. A satellite mapping cosmic microwave background radiation concluded, in 2001, that only four percent of the universe was made up of atoms, 23 percent was dark matter and 73 percent was something that was dubbed dark energy.

> "SCIENCE HASN'T ANSWERED ALL OUR QUESTIONS ABOUT DARK MATTER. WE DON'T KNOW WHAT DARK MATTER IS."

Dark energy is invisible, like dark matter, and must have a repulsive force, otherwise it would get sucked into galaxies and affect their motion. This antigravity force, by counteracting gravity, is helping to pull the universe apart. This has forced scientists to rethink the equations they use to predict the future of the universe. The three endgame options for the universe are: a **big freeze** in which space becomes a desolate wasteland of dying stars and black holes; a **pause** in which the universe is balanced, space survives but, eventually, slides into a big freeze; or a symmetrical echo of the Big Bang called the **Crunch**, in which galaxies collide and the universe turns into the mother of all black holes.

WAR OF THE WORLDS

"Nobody understands quantum theory," said Richard Feynman once. "Do not keep saying to yourself… 'But how can it be like that?' because you will go down

WORLD TOUR 2: THE MINOR WORLDS

Will and Lyra often have a quick pitstop in some odd little universes. Here's hoping we see more of the shaggy blue beast world in *The Book Of Dust*.

Beach world

Will escapes to a Mediterranean world of sand dunes and a glass-like sea when he and the angels Baruch and Balthamos are ambushed by Metatron. He and Lyra stay the night here. There is dense vegetation and trees here but, alas, no food or water.

Chained slave world

We glimpse this world in *The Amber Spyglass* when Will cuts through to it, testing his window-opening capabilities. All we see is a snapshot of a dirty factory full of chained slaves.

Desert world

This rocky, barren world with "bleached bone-white ground" is the only world from which Will can cut into Mrs Coulter's Himalayan cave. Though he worries the moonlight is so bright the "rocks would shine like a lantern once he opened the window into Mrs Coulter's cave", it comes in handy when he and Lyra flee the soldiers. The window is very easy to spot.

Holland world

Not to be confused with Holland, a country in Lyra's world, or with the 'Hollanders' who settled the Fens in Lyra's world. The Holland of *The Amber Spyglass* is so known because Will's first impression is that it looks just how he imagines Holland would look where a "stone-flagged yard was swept clean and a row of stable doors stood open".

Rainstorm world

This wet world appears near the end of *The Amber Spyglass*. Will accidentally opens this, his last window, in trying to destroy the subtle knife. After closing this window, Will says the name "Lyra" and presses the knife to the spot where her tear still lay on his cheek. The subtle knife shatters with the blade pieces left to "glitter on the stones that were still wet with the rain of another universe".

Shaggy blue beast world

While testing the feel of cutting windows as his hand recovers, Will walks into this grassy upland meadow in which a herd of "creatures the size of bison, with wide horns and shaggy blue fur" are grazing.

Uninhabited world

This almost undescribed world saves Lyra's life. When the ghost of John Parry tells Will a bomb is coming at Lyra, and that it's guided by a lock of her hair, Will quickly does as his dead father bids by cutting a window through which he shoves the strand before sealing it up again – thus averting disaster.

a blind alley from which no one has yet escaped. Nobody knows how it can be like that." That's a depressing thought for those of us who aren't scientists, because Feynman won a Nobel Prize in quantum physics.

This branch of modern science has two big drawbacks as far as most of us are concerned: it is extremely complicated and, as the Gribbins say, just plain weird.

How weird exactly? There are three basic experimental findings which demonstrate quantum theory's intrinsic oddness.

1 A wave and a particle

When straight waves pass through a slit (imagine a narrow harbour entrance) they come out as semicircles. Two slits make two sets of semicircles, and where a wave crest meets a wave trough, they cancel out. When you send light through two parallel slits and onto a screen, there are dark patches where peaks cancel out troughs. The waves from each slit have made an interference pattern. This shows that light travels in waves. But use a sensitive enough screen and you see that a single particle of light, a photon, goes through both slits at the same time and makes the same pattern. So a photon is a wave and a particle at the same time.

2 Looking changes things

Imagine a light bulb filament gives out a photon, seemingly in a random direction. **Erwin Schrödinger** came up with a nine-letter-long equation that correctly predicts the chances of finding that photon at any given point. He envisaged a kind of wave, like a ripple from a pebble dropped into a pond, spreading out from the filament. Once you look at the photon, this wave collapses into the single point. The wave becomes a particle. In other words, when we look at something like a photon or electron we may change it.

3 Schrödinger's cat

Schrödinger showed how crazy this duality is. He suggested you seal your pet cat in a box with a bottle of cyanide rigged up to a customized Geiger counter and some radioactive material. For an hour, the Geiger counter watches. If it detects a radioactive particle, it cracks open the cyanide. No particle, no cyanide. With a fifty-fifty chance of a particle being emitted as a quantum event, there's a fifty-fifty chance that your cat gets it.

Quantum physics started in the 1920s when scientists worked out the rules governing the behaviour of things like atoms and electrons. We know these rules are true because they can predict how atoms will behave. But the rules also suggest that in the quantum world, though nothing is certain, there are rules of chance that the Gribbins liken to throwing a die. There is always a one in six chance of your number coming up. But with two dice, you are twice as likely to get eleven (six on the first die, five on the second; and vice versa) as you are to get twelve. These rules, as interpreted by a group of eminent scientists in Copenhagen, say that nothing has really happened until you look at it. So Schrödinger's cat is neither dead nor alive until you open the door and find out which.

Quantum defence: is Rumsfeld a Schrödinger fan?

This idea has become so popular that the term **"Schrödinger's terrorist"** has been coined to describe famous people whose well-being is the subject of speculation and debate. **Donald Rumsfeld,** the former US Defense Secretary, helped popularize this variation on the theme when he said of Osama Bin Laden: "He's either alive, or he's alive and injured badly, or he's dead."

The interpretation that says the cat can be dead and alive actually help us understand how computers, lasers and DNA works. So we can't simply ignore them. This is where the **multiverse** – aka parallel universes and the **Many Worlds Interpretation** – comes in.

> "IN ONE WORLD, SCHRÖDINGER'S CAT GETS IT. IN THE OTHER, YOU ARE RELIEVED TO FIND THE FURBALL IS STILL BREATHING."

This ingenious solution suggests that the world splits into two and in one world, the cat gets it, while in another, the cat lives on. So, when you open the door to see the result of this experiment, there are suddenly two of you: one who guiltily finds a dead cat and one who is relieved to discover the little furball is still breathing after all.

The worlds keep splitting every time such a choice is faced, so there are millions of worlds, all subtly or dramatically different, that exist either side by side or on top of each other, or diverging like branches on a tree. Or, as **Serafina Pekkala** tells **Lyra**, millions of universes could be interpenetrating each other, yet unaware that any other universe exists. Oxford physicist **David Deutsch**, one of the most eloquent exponents of the Many Worlds Interpretation, says: "Physical reality is the set of all universes evolving together." He calls this concept the multiverse. Pullman has attended Deutsch's lectures and refers to the multiverse when Balthamos, the Kaisa and Asriel variously insist that there are myriad, millions or billions of other worlds.

This is a fantastically exciting conceit but it is not, as **Tony Watkins** points out in his book *Dark Matter*, without its problems, especially for a novelist. For him, the theory throws up four big questions:

1 How can we ever know?
Without our own subtle knife, how could we test the prediction that there are other universes and, if we can't test it, how can we prove or disprove it?

2 Where does the mass-energy for this rapidly increasing number of universes come from?
The short answer is we don't know. You can create another universe by simply deciding whether you will eat a biscuit now or later. Which raises another issue. You can usually see the point of scientific laws, discoveries and theories. But what purpose is served by creating another universe in which the major, initial, difference between the new universe and the old is that a biscuit is eaten at breakfast rather than dipped into your coffee during elevenses?

3 If there are countless billions of universes, what does that do to science?
Does it, for example, mean that everything we think we know scientifically applies only to particular universes?

4 If there are countless billions of universes, what happens to free will?
In this theory, you never make a choice, the universe just splits so that one is a universe where you opted to do A and another is a universe where you opted to do B. Or maybe you didn't opt. If there are an infinite number of universes, then you tick "all of the above" on every moral choice.

Parallel worlds have proved useful to many writers, especially to Michael Moorcock and Stephen King and filmmakers such as Peter Howitt (the director of the "what-if?" spectacular *Sliding Doors*), but an infinite number of universes could make character meaningless.

Asriel, for example, can decide not to kill Roger or build a bridge between worlds and simply beaver away happily in his icy fortress, leaving the Authority to do its worst. The multiverse, applied ruthlessly to the books, would destroy the very story of which, Pullman says, he was merely the humble servant. On the upside, many fans will be delighted to know that, in this theory, there would be many universes in which Lyra and Will are reunited.

> "SURELY it is EASIER TO BELIEVE iN ONE UNIVERSE CREATED BY GOD THAN TO BELIEVE iN BILLIONS OF WORLDS, ALWAYS INCREASING, CREATED BY NOBODY."

The scientific possibilities that spring from the Many Worlds Interpretation are so enormously mindboggling that it is easy to understand why the science writer Martin Gardner grumbled: "Surely the conjecture that there is just one universe and its Creator is infinitely simpler and easier to believe than that there are countless billions upon billions of worlds, constantly increasing in number and created by nobody."

The controversy may, though, just be proof that the problem of how the universe works is, at the moment, just too darn complicated for the human brain to comprehend and that we are all, as Feynman might say, stuck in a blind alley with, as yet, no sign of an escape route.

Our incomprehension might change. It was, after all, only ninety years ago that **Albert Einstein** did some fancy mathematics to try to reduce the dynamics of the universe to a set of numbers.

His sums showed that the universe expanded. But believing the universe was static, Einstein changed the equation. We'll probably have to alter ours a few times in the years to come.

TERMS OF ENTANGLEMENT

The **lodestone resonator** really shouldn't, as the Gribbins have pointed out, be made out of lodestone. This naturally magnetic mineral would be able to emit electromagnetic waves which 'only' travel at the speed of light – 186,000 miles a second – and would struggle to communicate between worlds. Still, you have to admire **Gallivespian** ingenuity. It is hard not to be impressed by a powerful device that looks like a short pencil, can be fitted into a violin-case no longer than a walnut and makes mobile phones in our world look as clunky and as functionally limited as the first computers seem to us today.

The lodestone resonator can communicate between worlds instantly – by comparison, NASA estimates the delay on a signal from Mars to Earth would be forty minutes. The resonator is very clever indeed and must, to the apparatchiks who work for **the Authority**, seem deeply suspicious.

A controversial theory called **entanglement** might explain how the Gallivespians' resonator can do this. In essence, this relies on the theory that, in the quantum world, once two things have interacted they are always aware of each other, even if they are separated. **Albert Einstein** didn't like this theory very much. He defined entanglement as "spooky action at a distance".

We think of electrons as particles, but they have a waviness about them. Entanglement – in quantum theory – happens when these waves get tangled up. Even though the particles might be separated, the waves stretch out very thin and, still tangled, can send out messages between these separated particles faster than you can say "lodestone generator". In fact, these messages take no time at all to travel between these particles, even if the particles are separated by vast distances.

> "ALBERT EINSTEIN DIDN'T LIKE ENTANGLEMENT THEORY. HE DESCRIBED IT AS 'SPOOKY ACTION AT A DISTANCE'."

The idea of entanglement is enormously exciting for scientists, but to the rest of mankind it sounds puzzling, disturbing and faintly subversive. Undeterred, physicists are now investigating something called **quantum teleportation**, which could, at some point in the future, enable us to transmit messages as instantaneously as the Gallivespians. One team, led by the Viennese physicist **Anton Zeilinger**, has transmitted such a message six hundred metres across the Danube.

Even in our world, there is evidence of entanglement, we just tend to call it different things. Think of the way **Balthamos**, in the Himalayas with Will, is instantly aware that his partner **Baruch** has been mortally wounded near Asriel's fortress. There is abundant anecdotal evidence that some lovers – and twins – behave like this. The idea that twins are telepathic is still deeply controversial. Studies that have tried to prove twins have such powers usually come up blank. Yet research suggests that the bond between twins is intense. The loss of a twin may leave the surviving sibling feeling the death has drained their soul away

– psychologists call this feeling 'halving'. This brings us on to **dæmons**, without whom none of the humans in *His Dark Materials* are complete.

Mind Games

In ancient Greece, dæmons were not all bad. **Socrates** had something he called a **daimonion** (a small demon), which he described as an inner voice that warned him against mistakes. In one baffling omission, it forgot to tell the shameless egotist to button it and just pay the fine rather than knock back a fatal dose of hemlock. Socrates' guardian angel was used against him at his trial. He was accused of treating it as if it were a new god. The misunderstandings worsened when Christianity came to power. Many Graeco-Roman sculptures were destroyed because they contained demonic images. It wasn't until the 19th century that **Cardinal Manning** decreed that Socrates' daimonion was really a divinely inspired conscience. By then, the devilish image of demons was so firmly fixed that even Manning's scholarship couldn't change it.

Pullman found Socrates' daimonion a "very fruitful metaphor", believing the "dæmon is the part of you that helps you grow towards wisdom". He probably also drew inspiration from the Norse legend of the **fylgja**, personal guardian

spirits in the shape of an animal who could jump into the future to make sure they gave their charges the very best advice. Such jumps did not, though, help them conquer death: a fylgja perished with its owner. Like the dæmons in *His Dark Materials*, the shape a fylgja chose was supposed to represent their owner's character – though the association in Norse mythology was much more obvious than in the novels.

William Blake had his own spin on this phenomenon: he believed people had a dual personality and were sometimes unnaturally separated from their opposite sides. For Blake, the separated part was an "emanation" and,

Greek icon: did Socrates have the first dæmon?

Jung at heart: Carl Jung was intrigued by alchemy, the *I Ching* and his own "spirit" Philemon

to him, Eve was an "emanation" of Adam. **Carl Jung** believed something similar. The psychologist argued that every psyche includes qualities from the opposite gender. This may be why most of the dæmons in *His Dark Materials* are a different sex to their human companion.

If Socrates had his guardian angel, Jung had, the Gribbins quipped, a garden angel, a spirit called **Philemon** that he used to walk down the garden with and talk to. Philemon first visited him when he was three. Nobody else could see this spirit, just as no one else ever saw the lanky, white palooka **Harvey** in the James Stewart movie. Jung often talked to Philemon at length, much as Lyra talks to Pantalaimon. Jung was never properly psychoanalysed, but a psychiatrist might say Jung was really talking to himself or that somehow his conscious and unconscious mind were talking to each other. Talking to characters no one else can see is also, of course, a classic symptom of schizophrenia.

Jung is an intriguing, often unacknowledged influence on *His Dark Materials*. He was interested in alchemy, liked to use the **I Ching** on his patients and was fascinated by different mythologies and religions that, to him, suggested that mankind had a **collective unconscious** – an idea echoed by the unifying magic of Dust in the books.

> "TALKING TO CHARACTERS NO ONE ELSE CAN SEE, AS CARL JUNG DID, IS A CLASSIC SYMPTOM OF SCHIZOPHRENIA."

If Jung could talk to his unconscious, he could have read the **alethiometer** as effectively as Lyra. The usual explanation for Lyra's ability to read such a bamboozling instrument is that she is, as a child, in a state of innocent grace.

But the alethiometer works rather like the Chinese system of the *I Ching*. In both cases, the user has to think about how to frame the questions properly. Then they have the truth meter or the system of hexagrams in the *I Ching* (see p.153) to concentrate on so their unconscious mind can find the right answer. This is why many devotees of the *I Ching* recommend you use stalks or sticks to choose the hexagrams that may guide your future. The theory is that, after grabbing a number of stalks from a bunch of 49, you have no idea how many you have in your hand. Not knowing helps you let go of rational thought and achieve a different, more spiritual state of mind where, deep down, you feel that some part of you really knows the number of stalks you are holding.

Some people find this business easier than others. Pullman suggests children are better than grown ups, at imagining and being open to new things in general, which is why, as Lyra gets older, she finds the instrument much harder to use. Losing contact with her unconscious mind is, Pullman suggests, part of the cost of growing up.

The psychological sub-texts of the books don't stop there. The **Spectres** do have a direct scientific significance, derived from superstring theory, but Nicholas Tucker makes a persuasive case in his book *Darkness Visible*, that the effect the Spectres have on their victims – in particular the witch Lena – also sounds like a terrible case of depression. Tucker draws a parallel with Joanne Greenberg's autobiographical novel *I Never Promised You A Rose Garden,* in which the mentally ill narrator, trying to recover her sanity, finds the imaginary friends who nourished her in her madness turning into pitiless tormentors as she strives to cure herself. For Tucker, the Spectres are both a consequence of man's intellectual hubris and a symbol of the kind of psychological forces that can threaten our will to live.

> "THE EFFECT THE SPECTRES HAVE ON THEIR VICTIMS SOUNDS LIKE A TERRIBLE CASE OF DEPRESSION."

PULLMAN'S THEORY OF EVOLUTION

Where did the **mulefa** come from? These horned invertebrates with trunks that look "like a cross between antelopes and motorcycles" had two sources. Walking around Lake Bled in Slovenia, Pullman was struck by the constant rumble of overtaking skateboarders. And then one day, he fleshed out the idea with his younger son (who was about fifteen at the time). "In two or three hours we had invented the mulefa. At least, we'd got the creatures and the trees and the seedpods and the wheels," he told Readerville.com. "But on their own they would have meant little and added nothing to the story, so then the connection had to be made with Dust and the basic theme of the story, which of course is the difference between innocence and experience."

The mulefa are like no creatures known to man. They have a diamond-framed skeleton, short horns and a trunk, but no hands. They communicate through flicks of their trunks, which have two finger-like appendages, and express interest with the position of their ears. But the really clever thing about them is the way they use the large round seed pods from the trees to travel around with. When each zalif – as individual mulefa are called – comes of age, the disc-shaped pods fit

IT ALL STARTED WITH A TORTOISE

Legend has it that the ancient divination tool the **I Ching** – or *The Book Of Changes* – started when the sage and first Chinese emperor **Fu Hsi** (who may, though history gets a bit spotty here, have ruled sometime around 2800BC) spotted eight three-line symbols on the shell of a tortoise.

He decided that these symbols, known as trigrams, actually represented eight elemental forces that help guide us through life.

Emperor Ching: Fu Hsi invented the *I Ching* almost 5000 years ago

His vision evolved into the *I Ching* as we know it today: 64 hexagrams (each made from two trigrams) arranged in a square surrounded by a circle. The *I Ching* can be consulted as an oracle, rather like the alethiometer.

First think of the question you want to ask and hold that thought. The question has to be about something you plan to do. Sadly, the *I Ching* won't help you with pub trivia questions or tell you if the Chicago White Sox will ever win the World Series again.

You can then use various random means to find out which hexagrams answer your question. Some people toss coins, which takes only two minutes, others use sticks or stalks, which takes twenty minutes. You can even, if you're not frightened of becoming a social outcast and likely facing prosecution, do it the old way and heat up a tortoise shell.

Each hexagram has a commentary attached, which you can look up to make sure you get the meaning.

When **Mary Malone** is told to stay put in the mulefa world by the *I Ching* she probably landed on hexagram 52, which uses the image of mountains standing together to caution the user: "The superior man does not permit his thoughts to go beyond his situation."

Anyone who watched the Shaolin monk dispense cryptic wisdom to David "Grasshopper" Carradine in the 1970s TV series *Kung Fu* will recognize the tone of these messages.

The most visible proof of the *I Ching*'s continuing influence is the South Korean flag, which surrounds the ying and yang symbol with four trigrams symbolizing heaven, water, earth and fire.

Pullman is one of many Westerners to acknowledge the *I Ching*. The psychologist **Carl Jung** used it to treat patients. **Philip K. Dick** employed it to decide some of the plot in his novel *The Man In The High Castle* and the technique has also influenced plenty of popular music, including the work of **Pink Floyd** and **George Harrison** (who wrote the song "While My Guitar Gently Weeps" after consulting the *I Ching* and seeing the hexagram "gently weeps").

THE BEAR FACTS

Armoured bears, Pullman said in an email, came easily to him. "When it was clear we were going to the north, I realized we needed something dangerous and threatening. Arctic – polar bears – armour – the rest was easy."

The creation of the bears wasn't quite that simple. A fencing bear has the starring role in Kleist's *On The Marionette Theatre* (see p.127). Kleist's creature can instinctively distinguish between a feint and a thrust in much the same way as **Iorek Byrnison** does with **Lyra**, proving, he tells her, that, "You cannot trick a bear" because bears "can see in a way that humans have forgotten".

The bears in *His Dark Materials* have a reasonably elaborate social structure, which doesn't square with the popular image of the creatures as prowling loners. Yet scientists who studied the species say the image is wrong. The researcher **N.G. Ovsyanikov**, after studying a community of bears on **Wrangel Island**, found that if a feed is big enough, up to one hundred and sixty bears may crowd around the same small lot, a gathering which forces them to regulate their social relationships.

They will spot another bear at six hundred metres, identify its social status and recognize it if they have seen it before - even if it was years ago. Although there is a social hierarchy – decided by strength, experience, confidence and size – adult bears will walk together and play together. They will also share meat – if another bear waits its turn politely – and are more likely, Ovsyanikov found, to adopt an orphaned cub than to eat one.

His research didn't, alas, settle the question of whether bears are left-handed as the Eskimos claim in Will's world. Anthropologist **Richard Nelson**, who spent a year living with the Inupiaq, was told by the locals that polar bears are left-handed so if you're about to get punched by one, try to make sure it's hitting you with its slower, less accurate, right paw. Others insist this is a myth. The belief certainly has a mythic source. Left-handedness is associated with femininity in some Inuit cultures, symbolizing what they believe is the bears' dual masculine/feminine nature.

This ancient tradition found surprising scientific support in 1986 when Canadian zoologist **Marc Cattet** found that at least a tenth of black, grizzly, and polar bears he studied were hermaphroditic but could still reproduce. The birth of their offspring, through the tip of their clitoris/penis, must be truly excruciating.

Scientists have recorded incidences of polar bears using tools. They are certainly more dextrous than their big paws might suggest. They can prise food from kelp, knock out a beluga whale, catch a lemming and flip a seal into the air. Using a weapon shouldn't pose much of a challenge. Surviving global warming will be a sterner test.

Polar opposites: the real polar bear is a social animal with a painful tendency to hermaphroditism

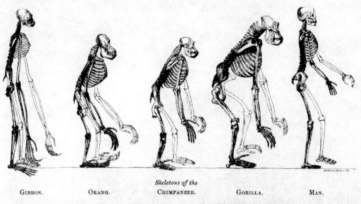

GIBBON. ORANG. CHIMPANZEE. GORILLA. MAN.

Skeletons of the
CHIMPANZEE.

Photographically reduced from Diagrams of the natural size (except that of the Gibbon, which was twice as large as nature),
drawn by Mr. Waterhouse Hawkins from specimens in the Museum of the Royal College of Surgeons.

Evolutionary wars: natural selection is not, Gould says, the be-all and end-all of Darwin's theory

neatly onto a spur on their front and rear legs. They push-start themselves with their side legs and, when they are on their way, they steer by leaning one way or another. They get around so easily because they are fortunate to live in a world of lava highways. When seated, they fold their legs under them. And, as if that doesn't make them weird enough, they smell of horse flesh and seedpods.

It's easy to dismiss the mulefa as primitive creatures. They live in a world without mechanization, in wattle-and-daub villages, use metal only for decoration, and make crude wooden and stone artefacts. Yet they also live in a state of **Edenic harmony** with their environment, efficiently cull the herds of grazer (to whom they are genetically related), minimizing any terror the beasts might feel, make lacquer from trees, distil acid from rocks and produce fishing nets so strong and light their gyptian guests have never seen the like. Their thought processes are slower than ours, but they have an incredible oral memory, remembering their 33,000-year history in such detail that Jung might say they have a collective consciousness.

The relationship between the mulefa and the trees is an example of the kind of symbiosis that keeps hummingbirds and the plants they feed on in harmony. Through natural selection, hummingbirds have evolved with longer beaks to probe deeply into the flowers to find their nectar. The deeper the birds probe, the more pollen they get dusted with and the more pollen they carry with them to fertilize the next flower they feed on. The mulefa need the trees, but the trees need the mulefa to crack open the seed pods and then plant the seeds.

Pullman finds the theory of evolution intellectually persuasive, so where do the mulefa – or the Gallivespians and the panserbjørne for that matter – fit into that theory? Even some fans have found the whole scientific premise for the mulefa laughable, and one reader complained on Amazon about having to wade through "endless pages on the mulefa-elephant aliens". But **Richard Dawkins**, in his book *The Ancestor's Tale*, mentions the mulefa in a footnote as an example of alternative yet realistic evolution, the result of a co-evolution between animals, plants and geology.

The trouble with the theory of natural selection – the process by which favourable traits become more common in successive generations of a species – is that it can narrow our view of evolution, leading us to assume that it is a simple sequential process and tempting us to make facile assumptions about which species are advanced (i.e. us) and which are primitive.

Dawkins uses the **duckbilled platypus** to make this very point. "A specimen sent to a museum was thought to be a hoax: bits of mammal and bird stitched together. Others have wondered whether God was having a bad day when he made the platypus: finding some parts left over on the workshop floor, he decided to unite rather than waste them." In fact, says Dawkins, that Donald Duck-bill contains 40,000 finely tuned sensors that electrolocate food beyond the range of sight, sound and touch. The platypus closes its ears, eyes and nostrils while foraging for prey, yet by detecting the faintest electrical signals made by the muscular twitch of a buried shrimp, it catches half its own weight in food every day. The platypus is also super-sensitive to the mechanical motion of water and uses the lapse between electrical signals and energy moving through water to calculate how far away its prey is. They also, like the Gallivespians, have poisonous spurs that unleash a substance toxic enough to kill small animals.

> "THE DUCKBILLED PLATYPUS CAN ELECTROLOCATE FOOD AND HAS, LIKE THE GALLIVESPIANS, POISONOUS SPURS."

Evolution works in so many unlikely ways that the mulefa don't seem quite so far fetched. The gender of a young crocodile, for example, is not determined by its genes but by how deep the eggs are buried in the nest and at what temperature they are kept. Low and high temperatures produce females, while eggs kept between 31C and 33C will hatch into males. Some scientists fear that the rise in global temperature triggered by **climate change** could damage the species, by changing the gender balance.

Sometimes, the shuffling of genes throws up an echo of a species' ancient heritage, in a process called **atavism**. Since medieval times, there have been around fifty recorded instances of people who were born covered with a thick coat of chimp-like hair. The most famous of these unfortunate souls was the Russian sideshow performer **Fedor Jeftichew** (1868–1904), who was billed as **Jo-Jo the Dog-Faced Boy**. Such a throwback may have inspired the hairy-bodied riders of the horse-people in *The Amber Spyglass*.

This doesn't just happen to humans. Suetonius wrote that **Caesar** "used to ride a remarkable horse, which had feet that were almost human, the hoofs being cleft like toes." The person who rode this horse was destined to rule the world – a superstition that probably reflects the fact that **Alexander the Great**'s horse Bucephalus was reputed to have toes too.

The American scientist **Stephen Jay Gould** argued that evolution was determined by structure, contingency and natural selection. The rules of structure say, for example, that an ape can never be as big as **King Kong** because its bones would crumble under its own weight. Contingency is almost a scientific word for accident. Entire species or families of species can become extinct, no matter how well adapted they are to their environment. And natural selection, Gould suggested, has no foresight.

The mammals who lived in the Cretaceous period managed to coexist with dinosaurs for a hundred million years but were so small that they were dominated by their gigantic neighbours. Only when a massive asteroid slammed into Mexico, triggering catastrophic climate change, did the mammals' lack of size become an advantage. The asteroid's impact is not an event that can be neatly fitted into the narrow sequential, gene-driven view of Darwinism.

And, as the mulefa have taught us, species are not passive receivers of their environment. They modify the environment – sometimes subtly, sometimes not so subtly – and leave the world a slightly different place for their offspring. Gould's thoughts on evolution have been viciously attacked – by creationists and such scientific foes as Dawkins – but they offer more scope for the novelist's imagination than the more deterministic strain of Darwinism.

··†··

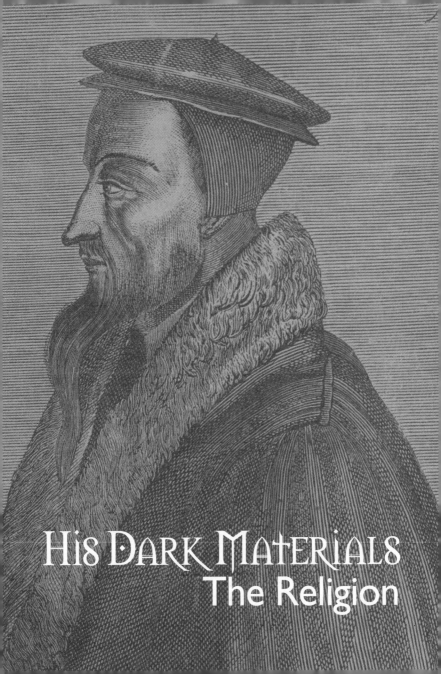

HIS DARK MATERIALS
The Religion

Reformed character? In *His Dark Materials*, John Calvin becomes Pope. In our world, he was so powerful he was dubbed the Pope of Geneva

CHURCH BUSINESS

The portrayal of religion in *His Dark Materials* has had many critics asking: what does Philip Pullman have against God?

A theism for kids. That's how one Christian critic dismissed *His Dark Materials*. British journalist **Peter Hitchens** has lamented: "In his worlds, the Church is wicked, cruel and child-hating; priests are sinister, murderous or drunk." Lapsed nun **Mary Malone** calls Christianity a powerful, convincing mistake – a view Pullman agrees with. When God appears, he is wicked and enfeebled by, Pullman said, "half a billion years of senile decay". This would have been enough, just five hundred years ago, to have him roasted at the stake for heresy.

New Line Cinema have assured America's unforgiving religious right that Pullman is not against religion per se but against cruelty, intolerance and fanatical zealotry. He recognizes **Jesus, Buddha** and **Mohammed** as "moral geniuses", a carefully chosen term, but feels that their messages have been abused by people who are determined to control and punish so that, in practice, "religions have a tendency to be less than divine". He has said in other interviews: "I'm not making an argument, or preaching a sermon or setting out a political tract: I'm telling a story."

Jesus the genius: but not, says Pullman, divine

It seems churlish to quibble with New Line but the books' portrayal of the Church does lack a little light and shade. Michael Billington complained in *The Guardian* that "in his didactic anti-clericalism, Pullman demonizes religion to the point of absurdity... it's hard to believe in a Church that has hardly moved forward since the days of the Inquisition."

And the "just telling a story" bit doesn't quite convince either. Read the books with their attitude to religion in mind and it's as if some fierce personal conviction had stifled, in this one area, Pullman's remarkably vivid and versatile imagination. Maybe the one thing he can't tolerate is intolerance. Yet, in attacking something he detests, he risks

RELIGIOUS DIFFERENCES

Your in-a-nutshell guide to five major faiths alluded to in *His Dark Materials*.

Christianity The belief that through the resurrection of **Jesus Christ**, the son of God, mankind can be absolved from sin and be resurrected to live forever. The books do not clearly indicate whether the Church is Catholic or Protestant.

Gnosticism The belief that human beings are divine souls trapped in a material world created by an evil spirit often called the **Demiurge**. To many Gnostics, Jesus was not the son of God but a teacher showing the way to true enlightenment, helping souls to free themselves from the material world.

Hermeticism An occult, mystical religion which argues that God is in all things. The Hermetic idea that all matter is part of a God they call "the All" sounds a bit like Pullman's Dust, only without the deity with a capital G.

Shamanism The belief that a spiritual leader, a shaman, can control and cooperate with the spirits that control human lives.

Zoroastrianism A monotheistic religion from ancient Persia which, in its most influential school, sees the world as the object of a cosmic duel between the forces of good and evil. The phrase "Zoroastrian heresy" is heard at Mrs Coulter's cocktail party.

sounding as dogmatic as his critics. The interesting question, which only he can really answer, is why the story so consistently condemns religion and not the ideologies that caused such immense suffering in the 20th century, and which he has, just as eloquently, publicly rubbished.

You can tell how important this theme is because twice in *His Dark Materials* he forgets his credo about trusting the story and puts his own thoughts in the mouths of his protagonists: Mary Malone's line about Christianity being a mistake and Lyra's rousing closing speech about the Republic of Heaven.

Interviewed by the Christian magazine *Third Way*, he reluctantly conceded that his treatment of the Church lacked subtlety. Asked why the servants of the Authority are so universally

> "OK, tHAt'S AN ARtiStIC FLAW. IF I'd HAd MORE tiME, I'd HAVE PUt A GOOd PRiESt iN tO SHOW tHEY'RE NOt ALL HORRiBLE."

reprehensible, he admitted: "OK, that's an artistic flaw. If I'd had more time to think about it no doubt I'd have put a good priest here or there, just to show they're not all horrible. But there we are. If you're writing a novel, especially a long story of thirteen hundred pages, there are always going to be things you wish you'd done differently. Artistic perfection is not achievable in anything much over the length of a sonnet." He went on to say that he could imagine writing a novel in which the Church did more good than harm.

To be honest, what he probably means is that he regrets the fact that this error has given critics an excuse to ignore his central argument. Just in case they need reminding what that argument is, he has helpfully declared: "My books are about killing God." That's some statement for an author who often reminds us to trust the tale, not the teller. What he's actually killing is the old idea of a God who looks after members of the human race, punishing us for our sins and rewarding us in heaven for our virtues. Instead of God, Pullman gives us that quasi-mystical mysterious enriching matter he calls **Dust**.

In 2003, Pullman explained: "In the sort of creation myth that underlies *His Dark Materials*, which is never fully explicit but which I was discovering as I was writing it, the notion is that there never was a Creator, instead there was matter, and this matter gradually became conscious of itself and developed into Dust. Dust sort of proceeds from matter as a way of understanding itself. The **Authority** was the first figure that condensed in this way, and from then on he was the oldest, the most powerful, the most authoritative. All the other angels at

IN HIS OWN WORDS

Philip Pullman has answered many – too many – questions about his views on religion. Here, for the record, are his more definitive remarks on the topic.

From his website:

"The religious impulse – which includes the sense of awe and mystery we feel when we look at the universe, the urge to find a meaning and a purpose in our lives, our sense of moral kinship with other human beings – is part of being human, and I value it. I'd be a damn fool not to. But organized religion is quite another thing. All too often in human history, churches and priesthoods have set themselves up to rule people's lives in the name of some invisible God (and they're all invisible, because they don't exist) – and done terrible damage. In the name of their God, they have burned, hanged, tortured, maimed, robbed, violated and enslaved millions of their fellow-creatures, and done so with the happy conviction that they were doing the will of God, and they would go to heaven for it. That is the religion I hate, and I'm happy to be known as its enemy."

From his interview with Third Way:

"The Christian story gives us human beings a very important and prominent part. We are the ones who Jesus came to redeem from the consequences of sin. It is a very dramatic story and we are right at the heart of it, and a great deal depends on what we decide. This is an exciting position to be in, but unfortunately it doesn't gel at all with the more convincing account that is given by Darwinian evolution – and the scientific account is far more persuasive intellectually. Far more persuasive."

From his website:

"I don't know whether there's a God or not. Nobody does, no matter what they say. I think it's perfectly possible to explain how the universe came about without bringing God into it, but I don't know everything, and there may well be a God somewhere, hiding away. Actually, if he is keeping out of sight, it's because he's ashamed of his followers and all the cruelty and ignorance they're responsible for promoting in his name."

From an interview with New Yorker:

"Although I call myself an atheist, I am a Church of England atheist and a 1662 Book Of Common Prayer atheist, because that's the tradition I was brought up in. I cannot escape those early influences."

From a debate with the Archbishop of Canterbury:

"If my religion is true, does that mean your religion is false, or are we worshipping the same God by different names? I'm temperamentally 'agin' the postmodernist position that there is no truth and it depends on where you are and it's all a result of the capitalist, imperialist hegemony of the bourgeois… all this sort of stuff. I'm agin that but I couldn't tell you why."

first believed he was the Creator and then some angels decided that he wasn't, so we had the temptation and the Fall – all that sort of stuff came from that."

No self-respecting when-you're-dead-you're-dead atheist would be convinced by Pullman's ideas on Dust for a nanosecond, but they are so crucial to *His Dark Materials* that it seems plain daft to say that the trilogy's attitude to religion, for all its flaws, begins and ends with deicide.

Two Cheers for Paganism

Trepanning would be too kind a fate for all but one of the Christian clerics in *His Dark Materials*. Yet as a self-confessed "tolerant, sceptical pagan", Pullman has much more time for pre-Christian religions, such as paganism, shamanism and witchcraft. The shaman **Stanislaus Grumman** is probably the only heroic, sympathetic, wise religious leader in the books.

Throughout the trilogy, Pullman enjoys working with dæmons (derived from the old idea that we all have guardian angels), harpies (influenced by the creatures of the same name in book three of Virgil's *Aeneid*), Spectres (who feast, vampire-like, on people's souls), headless ghosts, witches, zombies and the Black Shuck (a big ghostly dog, a recurring motif in English folklore). Spells, shamanic trances and divination (especially the **alethiometer** and the **I Ching**) pervade the novels.

> "THE BOOKS ARE FULL OF DÆMONS, ANGELS, HARPIES, SPECTRES, HEADLESS GHOSTS, WITCHES, ZOMBIES AND THE BLACK SHUCK, A BIG GHOSTLY DOG."

On a very literal level, the **pagan** influence can be traced through the named dæmons. Four of the most important dæmons have a symbolic meaning in ancient Celtic myth: **Pantalaimon**'s pine marten form is a symbol of grace and empathy, Will Parry's cat is a guardian, Serafina Pekkala's snow goose stands for vigilance and protection while Roger Parslow's terrier suggests fidelity. Asriel's snow leopard and Lee Scoresby's hare have pagan associations, while the raven, the Master of Jordan College's dæmon, features in Norse myths of Odin. To widen the frame of reference still further, John Faa's crow hints at alchemy and Mrs Coulter's golden monkey alludes to Chinese astrology.

Pullman's motifs reach out to such a vast, diverse body of belief it's as if he has absorbed, by osmosis, the works of **Joseph Campbell** and Sir James George

Fraser's *The Golden Bough*. To take just one example, the idea of a dæmon appears in Norse mythology as a **fylgia**, in Aztec myth as **Nahual**, as **aku-aku** in the legends of Easter Island and harks back to the age of Socrates (see p.149). With the rise of Christianity, demons began to be regarded as false gods and were soon held to be uniformly evil.

REWRITING GENESIS

When Pullman started writing *His Dark Materials* he jotted down an eight-page alternative version of **Genesis** to make sure that later in the trilogy, as he put it, the "scenery did not wobble". He gave *The Times* a condensed synopsis of his opening book of The Bible: "God was not the creator but the first. When other beings arose, the first angels, he told them He was the creator and they worshipped Him and obeyed Him because He told them to. One of them, Sophia, advised the being that called Himself God not to rule in this despotic, tyrannical way, to let everyone respect one another and be equal. But He wouldn't have it. So He threw her out of heaven, together with the other rebels, and she was one of the angels who tempted Adam and Eve. What the serpent was bringing Adam and Eve was wisdom."

> "PULLMAN WROTE AN ALTERNATIVE VERSION OF GENESIS TO MAKE SURE THAT LATER ON THE 'SCENERY DIDN'T WOBBLE'."

In the books, the Church doesn't want mankind to acquire wisdom. It is in deadly dispute with Asriel over his belief that there are other worlds, and it fears that Lyra, if she experiences love without guilt, could fatally damage its authority – which rests on the belief that sexuality is shameful and that only the Church can forgive sin. If sexuality is recognized as a natural state, humanity cannot be cowed by guilt or fear to obey the Church. If humanity can make that leap, Pullman suggests in a slightly didactic and out-of-character speech by **Lyra** in *The Amber Spyglass*, the human race can build a moral society – "the Republic of Heaven", a phrase associated with the English 16th-century radical **Gerrard Winstanley** (see p.169) – on Earth, rather than postponing such a society to an afterlife that does not exist.

Pullman has taken great pains to ensure that the Church in the books is not directly analogous to any church in our world. After the death of **Pope John Calvin**, the papacy was abolished, so the ultimate ecclesiastical authority is the

Divine shrine: the Hagia Sophia honours a Gnostic goddess who has much in common with Xaphania

Dead boring: Gustave Doré's idea of Purgatory

"tangle of courts, colleges and councils" known as the **Magisterium**. This rules through four slightly competing branches: the **Consistorial Court of Discipline**, the **General Oblation Board** (the gobblers), the **Society of the Work of the Holy Spirit** and the **College of Bishops**. The most powerful bodies are the Consistorial Court and the Oblation Board. Because the Church fears humanity is getting ideas above its station, it may reopen the **Office of the Inquisition**.

The Church is officially run by the Authority – who acts as God – but he is no longer the angelic dynamo that exiled Sophia. A demented being "of terrifying decrepitude" who dissolves in the wind and greets his demise with exhausted relief, he has, like many incompetent dictators in decline, ceded power to a functionary, the **Metatron**, who combines the cunning and efficiency of Martin Bormann with Hermann Goering's insatiable appetite for female flesh.

The papacy of **Pope John Calvin** is often seen as evidence that, in the books, the **Reformation** never happened. This would dovetail with the way some Oxford colleges have their old, pre-Henry VIII, names. But Calvin's papacy could equally imply that the Reformation did happen but didn't affect the Church's arrogant conduct. The slight disguise that turns what could easily have been a Catholic college of cardinals into the College of Bishops seems deliberate. Pullman's beef is with organized religion, not just with Catholicism.

Pullman may not believe in God, but he is thoroughly versed in Christian theology. This education started with his clergyman grandfather – hence his description of himself as "a Christian atheist, a Church of England atheist and a 1662 Book of Common Prayer atheist".

"LIKE MANY INCOMPETENT DICTATORS IN DECLINE, THE AUTHORITY HAS CEDED POWER TO A FUNCTIONARY."

A ROUGH GUIDE TO CHRISTIAN COMMUNISM

The Amber Spyglass ends with Lyra anticipating the Republic of Heaven, which is, the ghost of John Parry tells us, the paradise we must build in our own worlds. The phrase "Republic of Heaven" was popularized by the English radical **Gerrard Winstanley** (1609–76), a pioneer of Christian Communism, who criticized priests for living well on Earth but telling the poor their reward would only come in heaven.

In an email, Pullman said "I didn't come across Gerrard Winstanley till after I'd independently thought of the Republic of Heaven – though of course, as is almost always the case, I'd probably heard of it a long time before and simply forgotten."

Winstanley advocated a kind of Christian communism, believing God had created Earth as "a common treasury".

In the aftermath of the English Civil War and the execution of Charles I, some radicals believed it was enough to level society politically (by extending the vote), but Winstanley was convinced there had to be economic equality.

His followers became known as the **True Levellers** after they dug up land in Cobham Heath, Surrey, to set up their own commune. The Diggers inspired a few other communes, but they were soon harassed by hired thugs and the authorities made their lives as difficult as possible. By 1650, the Digger movement, which had led to communes in eight counties across England, had completely collapsed.

David Boulton, author of *Gerrard Winstanley And The Republic Of Heaven*, sees Winstanley as a liberation theologist ahead of his time. His legacy was largely forgotten until the 19th century, when the French Christian philosopher **Étienne Cabet** (1788–1856) called for a Christian Communist utopia, saying: "Communism is Christianity in its purest form before Christianity was corrupted by the Catholic Church."

Cabet can claim to have invented the word "**communisme**". Popular enough to be elected to the Chamber of Deputies, he despaired of reforming French society and emigrated to America, where he founded Icarian communities – the ideal society in one of his works had been called Icaria – in Texas, Illinois and Iowa.

His new societies lasted longer than Winstanley's – the last one, in Iowa, endured until 1898 – but he was expelled from the Illinois community in 1855 and lived, in exile, in St Louis. **Karl Marx** and **Friedrich Engels** were both heavily influenced by him – trying to meet him in 1848 in Paris – but ignored Cabet's Christian ethos.

In the 1950s, Cabet's writings helped inspire a doctrine called **liberation theology** which tried to combine social justice and Catholic theology and was especially influential in Central and South America in the 1960s and 1970s.

THE TALENTED MR CALVIN

The Protestant religious leader **John Calvin** (1509–64) is only mentioned twice in *His Dark Materials* but his influence runs far deeper.

In the first novel, Pullman tells us that Pope John Calvin had moved the seat of the papacy to Geneva. There, by setting up the **Consistorial Court of Discipline**, he established the Church's absolute authority over all aspects of life.

In *The Amber Spyglass*, Mrs Coulter hides Lyra in a Himalayan cave, trying to escape the Church's ruthless punishment. After all, she says: "Calvin himself ordered the deaths of the children." We are not explicitly told the two Calvins are one and the same, we just assume they are.

Why does Pullman single out Calvin? The real Calvin was a French Protestant Reformist theologian who taught, among other things, that mankind was naturally depraved and that certain men were predestined to go to heaven. He was exiled from Geneva because his accusers said he strove to create a new papacy, but he returned in the 1540s, ruling the city through a **Consistorial Court**, and became so powerful he was dubbed the "Pope of Geneva".

Although the *Catholic Herald* has found *His Dark Materials* especially offensive, the Calvinist brand of Protestantism offers a far more effective model for the books' powerful, sinister Church, with its pompously named bodies: the **Consistorial Court of Discipline** (an obvious homage to Calvin's governing body, though a formal meeting of the College of Cardinals is also called a consistory), the General Oblation Board, and the Magisterium.

Calvin symbolizes almost everything that Pullman despises about religion. He had opponents killed, more than twenty men and women were executed for witchcraft, women were imprisoned for dancing, a boy was whipped for calling his mother names and a girl was beheaded for striking her parents and breaking the Fifth Commandment – hence **Mrs Coulter**'s remark about children.

When Pullman said "**Jesus** set out a number of things in the Gospels which, if we all lived by them, we'd all do much better, what a pity the Church doesn't listen to them" he must have partly had leaders like Calvin in mind.

Calvin's defenders – he has some – paint him as a man who had some of the flaws of his time but praise him as a great Protestant thinker, a pioneer of education, a keen advocate of missionaries, a stern moral leader and the man who founded Geneva's silk industry. Though many women were punished for dancing and some burned as witches under his rule, his courts had no tolerance for spousal abuse and punished adultery among men as harshly as among women.

The bottom line, though, is that to live in Calvinist Geneva was to live in a **religious dictatorship**, where a stray remark could lead to imprisonment.

Pullman's knowledge of The Bible – "the old, authorized **King James Version** of The Bible" – informs the books. The novels allude to – or quote – Exodus, Ezekiel, Genesis, Daniel, Job, John, Kings, Luke, Mark, Matthew, Revelations and Paul's First Letter to the Thessalonians. Many biblical phrases – "ancient of days", "thief in the night", "Get thee behind me Satan" – are referenced. Serpents abound (at least three characters have them for dæmons) as do instances of temptation – usually as an allusion to the Fall but sometimes to Judas's betrayal of Jesus for thirty pieces of silver. The idea of Dust springs, in part, from God's rebuke to Adam and Eve: "for dust thou art and unto dust shalt thou return".

"INTERCISION ALLUDES TO THE CRUEL PRACTICE OF CASTRATING BOYS SO THEY COULD REMAIN SOPRANOS."

But Pullman's reading runs deeper and wider than that. Mary Malone quotes **St Augustine**'s thoughts on angels from the Catholic Catechism. The Authority's **land of the dead** reflects the nothingness of Catholic purgatory, especially as depicted by Gustave Doré. The Consistorial Court's doctrine of pre-emptive penance and absolution, granted to Father Gomez before he sets off on his mission, allows members to whip themselves (like the albino Opus Dei "monk" in *The Da Vinci Code*) before they kill, so they will be in a "state of grace". In the 16th century, priests did absolve, in advance, conquistadors who slaughtered thousands of indigenous people in Central and South America. Even today, in the Middle East, suicide bombers kill with the assurance that a place in heaven awaits.

Intercision alludes to the cruel practice of castrating boys so that, as **castrati**, they could remain sopranos. The practice wasn't invented by the Church – though Pope Sixtus V organized the Vatican choir in 1589 to include castrati – and was banned by **Pope Leo XIII** in 1878. Castration is one of the more recent offences by organized religion on Pullman's lengthy rap sheet.

THE HISTORY OF CHARISMATIC VILLAINY

Though many of the religious practices and doctrines in the books do have contemporary echoes, Michael Billington was right to point out that Pullman's Church has hardly changed since the Inquisition.

In the books, the Church has been cunningly crafted to embrace the worst attributes of the churches in medieval times and in the 16th century. The terminology (oblate, inquisition), the personnel (Calvin), the methodology (torture, assassination, persecution) and the attitude to science (the threats made against **Lord Asriel** and **Rusakov** recall Galileo's plight) all hail from those eras.

This may be Pullman's ingenious solution to a paradox that could have crippled the novels. His critique of organized religion seems central to his motivation and his story. Yet Western society is now so secular that he had to go back to the Middle Ages and the Reformation to find a Church with enough charismatic villainy to credibly menace Lyra and Will and threaten Asriel. In his defence, Pullman might argue that such horrors as the Inquisition are implicit in such organized religions as Christianity.

> "In a striking inversion of Christian tradition, Will shows mercy to a clapped-out God."

The criticism of Pullman's depiction of the Church can go too far. The use of rounded and flat characters is a tried-and-tested strategy for novelists, one that **Charles Dickens** perfected. We understand Oliver Twist and are perfectly happy to laugh at or despise his schoolmaster Wackford Squeers. Pullman's clerics are all flat. The eager assassin Father Gomez and the impatient, fanatical Father MacPhail are sinister enough, but **Father Borisovitch** is as easy to hate as Squeers. He stinks of tobacco, alcohol and sweat, likes playing cards and has paedophiliac tendencies, judging from the way he rests his "fat dirty fingers" on Will's knee. In another striking inversion of Christian tradition, Will shows mercy to a clapped-out God.

Peter Hitchens is right about one thing: the only truly sympathetic member of the clergy is **Mary Malone**, a fully rounded character who, in a true Hollywood cliché, is a lapsed nun.

Here come the Gnostics

In *The Da Vinci Code*, Dan Brown gives us an alternate secret history of Christianity. Pullman never planned to do anything that elaborate but, in fictionalizing his Church, he takes himself – and the reader – into far more diverse, exotic and esoteric theological realms than Brown's blockbuster.

Let's start with **Sophia**, the angel who has such a pivotal role in Pullman's variation on the Book of Genesis. She was sacred to Gnostic Christians and appears, loosely disguised, as the angel **Xaphania** in *The Amber Spyglass*.

REBEL REBEL

Considering one is a Greek god and the other a fictional aristocrat, Prometheus and Lord Asriel are almost two peas out of the same pod.

An intelligent, cunning, charismatic figure who, at a crucial point, sided with humanity and against religious authority. That description of **Prometheus** could just as easily be applied to **Lord Asriel**.

The name Prometheus means "foresight" although, as he completely failed to foresee how **Zeus** would react to his decision to give mankind fire, the name has a certain cruel irony. Fire wasn't his only gift to humanity: he taught the human race maths, writing, metalwork and architecture. In some myths, he created humanity.

There's general agreement that, as punishment for stealing fire for mankind, Prometheus was chained to a rock so an eagle could feast on his eternally regenerating liver.

The punishment was supposed to last 30,000 years – by which time the eagles would surely have been heartily sick of raw liver – but he was rescued by Hercules after twelve generations.

Prometheus was still legally obliged to be tied to a rock. But his defence team were even better than OJ Simpson's, and the letter – if not the spirit – of the law was fulfilled when he was given a ring with a rock in it to wear.

But the saga of Prometheus's defiance was not over. Deciding humanity had not been punished enough, Zeus tricked them into opening

Pandora's box and letting all kinds of bad stuff loose on the world.

The myth of Prometheus and the **Fall of Man** in Genesis are almost like rough drafts of the same tale. In both cases, mankind acquires forbidden knowledge and is swiftly punished by angry gods.

So what has all this do with Asriel? Prometheus is the only god who has the audacity, courage and intelligence to challenge Zeus on mankind's behalf, and **Dr Stanislaus Grumman** tells us: "If anyone could lead a rebellion against the Church in this world, or even further, it would be Asriel."

Both Prometheus and Asriel are feared by their enemies for their knowledge. One tradition says that all this stuff about fire was a sideshow and that Prometheus was really punished because he knew who would overthrow the gods, while Asriel's philosophical investigations earn him a death sentence.

Both the Greek god and Pullman's rebel are so convinced of their cause they don't worry about the chaos their rebellions might trigger.

Mankind pays for Promethean defiance with the arrival of evil and despair, while the hole Asriel rips in the sky triggers chronic cataclysmic climate change. Not a great argument for rebellion, is it?

The network of sects we now call **Gnosticism** flourished in the first and second century AD. "Gnostic" means "knowledge" in Greek but many believers used it to signify "revelation", often of some mysterious knowledge of salvation that others did not possess.

Though there were many strands of Gnosticism, there was a common idea that there were two worlds, good and evil, and that the body belonged to the evil, material world. For many Gnostics, Jesus was not the son of God but a teacher showing a select few the way to free themselves from the material world.

To the heirs of St Paul, who founded and ran the organization that became the Catholic Church, this was "wicked blasphemy". When Constantine made **Pauline Christianity** the Roman Empire's official religion, Gnostic heresies were severely punished. That may explain why 52 of their texts were stuck in a cave in **Nag Hammadi** in Upper Egypt. They were discovered, by accident, in 1945.

One of those texts, *The Testimony Of Truth*, retells the Fall. In this reworking, the serpent is a symbol of divine wisdom, trying to enlighten Adam and Eve while a jealous God tries to bully them into staying ignorant.

In Pullman's background story, **Sophia** fulfils the role of the serpent, as she does in some Gnostic allegories of the creation of mankind. Sophia was the pre-eminent figure in Gnostic

AIN'T THAT A HOLE IN THE HEAD

Trepanning – the practice of drilling a hole in the human skull – is pursued by **Siberian Tartar** tribes in *His Dark Materials* so that "the gods can talk to them". In our world, it often had a mystical, as well as a medical, purpose. The earliest evidence of trepanning was found at a burial site in France dating from the Neolithic period (about 6500 BC). Although post-mortem trepanning has been used for brain extraction and for making amulets and medicines, on many finds the bone has partially regrown, proving that the patient survived the operation.

As an operation to relieve pressure on the brain and to remove broken pieces of skull, **Hippocrates** (c.460–c.370BC) advises trepanning in his treatises on surgery, but in other early societies the distinction between medicines, ritual and religion is not so clearly drawn. To this day, trepanning is considered a cure for migraines and mental ailments among the **Kisii** of Kenya, who usually use a small saw or scrape away the bone until the dura mater is exposed.

The **Lugbara** of Uganda and the native people of British Columbia have, among others, trepanned to release evil spirits from the brain.

Fans might like to know that **Pullman** does not advocate the practice, telling *The Guardian*: "No one's coming near me with a drill."

Hole in one: drilling a hole in the skull was thought to ward off migraines and evil spirits

mythology, so pre-eminent, in fact, that she is hard to categorize. She was, at different times, a sacred, wise figure (her name means wisdom in Greek), a goddess who created the world by mistake, and Jesus' spiritual mate. Many Gnostics revered Sophia because she rebelled against the **Demiurge**, a figure they equated with the Old Testament God, who, just like the Authority, falsely claimed to be the true creator of the world.

Though she has a minor role in The Bible, her legend endures. The Russian Orthodox Church has a school of theology called **Sophiology** (in which adherents try to understand the wisdom of God), and her sacred shine, the Hagia Sophia in Istanbul, is one of the most beautiful buildings in the world.

In *His Dark Materials*, the very important angel **Xaphania**, one of Asriel's three high commanders, is austere, compassionate and inconceivably old, yet revered by Balthamos for much the same reasons the Gnostics worshipped Sophia. She advises Lyra and Will, who face the same Gnostic choice as Sophia: knowledge or obedience?

In a passing allusion to Gnostic history, Asriel's alethiometer reader, **Teukros Basilides**, takes his surname from the great Gnostic teacher who lived in Alexandria in the 2nd century. **Carl Jung** said that his book, *Seven Sermons To The Dead*, in which he lauds the serpent for helping mankind to discover knowledge, was a "translation" from Basilides. **Jorge Luis Borges** twice mentions the Gnostic teacher in his fiction. His 1944 story, *Three Versions Of Judas*, begins: "In Asia Minor or in Alexandria, in the second century of our faith, when Basilides published that the Cosmos was a reckless or evil improvisation by deficient angels".

It is not clear when Pullman decided to weave such themes into the books. But in the 1970s, he read **David Lindsay**'s *A Voyage To Arcturus* (1920) which, in the guise of a sci-fi novel about a trip to another planet, confronts the Gnostic idea that this world is the creation of a false God and that every Gnostic has a duty to find the one true God and their true home. Pullman hailed the book as a "crude, badly written, ignorant, work of genius" which was as visionary as Blake.

> "ALL THE GNOSTIC VARIANTS REJECT THE PHYSICAL UNIVERSE. I THINK THE EXISTENCE OF MATTER IS A BLESSING."

Asked for this Rough Guide if he believed in Gnosticism, Pullman replied: "I'm not a Gnostic, despite the intoxicating power of the Gnostic myth, because all the Gnostic variants involve a rejection of the physical universe. I love the physical universe. I think the existence of matter is a profound blessing, and not the terrible imprisoning evil Gnosticism makes it out to be."

Gnosticism is, however, an extremely handy source of ideas if, like Pullman, you intend to write a novel that will stand an awful lot of mainstream Christian theology on its head.

THE HIDDEN WISDOM OF HERMES

Lyra's **alethiometer** isn't just an instrument for measuring truth, it is a symbolic link to the submerged religious tradition we now call **Hermeticism** after **Hermes Trismegistus** ("Thrice-great Hermes"), a Greek god of magic and knowledge synonymous with the Egyptian god **Thoth**. In 1460, some old texts found by an agent of **Cosimo de' Medici** were attributed to Hermes and, as they were mistakenly thought to have come from ancient Egypt, believed to be the source of powerful, ancient, wisdom.

This was an important misconception because if the Church had realized, as was later proved, that these texts were from the early Christian era, they might have been discarded, censored or suppressed. Instead, in the intellectual ferment of Renaissance Europe, Hermeticism soon spread.

A CLASH OF SYMBOLS

The world's most famous fictional symbologist Dr Robert Langdon could write a book about the alethiometer. Some of the 36 symbols on it have many associations. There is a list of eighteen different meanings for the sun symbol on the Bridge To The Stars website, varying from kingship to homosexuality. Here are other intriguing, lesser-known resonances of the symbols.

Alpha and omega Taken together, the alpha and the omega represent the eternal nature of Jesus Christ. But omega, on its own, is an ancient symbol of the goddess Ishtar and once represented her headdress. Alpha comes from the ox-horn headdress worn by ancient kings.

Anchor An ancient symbol of hope, adopted by Christians.

Beehive A key symbol in Freemasonry, signifying industry and cooperation.

Bull A powerful Celtic symbol that could denote strength of will, virility and wealth, the bull was associated with storms in Mesopotamia and, in ancient Israel, with the God Yahweh.

Candle A humanist symbol of reason, but, in a pagan wicca service, a sign that the god and goddess are present.

Compass One of the three most powerful symbols in Freemasonry; the sign of a master mason.

Dolphin A symbol of resurrection – and of Christ – to Christians in Greek and Roman times.

Griffin As a unique blend of eagle and lion, the griffin has been seen as a symbol of Christ's resurrection. But before Dante's time, it was associated with the Antichrist and was also aligned with Apollo, the Greek god of fire.

Hourglass A common symbol of time running out, the hourglass is an emblem of human life for master masons.

Moon A pagan symbol for intuition, magic and mystery usually associated with womanhood or a goddess. Also a trump card in a deck of tarot cards and, in alchemy, a symbol of silver.

Owl Usually regarded in the West as a symbol of natural wisdom, the owl was regarded as a harbinger of death by the Mayans and the Aztecs. In Hopi native American mythology, the bird is surrounded by taboos because it is associated with evil and sorcery.

Tree To John Calvin, the tree was a symbol of the life mankind had received from God, but the tree has almost as many symbolic – and esoteric – associations as the sun.

In a Norse saga, an ash tree provides the magical springwater of knowledge, while in the Garden of Eden, Adam and Eve eat from the Tree of Life and the Tree of Knowledge. In Kabbalist and Hermeticist thought, the Tree of Life is a mystical concept used to explain the creation of the world.

Leonardo da Vinci praised "Hermes the philosopher", and many scholars, notably **John Dee**, Roger Fludd, **Heinrich Khunrath** and **Giordano Bruno** studied these works. All but Fludd were namechecked in *His Dark Materials* or in Pullman's invented back story for the alethiometer.

The historian **Frances Yates** even suggests that the renewed interest in the Hermetic tradition sparked a scientific revolution. By focusing on the power of numbers, glorifying mechanical inventiveness and creating a secretive world where hidden knowledge could be tested, the Hermetic tradition was, says Yates, the midwife at the birth of modern science. Hermeticism changed society in other ways, too, inspiring the esoteric order of the Rosicrucians, the Bavarian secret society known as the Illuminati and the Freemasons.

There is an argument over whether Hermeticism constitutes a religion. For true believers, it is *the* religion, the secret knowledge that lies at the inner core of such religions as Christianity and Islam. For others, it is a secretive, magical cult. *His Dark Materials* shares three motifs – angels, demons and magic – with one of the key Hermetic texts *The Emerald Tablet Of Hermes Trismegistus*.

This text celebrated three kinds of wisdom: alchemy (meaning the transformation of a soul, not metal), astrology and magic. The tablet proposes that magic could be divine – if performed in alliance with angels – or evil (*goetia*) – if carried out with demons.

Lyra's alethiometer may be likened to a compass or a clock, but it is an extraordinary instrument, full of allusions to all manner of arcane knowledge. Pullman's back story for the instrument acknowledges a debt to the memory theatre system of symbolic images devised in the 16th and early 17th century and it looks very much like the symbol-filled circles in Hermetic texts (for a fuller discussion of the alethiometer's secret history see p.49).

> "LYRA'S ALETHIOMETER LOOKS VERY MUCH LIKE THE SYMBOL-FILLED CIRCLES IN HERMETIC TEXTS."

But the most intriguing link is between Hermeticism and Dust. **Aldous Huxley**, in his book *The Perennial Philosophy*, identified four fundamental doctrines of Hermeticism. The first is especially relevant to *His Dark Materials*: "The phenomenal world of matter and of individualized consciousness – the world of things and animals and men and even gods – is the manifestation of a Divine Ground within which all partial realities have their being, and apart from which they would be non-existent." Stripped of the gobbledegook, this

Secret service: Hermes' cult of hidden knowledge sparked a scientific revolution

doctrine isn't really that far from Pullman's idea of **Dust** as the matter that keeps the universe alive.

The number of symbols on the alethiometer seems significant, alluding to another body of mystical teaching: the Kabbalah. There are 36 symbols on it, exactly half of 72. That happens to be the number of names God has in **Kabbalism**. The tradition is that these 72 names are the secret to immense power. Some traditions suggest **Moses** used one of these names to part the Red Sea. The most famous illustration of these names, reproduced in an esoteric tome called *Oedipus Aegyptiacus* (1652–54) by German Jesuit scholar **Athanasius Kircher** (credited as the author of a book advertised in *Lyra's Oxford*), looks uncannily like an alethiometer.

THE HEART OF THE MATTER

Gnosticism, Hermeticism, Kabbalism, shamanism, Christian Communism, where does this all take us? On one level, not very far. Pullman clearly doesn't believe in any of these "isms", any more than he believes in mainstream Christianity. They are, at the end of the day, just ideas he found useful or inspiring as he wrote the story.

But the painstaking care Pullman has put into the subtexts and symbols may explain why *His Dark Materials* has such authority as a work of fiction. By opening doors into many theologies, beliefs and practices, he has given his story extra resonance, a hinterland if you want to call it that, which makes the epic battle between good and evil that climaxes with *The Amber Spyglass* feel eternal, elemental and profound.

For all his knowledge of – and affection for – the King James Bible, Pullman makes it absolutely clear by the end of *The Amber Spyglass* that he does not believe in mainstream Christian theology. Though Dust offers some kind of mystical afterlife, even the angels long to have bodies. Physically existing seems the most desirable state of being. Anything else is a poor substitute.

Pullman does believe in human decency, which comes from our "accumulated human wisdom" and will help us build "the Republic of Heaven" on Earth. Though some religious writers have called his godless world nihilistic, Pullman believes we have reason enough to treat other people well, without the threat of punishment or the promise of reward. It is a courageous belief.

With the last century being marked by two world wars, several genocides, a succession of famines and mankind's seeming inability to change the behaviour that may destroy the planet it lives on, believing in "accumulated human wisdom" seems even more of a leap of faith than the conviction that Jesus came back from the dead to prove to us that he was the son of God. Presumably, humanity's rather dismal recent form is down to the fact that we haven't, yet, accumulated quite enough wisdom.

✢

His Dark Materials
The Politics

The man who changed the world: but would Lord Asriel's longed-for Republic of Heaven turn out as disappointingly as Lenin's Soviet Union?

"SOMETHING POLITICAL"

That's what Lyra says is going on in *Northern Lights*. And she's right – it's just that not many people have noticed

A sked whether, as the novelist **Robert McCrum** had suggested, *His Dark Materials* reflected "the atmosphere of 1970s socio-political crisis in which he first began to write", Pullman said, in an email: "Politics is a thing I'm very conscious of – it would be odd if my fiction didn't touch on it. The advantage of fantasy, of course, is that you can isolate and exaggerate things you want to focus on."

McCrum has written one half-decent political novel (*In The Secret State*) and his remark may have been prompted by the fact that, for him, Mrs Coulter "owes more than a little to Mrs Thatcher". *His Dark Materials* is about many things – most especially science and religion – but it is also about our place in the world(s) and what kind of society we ought to live in, both eminently political themes. The trilogy starts with Lyra noting: "I know there's something going on – something political" and ends with the heroine making an enormous sacrifice to dedicate herself to building the Republic of Heaven on Earth. This finale was so important to Pullman that he admitted, to Rough Guides, he considered calling the third novel *The Republic Of Heaven*. "But I was talked out of it by my publisher." The imaginative adventures are suffused with political intrigue, which erupts into bloody military conflict in *The Amber Spyglass*.

In this, Pullman is only being true to his word. He has chided English novelists – since the deaths of **William Golding** and **Graham Greene** – for avoiding the larger issues and preferring to dwell on the intricacies and professional mystifications of literary theory, declaring: "You can't leave morality out unless your work is so stupid and trivial and so worthless that [nobody] would want to read it anyway."

From his own remarks, his personal politics would seem to be an intriguing blend of left-wing radicalism and moralistic concern that hasn't really had a public voice since the assassination of **Robert Kennedy**. Pullman is disgusted by politicians' "desperately foolish" attitude to climate change, worried by the commercialization of everyday life, appalled by the marginalization of his old profession, teaching, and fearfully eloquent about free speech. In 2002, at the Edinburgh Festival, he defined his personal credo: "This is what I'm against. Every religion and fundamental organization where there is one truth and they will kill you if you don't believe it." That belief goes to the heart of the struggle between Lord Asriel and his allies and the Church. And we can't completely understand Asriel without exploring the books' political dimension. He is the politician we are, with a few hefty reservations, invited to empathize with.

GERRARD, LYRA AND BELINDA

A 17th-century Christian radical, the plucky heroine of *His Dark Materials* and the American pop temptress share one belief: that heaven is – or could be – a place on Earth. Belinda Carlisle's heaven is in the arms of a true love. For **Gerrard Winstanley** and **Lyra**, paradise on Earth is something much broader and harder to accomplish – the creation of a morally just society.

Winstanley (see p.169) campaigned for political and economic equality in the 1640s, digging up common land in various parts of southern England and living on it with his supporters, dubbed the Diggers. He coined the phrase "**the Republic of Heaven**" to describe the society he hoped to see on Earth.

He pointedly asked the wealthy clergy on the poor's behalf: "Why may we not have our heaven here (that is a comfortable livelihood in the Earth) and heaven hereafter too?" He believed that hopes of an unearthly paradise and fears of eternal Hell were blinding people to "what is done to them on Earth while they are living." In other words, two centuries before Karl Marx, he had effectively concluded that religion was the **opium of the masses**.

Winstanley is a charismatic, controversial figure from one of Pullman's favourite eras, the 17th century. His core beliefs were simple and lucid, especially when compared to most political thought at the time of the English Civil War. He argued that land belonged to everyone and that no one should be in power in any institution for very long because it bred arrogance.

He showed a Christ-like determination to turn the other cheek when his followers, the Diggers, were violently attacked. Ironically, the authority figure who presided over the destruction of his second community of Diggers in the rural Surrey town of **Cobham** was not a lord or a general, but a Puritan pastor called **John Platt**.

THE DIGGERS HAVE THEIR SAY

In 1649, Gerrard Winstanley explained why the Diggers were going to dig up St George's Hill in Weybridge, Surrey, and sow the land with parsnips, carrots and beans.

"The work we are going about is this, to dig up George's Hill and the waste grounds thereabouts, and sow corn, and to earn our bread together by the sweat of our brows. And the first reason is this, that we may work in righteousness, and lay the foundation of making the Earth a common treasury for all, both rich and poor, that everyone that is born in the land may be fed by the Earth his mother that brought him forth, according to the reason that rules in the creation."

When Winstanley all but retired from politics after 1650, the tradition of **pre-Marxist English socialism** went underground, though his legend lives on in the scholarship of historian Christopher Hill and in Kevin Brownlow's 1975 documentary styled movie **Winstanley** (the poster for which is shown above).

In 1988, the anarchist English group **Chumbawamba** recorded one of Winstanley's political songs, "The Diggers Song" on their album *English Rebel Songs 1381–1914*.

For Pullman, "the Republic of Heaven" would have sounded beautifully simple and pleasingly radical. Morality is too important to Pullman, for him to subscribe to the materialism of **Marxism**. And Winstanley is an intriguing hero for Pullman: an intelligent, eloquent, slightly batty spokesman for a strain of socialism that, unlike Marxism and its bastardized offshoots, has never been entirely discredited because it's never really been tested.

For all his radicalism, Winstanley still believed in God. Pullman doesn't. As he said to *Third Way* magazine: "The kingdom of heaven promised us certain things: happiness and a sense of purpose and a sense of having a place in the universe, of having a role and a destiny that were noble and splendid. We were not alienated. But now that, for me anyway, the King is dead, I still need these things that heaven promised. I don't think I will continue to live after I'm dead, so to achieve these things I must try to bring them about on Earth, in a republic in which we are all free and equal – and responsible – citizens."

> "I STILL NEED THE THINGS THAT HEAVEN PROMISED. TO ACHIEVE THEM, I MUST TRY TO BRING THEM ABOUT ON EARTH."

He sets out an idealistic manifesto for creating this paradise. "What does this involve? All the best qualities of things. We mustn't shut anything out. If the Church has told us that forgiving our enemies is good, and if that seems to be a good thing to do, we must do it. If, on the other hand, those who struggled against the Church have shown us that free enquiry and unfettered scientific exploration is good – and I believe they have – then we must hold this up as a good. Whatever good we can see with the accumulated wisdom we have as we grow up, and read about in history and learn from our experiences – wherever they come from, and whoever taught them in the first place, let's use them and do whatever we can do to make the world a little bit better."

Lyra says something similar, albeit in compressed form, to her sleepy dæmon at the end of *The Amber Spyglass*.

REBELS AND REPUBLICS

His Dark Materials is no monarchist fantasy. Instead of the fantasy genre's traditional conservative concern with the restoration of a line of fallen kings, the books are the product of a republican imagination. There are monarchs in the book but they either support or oppose Asriel's heavenly republic, the reason the rebellious aristocrat is at war with the Authority. But would his republic be the same as Lyra's or Pullman's? His right-hand man **King Ogunwe** certainly thinks so. He tells Mrs Coulter that his proudest task is to assist Asriel "in setting up a

HOW TO SPOT AN ABSOLUTIST REGIME

You don't have to rule in the name of God to exercise absolute power. It's enough, says Pullman, to have your own ideology that becomes a secular bible. On his website, he identified a number of traits theocratic regimes have in common.

"There is a holy book, a scripture, whose word is inerrant, whose authority is above dispute: as it might be, the works of Karl Marx.

⚜

There are prophets and doctors of the church, who interpret the holy book and pronounce on its meaning: as it might be, Lenin, Stalin, Mao.

⚜

There is a priesthood with special powers, which can confer blessings and privileges on the laity, or withdraw them, and in which authority tends to concentrate in the hands of elderly men: as it might be, the communist party.

⚜

There is the concept of heresy and its punishment: as it might be, Trotskyism.

⚜

There is an inquisition with the powers of a secret police force: as it might be, the Cheka, the NKVD, etc.

⚜

There is a complex procedural apparatus of betrayal, denunciation, confession, trial and execution: as it might be, the Stalinist terror under Yezhov and Beria and the other state inquisitors.

⚜

There is a teleological view of history, according to which human society moves inexorably towards a millennial fulfilment in a golden age: as it might be, the dictatorship of the proletariat, as described by dialectical materialism.

⚜

There is a fear and hatred of external unbelievers: as it might be, the imperialist capitalist powers.

⚜

There is a fear and hatred of internal demons and witches: as it might be, kulaks or bourgeois deviationists.

⚜

There is the notion of pilgrimage to sacred places and holy relics: as it might be, the birthplace of Stalin, or the embalmed corpses in Red Square.

⚜

And so on, ad nauseam. In fact, the Soviet Union was one of the most thoroughgoing theocracies the world has ever seen, and it was atheist to its marrow. In this respect, the most dogmatic materialist is functionally equivalent to the most fanatical believer; Stalin's Russia is exactly the same as Khomeini's Iran. It isn't belief in God that causes the problem. The root of the matter is quite different. It is that theocracies don't know how to read, and democracies do."

world where there are no kingdoms at all… we intend to be free citizens of the Republic of Heaven."

Asriel's character has been analysed with forensic intensity as if the proportions of good and bad could be determined with scientific rigour. But it is the ethical complexity of his character – and of the choices he faces as a leader – that intrigues Pullman.

Like his fellow foe of religion **Vladimir Lenin**, Asriel is engaged on a mission that should benefit the masses and, not entirely coincidentally, make him much more powerful. Thorold's remark that Asriel has a "way special to himself of bringing about what he wants" could equally apply to the Russian revolutionary. Asriel has rallied a diverse coalition around his cause, broader than that which took Lenin to power in 1917. Like the Bolshevik leader, Asriel believes the end justifies the means. He does not doubt that Roger Parslow's death serves the greater good, just as Lenin, once in power, never fretted over the executions of his erstwhile allies, the **Social Revolutionaries**. Asriel is unfazed by the environmental catastrophe wreaked by his gap in the sky, just as Lenin's heirs never worried about the ecological disaster triggered by rapid industrialization and nuclear arms testing.

> "ASRIEL SHOT THE WRONGED HUSBAND, PUT LYRA ON HIS SHOULDERS AND STRODE AROUND WHILE THE BODY LAY AT HIS FEET."

For impatient idealists like Lenin and Asriel, the future is so glorious that the damage they do today is utterly irrelevant. Just as Lenin disappointed those who hoped he would make Russia a socialist democracy, you wonder if Asriel – for all his talk of democracy and freedom – would ever have delivered Ogunwe's utopia.

Asriel had, like many arrogant politicians, committed adultery (even Lenin is rumoured to have had an affair with a French Communist). But Asriel deepens the stain on his reputation by cold-bloodedly shooting the wronged husband between the eyes and proceeds, in one of those weird changes of mood worthy of such dictatorial psychopaths as **Mao Zedong**, to put Lyra on his shoulders and stride up and down in glee, while the dead man lies at his feet. Such incidents remind us why Lyra finds it impossible not to admire him but hard to like or trust him – hardly an untypical response to a politician.

His autocratic behaviour, habit of rebuking manservants, and his suggestion that he and Marisa could reduce the universe to pieces and rebuild it suggest that his heroic rebellion is not against authority as such but, like Lenin's revolution, designed to replace an authority he despises with his own which he prefers ideologically. And the interim Republic of Heaven he creates at his basalt fortress seems, to connoisseurs of failed revolutions, wearily familiar. The most developed facilities seem to be arms factories, a preference for heavy industry that Stalin would approve of.

And yet, as with most political leaders – even **Lenin** – Asriel's legacy is too complex for him to be trashed as an outright villain. To simplify him is to miss Pullman's point: that any leader who tries to do something may end up with a record as complex as Lord Asriel's. Often vitriolic in his public remarks about politics, Pullman doesn't pretend in the books that leadership is a business where it's easy to be pure and virtuous. If Asriel wasn't an operator and an idealist, he wouldn't be such a threat to the Authority and such a hope to the armoured bears, gyptians and Gallivespians.

Asriel defeated anti-gyptian legislation in Parliament and lets them navigate through canals on his property. He is eloquent about the atrocities committed against humanity by the Church ("to rebel was right and just when you consider what the agents of the Authority did in his name"), leads his cause with Promethean audacity and courage – to the point of self-sacrifice – and, judged by the company he keeps, ought to be a better option for the world than Metatron. His struggle, though it does not transform society as radically as he had hoped, does achieve one unqualified good: dissolving the General Oblation Board and thereby ending the practice of intercision.

Ultimately, though more liberal factions have sway in the **Magisterium**, the Church remains strong and Asriel's vision is unfulfilled. His daughter **Lyra's** Republic of Heaven is not so overtly political as Asriel's, it is not as spelled out as his, but from what we can glean it seems more of a moral code.

The one character who does believe in the **Republic of Heaven** is shaman **Stanislaus Grumman**. He first mentions the phrase to Will and Lyra in *The Amber Spyglass* and correctly predicts Asriel's failure, saying that: "We have to build the republic of heaven where we are because there is no elsewhere."

The temptations of absolutism

In his University of East Anglia lecture *Miss Goddard's Grave*, Pullman attacked "theocratic absolutism" (the full lecture is on *www.philippullman.com)* in which he noted: "In fact, as far as the way they behaved in practice is concerned, there are remarkable similarities between the Spain of **Philip II**, the Iran of **Ayatollah Khomeini** and the Soviet Union under **Stalin**. We might see some parallels with the United States in the time of McCarthy."

Theocratic absolutism is probably as good a description as any of the power structure, represented in the books by the Church, the College of Bishops, the Consistorial Court of Discipline, the General Oblation Board, the Magisterium, the Office of Inquisition and the Society of the Work of the Holy Spirit. There is something terribly Venetian in the profusion of bodies and the way their roles and responsibilities apparently overlap.

The relationship of these ecclesiastical bodies with the organs of state is still more mysterious. The **General Oblation Board** is, the Master of Jordan College tells us, a "semi-private initiative, not entirely answerable" to the Consistorial Court, but, we assume, not entirely independent either. The GOB's headquarters are in the **Ministry of Theology** in White Hall. There is a parliament though, as it's mentioned just once, it could have been dissolved. Asriel and the Master sit on a cabinet council that advises the prime minister. This may or may not be the same as the council of state on which, in Lyra's world, the superbly connected **Lord Boreal** sits.

Boreal – or **Sir Charles Latrom** as he calls himself in Will's world – is a ubiquitous eminence grise. One of the GOB's top officials, he investigates the **Dark Matter Unit** and is in touch with the shadowy spooks searching for John Parry and Lyra and with the enigmatic Inspector Walters, who may be from Special Branch.

"THE VARIETY OF BODIES DEVOTED TO REPRESSION IN THE BOOKS IS SO GREAT AS TO BE ALMOST PYTHONESQUE."

No organogram could capture a theocracy that complex. But the variety of bodies devoted wholly, mainly or partly to repression is so great as to be almost Pythonesque. The Consistorial Court uses torture and **assassination** to protect its patch, the GOB is more interested in **abduction**, the Magisterium has two armies – Muscovy's Imperial Guard and the Swiss Guards – a corps of **censors** and an **Inquisition** to do its bidding. The censors behave like Communist **commissars** in Red Army units, sniffing out heresy whether it has occurred in scientific research institutes or on expeditions.

In the fruitier regions of cyberspace, the Jesuits are the assassination squad of the Catholic Church. In the books, the mission – and self-certainty – of **Father Gomez**, the Church assassin, may be inspired by Balthasar Gerárd, the Catholic

Modern witchhunter: Senator McCarthy is a symbol of the absolutism Pullman's novels condemn

fanatic who shot **Prince William the Silent** (1533–84) with a pistol. William's religious tolerance so incensed King Philip II that the Spanish Bourbon offered 25,000 crowns to anyone who would murder this troublesome prince. Gerárd obliged and made William a Protestant martyr in the Netherlands.

Not to be left out, the state has at least one security service – Will kills one of their spies at the start of *The Subtle Knife* – and Special Branch. Boreal/Latrom says the men who persecute Will's mother work for the Secret Service. Their arrogance, boorish harassment and constant intrusions are reminiscent of the **FBI** goon squads that, in the early 1950s, so enthusiastically investigated suspected Communists accused, often with the flimsiest evidence, by the paranoid, alcoholic **Senator Joe McCarthy** in a hysterical witchhunt that did more damage to America than anything the Communist Party ever achieved.

"To isolate and exaggerate"

Global warming is a recurring theme in Pullman's journalism and in the books, with the environment under serious threat even before **Asriel** opens the bridge between two worlds with such disastrous consequences.

Global warning: the Alaskan city of Shismaref may soon be utterly destroyed by climate change

The habit of cutting **windows** from one world to another has, after three hundred years, left the **mulefa** facing ecological chaos. Dust is drifting out to sea, the seed-pod trees are dying and the mulefa's tradition of living "in perpetual joy" with trees is in danger. The mulefa are a metaphor for humanity, though, unlike us, they are responsible environmental stewards. (They are not perfect: the fact that they try not to scare the grazers while killing them for food won't impress many vegans.) **Mary Malone**, a scientist who has none of Asriel's recklessness, realizes why the seed-pod trees are dying and tries to solve the problem. Ultimately, it takes Lyra and Will to reverse the flow of Dust.

Asriel's bridge is an unmitigated environmental disaster. With rivers flowing in the wrong direction and animals forgetting where they are migrating to, Will tells Lyra: "People have been interfering with the atmosphere by putting chemicals in it, and the weather's going out of control." Luckily, in context on the printed page, this doesn't seem as corny and message-laden.

Though environmental apocalypse is just averted in the books, we are left to ponder that it won't be so easy in our world. The tragedy has already begun in one of Pullman's favourite parts of the world, the Bering Straits.

The Alaskan city of **Shismaref**, inhabited for 4000 years, will, barring a miracle, have to be completely evacuated within a few years as global warming melts the permafrost that has, for so long, supported it. Most of the locals are Inupiats, the kind of Inuit people the barman at Nova Zembla is referring to when he talks of the inhabitants of **Beringland**.

The books confront another political evil – that of **racism** – with less fanfare and more stealth. The **gyptians** – though Pullman has muddied their gene pool with some Dutch – are clearly meant to be gypsies (the two words derive from Egyptians, which is how the English used to refer to the Roma), and their persecution by the authorities and the whispered allegations of horse stealing are not far removed from the kind of petty harassment faced today by **Roma** – or those who are simply known as travellers.

The proposal for a "**continuous cruising license**", which would force boat dwellers to travel a minimum of 120 miles every three months or rent expensive docking space, is analogous to many councils' efforts to constantly move travellers on. Yet the gyptians are arguably the most democratic race in the books, with a habit of communal decision making matched only by witches.

Like the gyptians, the **Gallivespians** have special reason for joining Asriel's rebellion. They are regarded as "diabolic" by humans who, Ogunwe says, "have been trying to exterminate the small people since the earliest time anyone can remember." Hated by the Authority's supporters, the diminutive creatures rally to Asriel's side.

Humanity represents a different kind of danger to the armoured bears. Iofur Raknison is deservedly defeated by **Iorek Byrnison** because, as king, he betrayed his race, encouraging them to ape humans. The issue here is not maintaining the panserbjørne's racial purity but preventing their native culture from being diluted or absorbed by a more powerful and glamorous one.

> "THE CONTINUOUS CRUISING LICENCE IS A METAPHOR FOR THE KIND OF PETTY HARASSMENT THE ROMA FACE EVERY DAY."

SUFFER LITTLE CHILDREN...

The **intercision** that separates children from their dæmons and turns them into **zombi** is a brutal business that makes for very uncomfortable reading. One method of intercision, the ambiguous operation involving a scalpel known as the **Maystadt process**, cannot be done when the child is conscious. Alternatively, child and dæmon are placed in two separate cages so a special silver guillotine

– another quick reference to another bloody revolution? – can sever the invisible link between them. Intercision, the Church's desperate bid to stop children having sinful thoughts, leaves victims traumatized, sickly and nearly dead.

The rationale for this practice isn't purely theological. The fact that the gyptians suffer disproportionately from the Gobblers suggests there is racism at work, too, and the way the process is organized, described, and discussed has chilling echoes of Nazi Germany and the practices of **Dr Josef Mengele**.

Intercision is carried out at a remote experimental station – even further away from the rest of society than Mengele's unit at Auschwitz was. The "doctors" at Bolvangar are, in a similarly crazed way to Mengele, perfectionists. They don't think intercision is as smooth technically as it could be. So they look at ways of ensuring the process becomes less stressful for them as operators and that fewer children die of shock during the operation.

The staff at Bolvangar deal in statistics of death, calculating that nearly one in twenty children die from shock under the Maystadt process. But deliverance, as with the doctor who became known as the Angel of Death is only temporary. Most of the children who survive intercision get sick and die anyway. Just as Mengele's sadistic experiments were cloaked in scientific mumbo jumbo, the burst of energy that intercision releases gives the **Consistorial Court** a bizarre scientific rationale for the practice.

··†··

His Dark Materials
The Magic

Tricky business: Pullman's magic stretches back much further than light entertainment, to a pre-Christian time when spells were about life and death

THE SECRETS OF SORCERY

Magic in *His Dark Materials* isn't there to baffle or delight, it's a costly business that points towards ancient wisdom

I f you asked people to picture a magician, they might think of **David Blaine** nearly drowning alive, or someone in top hat and tails pulling a suspiciously content white rabbit out of a hat. Asked the same question, **Philip Pullman** would probably imagine a **shaman** or **John Dee** who, Will learns, developed "Enochian magick". For Pullman, magic is not a matter of stunts, tricks and shuffling cards. In an email for this book, he noted: "Magic is costly. It has to be if it's going to be interesting. If you give someone a magic wand with which they can do anything, it simply ceases to have any tension or any cost. So the witches' invisibility spell, for instance, involves prolonged and intense effort, and then isn't always successful. Nor can they cure Will's wound. Only his father can do that." The remark about Will's father – and its suggestive link to the author's childhood loss – does suggest magic is a profound force in the books, though its role has not hitherto been analysed in much detail.

In his book *Dark Matter*, Tony Watkins observes that Pullman's witches and gyptians "have authentic traditions that go back centuries to a time before – in Pullman's view – all the extraneous nonsense of Christianity came in and cut people off from their deep roots". The ideas expressed in *His Dark Materials* are often very new – such as quantum theory and multiple universes – but just as often they are very, very old.

Take the bomb developed on the order of Father MacPhail to kill **Lyra**. This is powered by a "hydro-anbaric" power station and intercision, and at its heart is a resonating chamber where the target's "genetic particles" are analysed and transformed into a series of "anbaric pulses", which then cause an explosion at "the origin of the materials" – even in another world.

On the face of it this is cutting-edge science, but essentially it is sympathetic – or, to be more precise, contagious – magic. **Contagious magic** is a pre-religious belief, common to all humanity, that things that were once in contact continue to have an effect on one another, regardless of the distance. In *His Dark Materials*, the object placed in the resonating chamber is a lock of Lyra's hair – resulting in an explosion at the point the hair was cut from.

Like the principle, the use of hair is an ancient aspect of sorcery. For example, the **Nandi** in western Kenya would traditionally shave the heads of their prisoners and keep the hair to ensure that they did not escape – since they had merely to injure the hair to injure the prisoner, no matter where he was. When the prisoner was ransomed, the hair would be returned.

A similar principle helps the **lodestone resonator** communicate between worlds. This is explained as quantum entanglement: "a way of taking a common lodestone and entangling all its particles, and splitting it in two so that both parts resonate together". The rationale is modern but the idea is contagious magic.

His Dark Materials is thick with magical roots. In Cittàgazze, Will and Lyra meet **Giacomo Paradisi** at the top of the Torre degli Angeli. Paradisi is the bearer of the subtle knife, a priest-like position that he took up when, many years earlier, he "fought and lost the same fingers" as Will lost in his fight with Tullio. From his account, people often come to Cittàgazze to challenge him for the knife, and when Will and Lyra find him he is tied up, "battered and bruised" – having finally been defeated. Paradisi says that he must now die.

> "THE BOMB TO KILL LYRA USES HER HAIR, AN ANCIENT ASPECT OF SORCERY USED BY THE NANDI IN WESTERN KENYA."

Hair apparent: did hair oil help Chaka reign?

The position of knife-bearer has many echoes in pre-religious culture. In Cambodia, for instance, there were until recently two sacred kings, the **King of the Fire** and the **King of the Water**, who inhabited seven towers in succession and were killed and replaced if their strength failed.

The King of Fire had three talismans of his office – including a miraculous sword, which would bring the world to an end were he ever to draw it, or put out the sun and send all men and animals to sleep if he exposed a few inches of the blade.

The principle of killing sacred figures when their strength fails has been practised throughout the world and forms a major motif in Fraser's classic of mythology *The Golden Bough*.

The **Chollo** people of Sudan would kill their king at the first signs of decay, but he could also expect to be attacked at any time, without warning, by the son of another king and have to defend his position in single combat.

As late as the 19th century, the chieftain **Chaka**, the cruel, powerful leader credited with almost single-handedly founding the Zulu nation, was livid when a hair oil touted as having the same effects as Grecian 2000 didn't work, because the custom was to execute a king with wrinkled skin or grey hair.

The origins of this practice are explained by **sympathetic magic**. In this case, the vitality of the king – which must be continually proven by his fitness in battle – ensures the vitality of his kingdom, and his sacrifice or defeat allows the transference of his spirit to a more vigorous candidate. This idea underpins the knife-bearer's position – as the derelict condition of both Cittàgazze and the white-haired Paradisi reflects.

The best-known application of sympathetic magic is **voodoo**. Beneath all the B-movie caricatures, however, voodoo (or "vodou") is a spiritual tradition from West Africa, which spread to the Caribbean with the African diaspora, and it has influenced Pullman in numerous ways. **Zombi** were first encountered by **Mrs Coulter** in Africa, and, as people without dæmons and therefore with "no fear and no imagination and no free will", they gave her the idea for intercision. In the voodoo traditions of **Haiti**, zombies are people whose soul or spirit has been stolen by a sorceror or who have been revived from the dead and kept under a sorceror's control. Since **Spectres** reduce people to zombi – eating their dæmons and leaving "nothing there" – they owe something to the same source.

Spy-flies, meanwhile, straddle the old and the new, coupling nanotechnology and voodoo. These "Afric things" are mechanical flies whose momentum is provided by "a bad spirit with a spell through its heart".

SOULS, SHAMANS AND DÆMONS

Another magical concept running through *His Dark Materials* is that of external souls, which underpins the notion of dæmons. External souls pervade folk culture from Mongolia to the Hebrides. In the Egyptian tale *The Two Brothers*, written down around 1300BC in the reign of **Ramses II**, a brother's enchanted heart is placed in the flower of an acacia tree and, when the tree is cut, he falls down dead, only to revive when the flower is watered.

The idea of killing someone by destroying their external soul is very common. In one old Indian folk tale, Ravana, the **King of Ceylon**, magically takes his soul out of his body and leaves it in a box with a hermit for safekeeping. This wheeze makes him invulnerable in battle until a wily opponent tricks the hermit and squeezes the box until it breaks, killing the king.

The soul in the form of an animal is one of the most common motifs in folklore. In a traditional **Malay poem**, a girl named Bidasari has a soul in the form of a golden fish. Jealous of her beauty, the queen of Indrapoora seizes the fish, which has a sympathetic connection with the girl, allowing her to control her.

> "WHEN IT COMES DOWN TO IT, I'M A SCEPTICAL PAGAN. I FIND SHAMANISM VERY SYMPATHETIC, BUT I DON'T BELIEVE IN IT."

In Siberia, the shamans of the **Yakuts** are supposed to keep their soul (or one of several souls) in an animal, which they conceal to guarantee their personal safety. Only the shaman can see this animal, and, as with dæmons, the status of the animal depends upon the status of the dæmon. A weak shaman will have a dog for a soul, which will torture him by tearing at his innards. A bolder, more powerful shaman will have an a stallion, bear or eagle.

Shamanism is a brand of religion that Pullman seems actively to endorse in the books. In its most general sense, shamanism is very much like **animism**,

Unsympathetic magic: Voodoo dolls and pins make for a powerful, scary spell

House call: an Inuit shaman heals a patient

a range of traditional beliefs and practises that may date back to the Upper Palaeolithic period (about 40,000 years ago) and involves a shaman or healer mediating between this world and the spirit world to help in hunting, the treatment of sickness and the altering of weather.

Animism of some form has been a feature of all races and cultures, but in *His Dark Materials* Pullman focuses principally on the Siberian tradition that produced the word "shaman" (literally, "he/she who knows" in Turkic-Tungus). In regions such as Tuva, on the Russian-Mongolian border, this continues to be practised today.

Stanislaus Grumman (John Parry) is a shaman in a Siberian Tartar tribe, the Yenisei Pakhtars. He wears a cloak trimmed with feathers and fastened at the neck with a brass buckle, and, in order to perform his function, he enters a trance assisted by a hand-rattle. In our world, the hand-rattle is more characteristic of North American Arctic shamans – Siberian shamans tend to use a drum – but Grumman's appearance is otherwise true to life. His powers, too, are typical of the tradition. In **Lee Scoresby**'s balloon, he summons a storm to help them escape the Church zeppelins, and, in the land of the dead, his ghost still has the foresight to see the bomb intended to kill Lyra.

Shamanism has had an influence elsewhere in the books. The priest-like position of shaman is, for instance, one for which people are chosen – by dreams or spirit possession – and this has informed the idea of the knife-bearer, chosen by the **subtle knife** itself.

As a "shaman-academic" and long-lost father, **Stanislaus Grumman** embodies ancient and modern in the books, and seems to come close to a Pullman ideal. It is easy to see why this might be. On a narrative level, the mysticism of *His Dark Materials* is one of its most appealing aspects – key to its sense of wonder – but the shamanic outlook also chimes closely with Pullman's own. Among their other roles, shamans are traditional story-tellers, and in some tribes (such as the South American Tukano) they help to maintain an environmental balance by regulating hunting and other natural resources. There is no doubt that an integrated relationship with the environment – as demonstrated by Grumman – contains valuable lessons for humanity, but it must be remembered that shamanism considers illness to be the result of malicious spirits or witchcraft and has, in some cultures, used psychedelic plants to acquire secret knowledge.

Pullman, in an email, cautioned against reading too much into his treatment of shamanism: "When it comes down to it, I am a sceptical and tolerant pagan more than I'm anything else. I find it very sympathetic. But I don't believe in it. Unlike (say) Richard Dawkins, I am prepared to indulge and enjoy things I don't believe in – in fact I find them necessary: I couldn't work without them."

BURNING WITCHES AND INVISIBLE HEADGEAR

In medieval times, at least three out of every four people burned at the stake for **witchcraft** were women. The Church supported and organized this persecution, and as so much of *His Dark Materials* is about inverting traditional Christian motifs, there is a certain inevitability about the way they become, essentially, heroines. Our images of witchcraft are conditioned by the hags of *Macbeth*, but in pre-Christian times, witches were often regarded as wise women who could heal magically and were so close to nature they could deduce information from it – much as, in Lyra's world, they can discern meaning in pine marten trails, perch's scales and crocus pollen. They were not at all devilish.

To a male priesthood in an increasingly patriarchal world, these women were a threat that had to be confronted, and the easiest way to do that, various historians have suggested, was to demonize them. As early as 906, the Catholic Church was condemning "**wicked women**" for riding animals in nocturnal flights. Pullman's witches are not uniformly good, but they are presented sympathetically enough to challenge centuries of propaganda.

In the books, witches live for centuries, enjoy superhuman strength and can, by "mental magic" achieve a "fiercely-held modesty that could make the spell-worker not invisible but simply unnoticed". The idea of invisibility goes back to Greek myth. **Perseus** famously wore a cap that made him invisible. **Proteus** could make himself 'vanish' by assuming another shape – and owes something to the **Brothers Grimm**. In their story *Twelve Dancing Princesses*, a soldier uses an invisibility cloak to avoid being beheaded. But Pullman's version of invisibility has much more to do with the audience than the spell worker. It works primarily because humanity's powers of observation, as Will understands and often turns to his advantage, are so incredibly limited.

THE SECRET MAGIC OF THE ALETHIOMETER

The **alethiometer** is such an intriguing device that Pullman couldn't resist creating a back story for it. In an invented history written for the website of his American publisher Random House, Pullman says the first ever alethiometer was "constructed in Prague during the reign of **Rudolf II** by a scholar named **Pavel Khunrath**." The facts behind this fiction unlock some of the trilogy's most intriguing references, open the door to a strange kind of magic – it almost demands to be called magick – and introduce us to a mystical emperor, a spy for **Queen Elizabeth I** and an eloquent heretic who burned for his beliefs.

If you want to explore the intricate history of esoteric thought in the 16th and 17th centuries, you could do worse than emulate Pullman and read the works of the historian **Frances Yates**. The three books that are most relevant to *His Dark Materials* are *The Rosicrucian Enlightenment*, *The Art Of Memory* and *Giordano Bruno And The Hermetic Tradition*.

"THE HISTORY OF THE ALETHIOMETER STARS A MYSTICAL EMPEROR, A ROYAL SPY AND A HERETIC WHO WAS BURNT AT THE STAKE FOR HIS BELIEFS."

In an email, Pullman revealed: "I found *Giordano Bruno And The Hermetic Tradition* on the shelves of Oxford public library in May 1968, when I should have been revising for my university final examinations. Yates blew all of my proper work away. I could think of nothing else." Her work has had a serious, if often unacknowledged, influence on the trilogy.

King Rudolf II (1552–1612) really did reign over the Holy Roman Empire from 1576 to 1612. His court in Prague was the centre of intellectual intrigue and a haven for alchemists, who flocked there from across the world as the king sought to find the **philosopher's stone**, a legendary substance reputed to turn lead into gold.

Like many mystically minded folk, Rudolf II wasn't that good at the practical day-to-day stuff and, after trying to launch a Crusade against the Turks and giving Bohemian Protestants freedom of expression, he was stripped of his power by his brother Matthias.

Heretical hero: Giordano Bruno dreamed of Dust

One of the alchemists attracted to Prague was **Heinrich Khunrath** (Pullman presumably changed the name to tell us he's fictionalizing history, not reproducing it) who tried to develop a system that would reveal divine eternal truths – much like the alethiometer. The circular designs in Khunrath's book *Amphitheatre Of Eternal Wisdom* (1595) are suggestive of the alethiometer (see p.49).

Khunrath's real life is mysterious. He was born in Germany (probably in Leipzig or Dresden) in 1560 and died poor in one of those two cities in 1605. He studied alchemy and, like Pullman's fictional Khunrath, explored what the novelist describes as a "memory-theatre system of symbolic images" – in effect, a more elaborate system of the technique many people use to remember things by associating them with a certain image.

Pullman's fictional history credits a real scholar called **Giulio Camillo** (1480–1544) with interesting Khunrath in memory theatres. Camillo claimed to have built one that contained all human knowledge.

There is no compelling proof that he actually had done so. Camillo's most famous work, *L'Idea del Theatro* was found in the library of the Elizabethan philosopher, mathematician, occultist and royal spy **John Dee** (1527–1608). Yates suggests that through Dee and hermetic philosopher **Robert Fludd** (1574–1637), Camillo's ideas probably influenced the design of Shakespeare's **Globe Theatre**.

Dee is much more intriguing than either the real Khunrath or Camillo, which may be why, unlike them, he is mentioned, albeit briefly, as a "legendary magician" in an alternate Elizabethan England in *Northern Lights*. So trusted by **Elizabeth I** that he helped decide the date of her coronation, he met Khunrath at Rudolf II's court and may have become his hermetic mentor. He sought to contact angels through an intermediary and wrote several books that he said had been dictated to him by angels and were written in a language called Enochian. **Enoch** is, of course, the man who becomes the angel **Metatron** in *His*

Dark Materials and that may explain why, in Will's world, Dee is credited as the developer of "Enochian Magick".

In the 1580s, Dee's circle came into contact with a Italian philosopher called **Giordano Bruno** (1548–1600), also mentioned by Pullman in his back story for the alethiometer. Bruno's life is rich with themes that resound in *His Dark Materials*. Like Pullman and Lyra, he spent some time in **Oxford** (and, also like Pullman, he wasn't impressed by the university academics). Bruno studied to be a priest, but his lifelong conflict with the Church culminated in him being burned at the stake in Rome on the Pope's orders. Pullman had that unhappy end in mind when, in his invented history, he has Khunrath coming to an equally fiery end on the orders of the **Magisterium**.

Bruno had been intrigued by **John Calvin** but, after daring to criticize Calvinism, had to flee Geneva. In France, he started studying memory devices and came to the shocking – for the 16th century – conclusion that there was an infinite number of stars and hence an infinite number of worlds. He also believed that all matter came from the same elements and that those elements have an energy or life force – which is very close to Pullman's idea of **Dust**. He held so fiercely to his belief in multiple worlds that he didn't abandon it, even when on trial for his life in Rome before the Inquisition – an ordeal that parallels **Boris Mikhailovitch Rusakov**'s suffering in the books.

Some have hailed Bruno as a martyr to science, others say he was condemned for his religious views (notably the suggestion that Jesus was a magician). As Pullman said once when discussing the Inquisition, the distinction probably didn't seem that important as the flames started licking around Bruno's feet. Bruno's biographer Dorothea Walsey Singer said of this troublesome pioneer: "Unsuccessful in human relations, devoid of social tact or worldly wisdom, unpractical to an almost insane degree, he yet played a crucial part in the reshaping of European thought that began in the sixteenth and took form in the subsequent century." Today, a statue of Bruno stands on the spot, in the Roman square Campo de Fiori, where he was burned to death.

The real Khunrath, Camillo, Dee and Bruno were far ahead of their time, yet believed that they were reconnecting with ancient wisdom. You can read *His Dark Materials* and hardly notice they exist – only Dee is named in the books – but their lives, their ideas and their schemes are directly relevant to the alethiometer, the conflict between religion and science in the books and the business of Dust.

···†···

HIS DARK MATERIALS
The Victorian World

The golden age of air travel? The hydrogen-filled zeppelins of World War I were the models for the Consistorial Count's favoured vehicles

PERIOD CHARM

The most influential monarch in *His Dark Materials* isn't King Ogunwe or a witch queen, it's Queen Victoria

The Victorian world is one of Pullman's great passions, and appears throughout his work. His **Sally Lockhart** novels are set entirely in late 19th century London – a world of slums and opium dens any **Sherlock Holmes** fan would recognize – while *Spring-Heeled Jack* is based on a character from the Victorian "penny dreadfuls" and both of his **New Cut Gang** novels take place in South London in 1894: a hundred years before the first, *Thunderbolt's Waxwork*, was published. It was in the Victorian era that **Lewis Carroll** and **George Macdonald** (with his neglected masterpiece *Lilith*) first suggested that children's novels needn't just be for children. What's more, from 1988 to 1996 Pullman taught the **Victorian novel** part-time at Westminster College, Oxford (along with courses on folk tales and how words and pictures fit together), so it is no surprise to find that Lyra's world is so thoroughly Victorian – albeit with plenty of anachronisms.

"The Victorian period is fascinating," Pullman has said, "because there's so much material available – especially photographs – and it's close enough to the present day for the language to be not too different… Besides that, it's on the

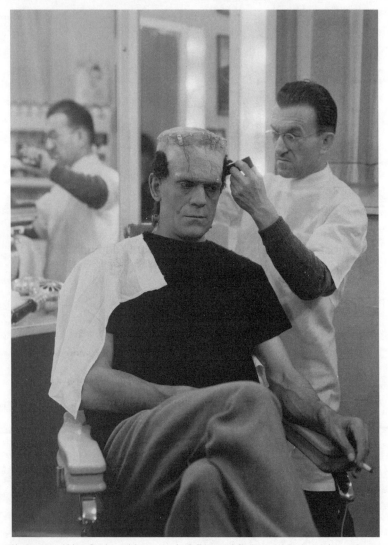

Monstrous ambition: Frankenstein's monster is, Pullman and Shelley suggest, the result of human arrogance

cusp of the modern world, with things like telephones and careers for women just coming in." When asked, Pullman finds it hard to say precisely why he was so fascinated by the 19th and 17th centuries, "Perhaps it's the intellectual ferment that characterized both periods."

The central narrative of the Victorian age was a coming together of the old and the new, the agrarian and the industrial – in a sense, of innocence and experience – and this is vital to the backdrop of *His Dark Materials*.

> "THE VICTORIAN ERA IS ON THE CUSP OF OUR WORLD. PHONES AND CAREERS FOR WOMEN ARE JUST COMING IN."

In Lyra's world, for instance, society is still rigidly defined by **class** and **sex**. Attended by his batman, the aristocratic Lord Asriel hunts on horseback at his estate, whereas, at twelve, Roger Parslow is already the sixth generation of his family to work in the Jordan College kitchen. The Retiring Room at Jordan is strictly out-of-bounds to women, even maids: a sanctuary of poppy heads and 1898 Tokay. Similarly, all twelve members of the Consistorial Court of Discipline are male. And yet, the Court's dominance is under threat by the General Oblation Board, led by the young, disconcertingly beautiful **Mrs Coulter**. The traditions of **Brytish** society are well-rooted – the Church all-powerful and the calendar still determined by Spring and Autumn fairs – but change is most definitely on its way.

ANBARIC LIGHTS AND HAND-CRANKED PHONES

Nothing identifies the late-Victorianness of Lyra's world quite so clearly as the **technology**. Although atomcraft and gyropters are mentioned, science is mostly at a very specific stage.

Naphtha still provides the lighting in Jordan's Retiring Room – that haven of tradition – but **anbaric** (amber) lights have taken over on the streets outside, and the Experiment Station at Bolvangar is, of course, "brilliantly lit". There are **telephones** but, at both the College of St Jerome and Asriel's basalt fortress, they are the hand-cranked variety. There are **photograms**, but when **Asriel** shows his slides to the scholars of Jordan College, he uses a projecting lantern – effectively, a magic lantern: oil-lit and requiring constant pumping to circulate the air. His first picture shows a "man in furs, his face hardly visible in the deep hood". Later, in the North, characters appear in coal-silk anoraks, but man-made insulation is obviously not very developed. Wealthy explorers still dress like **Ernest Shackleton**, in seal-skin boots and waterproof capes, and travel by dog sledge – although, characteristically, **Mrs Coulter** appears at Bolvangar on a **motorized sledge** with anbaric headlights.

Technology in travel is similarly caught between eras. Lee Scoresby's **balloon** is deemed a major asset to the Bolvangar expedition, with its criss-crossed ropes, leather-rimmed basket, altimeter and oxygen tanks. Like the **zeppelins** of the Magisterium, it is filled with (highly flammable) hydrogen – which, in the technological evolution of our world, places it near World War I, when zeppelin bombers were trying to reach ever-greater heights to avoid ack-ack guns. The aëronaut and the out-of-time zeppelins recall the films of the great Japanese animator Hayao Miyazaki, most notably *Castles In The Sky*. When Asriel returns to London from Oxford he takes a **steam train**, but when he travels from his fortress to the armoury his train is anbaric. On their journey to Norroway, the gyptians charter a timber ship with engines, masts and a crow's nest; apparently one of the hybrid vessels characteristic of the late 19th century.

TOO ADVENTUROUS FOR THEIR OWN GOOD?

With all this Victorian technology comes a Victorian attitude to science and exploration. Lyra's world is not somewhere known by satellite photographs, but somewhere still to be discovered. Nor is there only one world. Exploration and inventiveness is a trait of many of the books' major characters. They are, as the poet Ogden Nash might say, altogether too adventury.

Mrs Coulter has been to Africa and the North, using her experiences to invent intercision. Lord Asriel has manipulated silver nitrate preparation to reveal **Dust** in photograms, developed "an alloy of manganese and titanium" to insulate human from dæmon and worked out how to blast a hole in the sky, betraying no qualms as he continues his adventures into Cittàgazze.

Even **John Parry**, who comes from Will's world, has a Victorian/Edwardian quality about him, with his Arctic experience, theory of magnetic polarities and history as a Boy Scout. Given Pullman's magpie habits when naming his characters, Will's father must owe something to his near-namesake **Sir William Edward Parry** (1790–1855), who tried to reach the North Pole from the northern shores of Spitsbergen, the largest island in the archipelago of Svalbard.

In contrast with this scientific relish, there is a growing sense of science's dangers. Science in 19th century literature can be roughly divided into two camps. On the one hand, you have **Jules Verne**, whose colonial-era characters, with the boldness of Asriel, develop enormous guns to fire themselves to the moon. On the other, you have the concerns expressed by **Mary Shelley**. Pullman chose her most famous novel *Frankenstein* as a favourite book on the BBC Radio 4 programme *With Great Pleasure* and adapted it for the stage in 1990.

> "ASRIEL'S BLIND AMBITION LEADS TO CATASTROPHIC CLIMATE CHANGE: THE LESSON FOR THE 'MODERN PROMETHEUS' IS PERTINENT TODAY."

Echoing the creation myth, *Frankenstein* tells the story of **Victor Frankenstein**, his animated "creature" and the terrifying result of his amoral behaviour. Through *His Dark Materials* – and particularly *Northern Lights* – there is a growing sense of the perils of human arrogance. When Lyra arrives in the North, the initial romance of her adventure soon segues into the horrors of Bolvangar. Amid the Arctic desolation, Asriel too is a more stark and ruthless figure. His prison-laboratory is poised on a crag amid "thigh-deep snow" – it could hardly be more **Gothic** – and the result of his blind ambition is catastrophic climate change: the lesson for "the modern Prometheus", Pullman suggests, is just as pertinent today.

GOTHIC TRICKS AND UNFASHIONABLE MORALS

The 19th century influence on *His Dark Materials* is everywhere filtered through the prism of 19th century literature. **Gothic** is one important influence: an offshoot of **Romanticism**, revived during the Victorian era and specializing in terror, mystery, ghosts, vampires, castles, gloom, madness and death – all of which find their way into the books, in some shape or form. It also tends to feature tyrants, magicians, Asriel-like Byronic heroes, the devil and, in novels like **Edgar Allan Poe**'s *The Pit And The Pendulum*, with its horrifying scenes of the Spanish Inquisition, a strong anti-Catholic bias. One of the most important ways in which **Lyra's Brytain** differs from Victorian Britain (together with the absence of an Empire) is in the dominance of **Catholicism**. And yet, in the world of Victorian literature, tyrannical Catholics are more than familiar figures.

Northern Lights has a Gothic tone about it right from the start. **Jordan College**, with its roots in the Middle Ages, its pinnacles and "netherworld" of vaults, cellars and catacombs is an ideal setting for some Gothic intrigue, and

Pullman uses these presumptions cleverly. At first you are led to assume that Lyra's dæmon is some dark aspect of the "darkening Hall" with its portraits of former Masters – only to find him nervously instructing her to behave herself. The contrast of masculine rules and tradition with the girl's unruly exuberance has you backing her immediately.

Pullman plays strangeness and familiarity off against one another repeatedly in the books. The unnamed Mrs Coulter prowling around Limehouse is another good example. For a novelist, as Pullman has said, "**Wapping** and **Limehouse** and so on are attractive because of their long-standing associations with crime, foreign sailors, opium dens, etc."

At this stage of the story, the reader knows nothing of intercision, only that children are disappearing, but here we have a **Victorian slum** straight out of those cheap serials known as the "penny dreadfuls": all fortune-paper stalls and fried fish carts. Tony Makarios is a pie-stealing, not-so-artful dodger with a shilling in his pocket, an alcoholic mother and the scrambled racial background of the docks. The lady with the golden monkey dæmon (Mrs Coulter) is young, beautiful and glamorous, but, to the reader, she is already **Jack the Ripper**, and Tony is in for a fate too awful to contemplate.

> "MRS COULTER IS YOUNG, BEAUTIFUL AND GLAMOROUS BUT TO THE READER SHE IS JACK THE RIPPER. TONY IS IN FOR A FATE TOO AWFUL TO CONTEMPLATE."

Pullman takes great care over his **Brytish London**: a city that still revolves around its river in a way that recalls Dickens or Conrad. It is a place of unremitting danger – from the glamorous cocktail parties in Mrs Coulter's apartment, where smiling faces conceal journalists and Oblation Board apparatchiks, to the smog-ridden streets, "laden with fumes and soot and clangorous with noise".

Lyra has barely escaped her mother before she comes to a coffee stall, where "a gentleman in a top hat and white silk muffler" attempts to get her drunk, and she has no sooner left the world of theatres and department stores for a scramble of canals, warehouses and the occasional "dismal oratory" before two Gobblers catch her with a net. The London passage spans only a few pages, but it packs in enough smoke and terror for a book of its own.

Still, the Victorian feel of *His Dark Materials* isn't just about its setting. The books are written in the third-person, with the kind of omniscient narrator

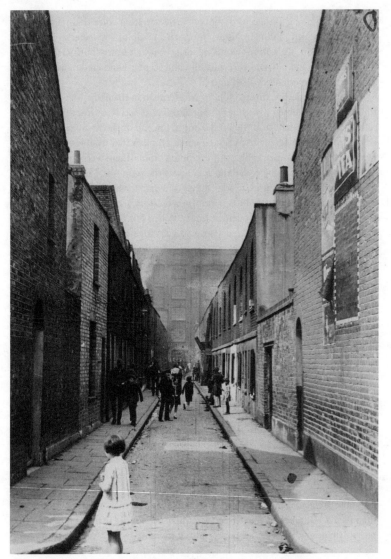

Pullman's Brytish London, like the real Victorian city, is full of soot, smog and noise

familiar from much 19th-century fiction. "The narrating voice that tells **Middlemarch**," says Pullman, "is just as much a made-up character as Dorothea or Mr Casaubon." It is, in his words, a "sprite" without limits, both male and female, "young and old, and wise and silly, and sceptical and credulous, and innocent and experienced, all at once".

As a fictional device, this fell foul of **Modernism** in the early 20th century. Pullman has reclaimed it with relish but also out of necessity. Recalling his first stab at a novel, he has said: "Before I'd got to the end of the first paragraph, I'd come up slap bang against a fundamental problem that troubles me today whenever I begin a story: where am I telling it from? There were so many possibilities, and nothing to tell me which was the right one." The narrating voice of *Middlemarch* has since solved that dilemma for him.

More important still is Pullman's emphasis on **story** and **morality** – both, again, reclaimed from the Modernist legacy. When *Northern Lights* won the Carnegie Medal in 1995, Pullman gave a speech lamenting that "technique, style, literary knowingness" are all-important in adult fiction, and that the "present-day would-be George Eliots take up their stories as if with a pair of tongs. They're embarrassed by them". In an email, Pullman said things might have changed a bit since, but he doesn't think it has anything to do with *His Dark Materials*: "Tastes change naturally and things go in and out of fashion. Having been unfashionable for quite a while, perhaps storytelling is coming back in."

Pullman is proudly, defiantly a storyteller, and describes his ideal as sitting on a carpet in a market, telling his stories among other stall-holders. He sees stories as a pleasure and a need – containing "more wisdom than volumes of philosophy". In his 2005 lecture, *Miss Goddard's Grave*, at the University of East Anglia, Pullman read an extract from Jane Austen's 1816 novel *Emma*, in which Mr Knightley reproves the heroine for thoughtlessly insulting Miss Bates which, he said, showed how "we can learn what's good and what's bad, what's generous and unselfish, what's cruel and mean, from fiction".

Lyra learns these lessons in *His Dark Materials*. From her row with Pan about whether to stay in the Retiring Room wardrobe and warn Asriel to the necessity of abandoning Will in the world of the mulefa, Lyra faces many moral choices. This approach is far more closely associated with Christian Victorian novels than secular 20th century novels, and, Pullman's attitudes towards religion notwithstanding, represents a reassertion of morality in the world of fiction.

··†··

PART III
THE WORLD OF
HIS DARK MATERIALS

HIS DARK MATERIALS
The Gazetteer

A towering source of inspiration: St Mark's Campanile in Venice is clearly the model for the Torre degli Angeli where Will finds the subtle knife

Mapping Pullman

Your guide to the strange geography of *His Dark Materials*,
where the North is everything and America barely exists

Every novelist reimagines the world for their own ends. In *His Dark Materials*, Pullman has been almost insanely ambitious, creating a fictional geography so detailed it is impossible not to ponder its significance. Laurie Frost's painstaking plotting of the trilogy's geography in her book *The Elements Of His Dark Materials* brings many of the peculiarities into focus. As you might expect from *Northern Lights*, his preferred title for the first novel in the trilogy, Pullman ignores much of the South. Australia, Benin, Brazil, Madagascar, Morocco, New Zealand, Sumatra and Zaire merit passing mentions. But it is Oxford and the North – and in the trilogy the region most definitely has a capital N – that fire his imagination. He has lived in Oxford for decades. It is harder to determine quite why the **North** holds his imagination in such thrall.

In part, it may be, as he said once at a conference in Sweden, that the North was a massive blank canvas onto which he could project his story. That doesn't though, explain why he applied for a travel grant to research **Svalbard** as a location in the 1970s and why, when he was turned down, he consulted photographs of the island while writing about it. The clue may lie in the epigraph that starts Chapter 21 of *The Amber Spyglass* which reads: "But I hate things that are all fiction. There should always be some foundation in fact".

Pullman's North may be a fantastic realm where witches fly and bears forge iron, but the fantasy is fired by reality. The appropriate amount of the right kind of facts can prove useful for any novelist and Pullman grounds his imaginary regions in real, geographic entities.

To give one small example, on his expedition, John Parry writes a letter from a campsite near a place in Alaska called **Umiat**. Such a place – a settlement on the Colville River with a permanent population of about five people – does exist, 140 miles south of the wonderfully named town of Deadhorse, and is one of the coldest parts of the state.

THE NORTH-SOUTH DIVIDE

The North gets a bum rap in The Bible and Pullman will have enjoyed inverting this stereotype. In the Book of Jeremiah we are warned that "Evil threatens from the north" while, in Isaiah, Lucifer vows to set up his throne "in the recesses of the north", a theme referenced in *Paradise Lost* where Satan calls his troops to "the quarters of the north" to prepare. Milton also mentions "Lapland witches" although in his poem these were not sympathetic figures but evil creatures who rode through the air looking for infant's blood.

The mysteries of the books' geography don't end with the North. In Pullman's Europe, nothing good comes out of **Switzerland**, Hungary's main contribution to the world is to make **Tokay** wine, the Dutch have settled in the **Fens** of East Anglia and the North Sea is the **German Ocean** (as it was sometimes known, even in Britain, until 1914).

Pullman's New World is even more intriguing. Canada and the United States are simply not mentioned, the landmass seems to be called **New Denmark**, an allusion to the Viking discovery of the continent centuries before Columbus. America is no nation of united states but a region ruled uneasily, in part, by New France and New Denmark. These competing colonial powers fought the battle of the **Alamo**, watched by the young Lee Scoresby. The most significant places in New Denmark – Alaska, California, the Mississippi river, the "country of Texas" – hark back to a wilder, older pre-industrial West. The native population – the Skrælings, the Inuit and the Navajo – seems unconquered, though the New Danes are trying to stop the Skrælings from scalping people.

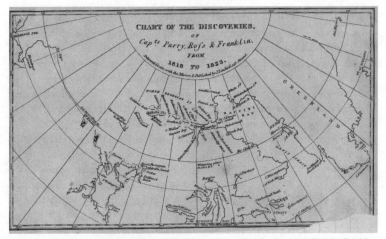

Arctic voyages: the explorations of Sir William Edward Parry, Sir John Ross and Sir John Franklin

Pullman is a huge fan of Westerns, admitting, in research for this book, that he can recite much of the *The Magnificent Seven* script. And the North in the books has certain similarities to the **Wild West**. Both regions are mythologized as lands of excitement, mystery and danger where journeys often turn into odysseys of hardship and heroism. The two landscapes – one fictional, the other a mythic twist on historical reality – share many other themes: scalping, violent conflict, drunken clerics, mining and environmental degradation.

The geography of *His Dark Materials* seems determined largely by what Pullman found useful to do his job. Once he had identified the North as the setting for his most ambitious novel, many other things quickly fell into place. The North was so vast and dotted with so many evocative, almost musical, place names that he didn't need the South, most of the US, Africa, the middle East or many parts of Europe.

The North made his archaic names (Muscovy, New Denmark, New France) feel mysteriously appropriate. Once Pullman had Oxford and the North, his fictional world was almost complete, apart from the sinister glitter of **Cittàgazze**. Travelling between worlds was more important, as he wrote, than circumnavigating the globe.

In the books, travel is never something to be taken for granted. This is partly because of the characters' modes of transport. A few – like **Sir Charles Latrom**

– drive cars while Will and Lyra get the bus once. For the most part, the characters use such an incredible array of machines and contraptions that even Jules Verne would be impressed. Balloons, barges, bikes, boats, canoes, carts, frigates, gyropters, kayaks, lifeboats, pedal boats, punts, ships, sledges, tractors, trains, tramcars, tugs, vans, wagons, wings and zeppelins are all brought into action. The most elaborate modes of transport are the mobile citadel, the **Clouded Mountain** and the magnificent flying machine that is the **Intention Craft**. With bug-like legs, string and laser beams, Asriel's craft could have leapt from the pages of Verne's fiction or from the imagination of the English illustrator **Heath Robinson** (1872–1944), famous for his cartoons of rickety machines.

"THE INTERNAL COMBUSTION ENGINE IS A MENACE. LATROM'S ROLLS-ROYCE IS A SYMBOL OF HIS SMUGNESS, TRUCKS SPIRIT BOYS AWAY FROM BANBURY."

The internal combustion engine is usually depicted as a source of menace. Latrom's gleaming **Rolls-Royce** is a symbol of his self-satisfaction, trucks are used to spirit away boys from Banbury and a car very nearly runs Lyra over when she enters Will's Oxford.

Driving is too advanced, too perilous for the environment and too safe for the travellers to be of use to Pullman. The characters often embark on their hazardous journeys with the curiosity and self-confidence of the great 19th century explorers in our world. The fathers of Lyra and Will set off on expeditions which are, notes novelist Michael Chabon, "lovingly outfitted by Pullman with the full Shackletonian panoply of Victorian explorers' gear". Veterans who have explored and survived are held up as icons to Lyra by Mrs Coulter at the **Royal Arctic Institute**.

The novels are littered with artefacts from distant lands – harpoons, stones, scalped heads, trepanned skulls, letters, and Samoyed photos to name but a few – that conjure up the intrigue, glamour and romance of a golden age of travel. Pullman's own golden age of travel came when he was a boy. As a man, he prefers to travel in his imagination with the aid of the **Bodleian Library**.

Pullman's reluctance has, of late, become a point of principle. Worried about the environment, he vowed, at the start of 2006: "From now on I stay on the ground. This means no long-distance travel unless I can find a ship going where I want to; no flying within Europe, and certainly none inside Britain. All unnecessary. Festivals? Conferences? The days when we could thoughtlessly

LORD ASRIEL'S AMBER TIPPLE

As fictional vintage wines go, Lord Asriel's preference for a bottle of **1898 Tokay** isn't exactly up there with James Bond's favourite Dom Perignon (007 was especially partial to the 1952 and 1953 vintages).

The late-harvest dessert wine has been produced in a small plateau near the Carpathian mountains in Hungary since the 1300s and might seem an odd choice for a Lord who, Pullman indicates, has a Bondian taste for luxury. It does suggest that if Asriel ever came to dinner at your house, the wine he brought might end up on the tombola stand at the school fair.

But tokay – tokaj as the Hungarians call it – was once a hugely prestigious wine. Tokay was much favoured by Queen Victoria, Louis XIV, Napoleon III and Gustav III of Sweden who refused to drink any other wine.

It probably helped that the **Habsburgs** owned the estates for centuries. The wine is even mentioned in the Hungarian national anthem ("Thou hast made nectar drip out of the vines of Tokaj"). **Voltaire** dedicated a poem to the "amber beverage with gleaming hues that makes the wittiest of words scintillate".

Amber may be part of the attraction for Pullman. The wine first appeared in his fiction in *The Tiger In The Well*, the third Sally Lockhart novel.

get on a plane and fly across the Atlantic to deliver one lecture are over. Tours to publicize a new book? Only by ship and by train."

Many places are namechecked in the books but only a few – most especially **Oxford** – are truly significant. The most obvious place to start on this geographic guide is with the city Pullman, Lyra and Will all call home: Oxford.

OꝪFORꝺ

The city of Oxford, says Pullman, is an unbeatable place to write: "I put it down to the mists from the river, which have a solvent effect on reality."

In much of *His Dark Materials*, he has used his home city as the basis for his imaginings. So, in Lyra's world, he has built an alternative Oxford around the city's frame, while in Will's world he presents very much the real place – albeit with a **Dark Matter Research Unit**, in a Department of Physical Sciences, plus one or two other amendments. The final decisive proof of his enduring fascination with the place came with the publication, in **Lyra's Oxford**, of an annotated fold out map of Oxford "by train, river and zeppelin", apparently designed to help the reader plot the stories. Although Pullman has occasionally disguised places, the locations and inspirations in our world can be easily tracked down.

THE ASHMOLEAN

Pretending to be a tourist in *The Subtle Knife* **Lyra** asks a couple of policemen the way to "the Museum", and is given directions to the **Ashmolean**. This is probably also the "large museum" that Will visits after leaving the Institute of Archaeology which is on the same street.

The Ashmolean Museum of Art and Archaeology, on Beaumont Street, was the world's first university museum. It was built between 1678 and 1683 to house a collection of books, coins, engravings, and geological and zoological specimens presented to the University of Oxford by **Elias Ashmole** in 1677.

Among its early exhibits was a stuffed dodo – the last of its kind ever seen in Europe – although, because of moth damage, only its head and one claw remain. The Ashmolean now contains a library specialising in the classical world, archaeology and art history, and collections ranging from Greek and Minoan pottery to Pre-Raphaelite paintings. Among its most famous exhibits are drawings by **Leonardo da Vinci**, **Raphael** and **Michelangelo**, the very lantern used by **Guy Fawkes** during the Gunpowder Plot of 1605 and a death mask of **Oliver Cromwell**.

The Ashmolean is shut on Mondays and from 2–4 September for St Giles Fair but is otherwise open all year around (Tue–Sat 10am–5pm; Sun, bank holidays 12pm–5pm). Times vary over Easter, so check *www.ashmolean.org* for details.

Think bike: Oxford students' cycling experience would come in handy for riding mulefa

BALLIOL COLLEGE

Balliol – it is pronounced Bailey'll – is one of only three Oxford colleges mentioned in *His Dark Materials* that are the same in both Will and Lyra's worlds.

It is arguably the oldest Oxford college, having been founded in 1263 by **John de Balliol** (1212–69), the father of King John of Scotland, and can be found on the far side of Broad Street from Exeter College.

The college, which has appeared in the fiction of Anthony Trollope, Jerome K. Jerome, Rudyard Kipling and Dorothy L. Sayers, takes great pride in having a tortoise, **Rosa**, named after the German revolutionary Rosa Luxemburg.

THE BODLEIAN LIBRARY

The **Bodleian Library** provides another important inspiration for Jordan College. As a student, Pullman had the notion that its "stacks extended for untold miles in every direction" underground, which prompted the idea of the college's subterranean "froth of stone". But the actual library also appears in both Will and Lyra's Oxford, where it has retained its official name, **Bodley's Library**.

The roots of the Bodleian lie in the 14th century, with a collection of "chained books" which, by 1437, had grown large enough to demand a library of their own. The result, Duke Humfrey's Library, still exists, and despite lean times in the 16th century (all of the furniture had to be sold, along with all but three books in the collection), it became the basis of the library which was refitted, restocked and funded by **Thomas Bodley** and reopened in 1602.

Ever since, the history of the Bodleian has been characterized by enormous expansion. The 17th century saw the building of both the Schools Quadrangle and the Tower of the Five Orders, but by far the most recognisable Bodleian building is the **Radcliffe Camera** on Catte Street: the "round building with a great leaden dome" or "university library" where Will and Lyra plan to meet in *The Subtle Knife*. This was built between 1737 and 1749 to house the Radcliffe Science Library, but became part of the Bodleian in 1860 and now houses part of the theology, English and history collections.

These days, the Bodleian is perhaps best known as one of the six libraries in the UK entitled to a free copy of every new copyrighted book. Although the "race of sub-human creatures" imagined on the lowest level by the young Pullman remain undiscovered, the library contains over eight million items and 117 miles of shelves, and includes Shakespeare's **First Folio** among its numerous rarities.

The Divinity School and exhibition room are open all year round. Check *www.bodley.ox.ac.uk* for opening hours.

THE BOTANIC GARDEN

The **Botanic Garden** is a key location in both **Will** and **Lyra**'s worlds, and gives its name to the last chapter of *The Amber Spyglass*. Here the two children spend their final moments together – Will cuts a window back to his home at the garden's gate – and find "a wooden seat under a spreading low-branched tree" where they pledge to sit, in their own worlds, for an hour every Midsummer's Day.

The garden is a symbol of the pair's ongoing love, and it is embraced as such by fans. "Once, I saw something on one of the benches," says **Pullman**. "It turned out to be a little wooden heart with 'For Will and Lyra' written on it. Isn't that nice?"

As you might expect, the garden is a part of the University. Founded in 1621 by **Sir Henry Danvers**, Britain's oldest botanic garden was intended to grow plants for medical research.

The garden sits on the bank of the river Cherwell, facing Magdalen College, and contains more than 8,000 species. There are three areas: the walled garden with its 17th century stonework, the glasshouses for plants that like a warmer climate, and the area between the walled garden and the Cherwell. Will and Lyra's bench, pictured below, is near the back of the **walled garden**, just as Pullman describes. The gardens usually open at 9am but closing times do vary so check *www.botanic-garden.ox.ac.uk*.

The garden where Will and Lyra sit, in their separate worlds, to remember each other

BURGER KING

Having fled Winchester, Will arrives in Oxford hungry and tired, and eats at a Burger King before going to hide in a cinema. There are two Burger Kings in Oxford, but one is in the retail park in Cowley, and Will probably visited the branch on **Cornmarket Street** which is on the direct route from Winchester.

CATTE STREET

Catte Street is another location common to Will and Lyra's worlds. Running along the eastern side of Radcliffe Square, it is home to the **Radcliffe Camera** (see Bodleian Library) and in both worlds the initials "SP" have been carved into a stone on the corner. **Simon Parslow** did the carving in Lyra's world.

COVERED MARKET

In *Northern Lights*, Jessie Reynolds, the daughter of the saddler in the covered market, is abducted by the Gobblers, while, in Will's world, Lyra goes there to buy an apple – deeming it "much more like the proper Oxford" than the rest of the city she has encountered so far.

Though there have been shops on or near the site since the Middle Ages, the covered market was built on the High Street, between Cornmarket Street and Turl Street in 1774, to help clear the messier stalls from the city streets. Designed by **John Gwynn**, also architect of Magdalen Bridge, the market first sold fresh food, although the butchers and greengrocers have now been joined by gift shops and the like.

EXETER COLLEGE

Exeter College is the model for **Jordan College** in Lyra's world, the place that, more than any other, she calls home, and Pullman's own alma mater. Other alumni include Alan Bennett, Richard Burton, and **J.R.R. Tolkien**. Founded in 1314 by Walter de Stapeldon, Bishop of Exeter, it was meant as a school for the clergy – at first, it had only twelve students – but it grew rapidly in the 15th century, acquiring its gatehouse, Palmer's Tower, in 1432, and by 1710 the college was in its present form – although the chapel, the library and the Rector's Lodgings were added in the 1850s, along with further student accommodation in the 20th century.

Exeter, like Jordan, can be found on

Turl Street, with its back to the University library. To either side are Wadham and Jesus Colleges, which, in Lyra's world, become **Gabriel** and **St Michael's**. While it occupies the same location as Jordan, when Lyra arrives in Will's Oxford she finds "an entirely different building" in Jordan's place.

Exeter is not the oldest college in Oxford nor is it the most academically prestigious. Essentially, Jordan is Exeter with its "grandness and richness" enhanced. The tradition about being able to walk on Jordan's land from London to Bristol is an urban legend often told about **St John's College,** Oxford and **Trinity College**, Cambridge. Both Pullman's alma mater and Lyra's home have a Palmer's Tower. Exeter has its share of "tunnels, shafts, vaults and cellars", but has only one central quadrangle while Jordan is built around three.

HEADINGTON

Headington is the wealthy Oxford suburb where **Sir Charles Latrom** lives in Limefield House: a large, creeper-covered property which "spoke of wealth and power". There is no Limefield House in our world, but the Headington area lies to the east of Oxford, on Headington Hill. Its former residents include Robert Maxwell, J.R.R. Tolkien and **C.S. Lewis**, while the writer **Brian Aldiss** (whose novel *The Malacia Tapestry* inspired Cittàgazze) lives there today. But the area's best-known landmark is the **Headington Shark**: John Buckley's 25-foot fibreglass sculpture of a shark buried head-first in the roof of 2 New High Street.

JERICHO

In our world, Jericho is a respectable area of Victorian terraced houses, but, to Pullman, it has always had "a hidden character, more raffish and jaunty altogether, with an air of horse-trading, minor crime and a sort of fairground Bohemianism."

This is the Jericho that appears in Lyra's world, both in *His Dark Materials* and *Lyra's Oxford*: a maze of little streets around the **Oxford Canal**, where the gyptians dock for their seasonal horse fairs. The name Jericho also suggested that of **Jordan College**.

THE PITT RIVERS MUSEUM

Wandering in Will's Oxford, Lyra enters the **Pitt Rivers Museum** because it is a "real, Oxford-looking building" – even though it doesn't exist in her own world.

Here she finds "stuffed animals and fossil skeletons", **Samoyed** clothing and trepanned skulls, and much the same things can be found there in reality.

The museum was established in 1884 by **General Augustus Pitt Rivers**, a passionate anthropologist who donated his collection of about 20,000 items – shrunken heads and Buddhist skull bowls among them – to Oxford University. Since then, the collection has swollen to more than 500,000 artefacts.

The **Pitt Rivers** is on Parks Road and can be entered via the Oxford University Museum of Natural History. The place retains its Victorian atmosphere, with cluttered wooden cabinets, handwritten labels and, at the founder's behest, a layout intended to show how different peoples addressed the same problems at different times. Exhibits include a mourner's costume from Tahiti collected by **Captain Cook**, ceremonial ivories and brasses from the **Kingdom of Benin**, and every imaginable type of jewellery, charm, instrument, tool and weapon. They also include Inuit parkas made of reindeer skin and **trepanned skulls** – as Lyra discovers.

RIVER THAMES / ISIS

Traditionally, the stretch of the Thames that runs through Oxford is called the Isis, but in Lyra's world the name extends to the whole river, which is the principal means of transport to London – "thronged with slow-moving brick-barges and asphalt-boats and corn-tankers". Isis is probably a contraction of the river's Latin (or Celtic) name, Tamesis, not derived from the Egyptian goddess.

ST JOHN'S COLLEGE

In Will's Oxford, Lyra is surprised to find the **St John's College** gates, which she once climbed with **Roger Parslow**, exactly as she remembered them. In our world, the college was founded in 1555 by Sir Thomas White, a Catholic merchant, and although initially small and poorly endowed, it has since become the richest in Oxford, owning most of the north of the city. St John's is located between St Giles and Parks Road, and its alumni include Tony Blair, Kingsley Amis and Philip Larkin.

SUNDERLAND AVENUE

Sunderland Avenue is the site of the window to **Cittàgazze** discovered first by a cat, and then by intrepid Will. It is lined with hornbeam trees, which feature in the woodcut at the start of The Cat and the Hornbeam Trees: Chapter 1 of *The Subtle Knife* and helps them remember where the window is. The house where Pullman wrote the trilogy in the legendary garden shed is just a few streets from here. In our world, the avenue is home to car hire firms, apartments and a bed and breakfast.

ALASKA

On one very basic level, the American success of *His Dark Materials* is surprising. Pullman's imagination seems, if not decisively anti-American, determinedly un-American. It can be no coincidence that the three US states that play the most significant role in the trilogy – **Alaska**, California and Texas – all originally belonged to someone else. Alaska was bought from Russia for a pittance, California – where Mary Malone learned to climb trees and make margaritas – was once a Spanish colony and Texas belonged initially to Mexico and then, briefly, to itself.

Though Alaska, the 49th state, exists in its own right in Will's world, in Lyra's world it is also known as **Beringland**, a reminder that the Dutch explorer **Vitus Bering** sailed past this state in 1728, though as his ship was embroiled in fog, he probably didn't realize that the first time around. He came back in 1741, found Kayak Island but refused to go ashore on the mainland. The straits and the state were probably first discovered by an explorer in 1645 by Cossack navigator Semen Dezhnev.

Will's father **John Parry** disappears in Alaska on an expedition somewhere near the North American Arctic Survey Station at **Noatak** in the remote Brooks mountain range. The goal of the expedition was to investigate the **Aurora Borealis**, an eerie, much

WHERE TO SEE THE AURORA

You can see the **northern lights** regularly within a 1500km radius of the magnetic North Pole in a zone that includes northern Scandinavia, Iceland, the southern tip of Greenland (where Mrs Coulter studied the phenomenon), northern Canada, Alaska and the northern coast of Siberia.

The Aurora, named after the Roman goddess of dawn, are especially common in the Norwegian counties of **Troms** (your best bet is to fly to Tromso airport) and **Finnmark** (the nearest airport is Vadsø) where they can be seen on half the clear nights. Visibility is at its best between early September and the middle of April.

The peak season in **Fairbanks**, Alaska (a short flight – or a 358 mile drive – from Anchorage) runs from December to March. The lights shows can last for hours, with the sky looking as if it's full of glowing, dancing, green, orange, yellow or dark red curtains or be over in 10–15 minutes, with coloured rayed bands whirling into a giant green corona.

Fairbanks is so geared up to the Aurora, you can telephone (907) 474–7558 for a daily forecast.

If you don't have the time or the money to see the Aurora in person, try a quick Google search for aurora cams. There seems to be a new crop of these every season.

mythologized, natural phenomenon that – many characters believe – has something to do with the mystery of Dust.

Their ill-fated expedition started in **Fairbanks** which, in real life, is the largest city in the Alaskan interior, famed for its extreme weather. The main attractions in Fairbanks are the Aurora, the native villages nearby and the surrounding wilderness (see *http://explorefairbanks.com*).

Noatak is real too. This small settlement, 70 miles north of the Arctic circle, was founded as a fishing and hunting camp and is the only community on the banks of the Noatak river, the source of which lies in the **Brooks mountain range** where John Parry disappeared. The Brooks mountains are not especially high – the tallest peak is 9,020ft high – but they are mostly uninhabited and undisturbed, a haven for caribou, sheep and grizzly bears.

Parry's journey from one world to another – via a "doorway into the spirit world" – would not have shocked the native **Inupiat** who, in the real Alaska, live in Noatak. Paul Ongtooguk, one of the founders of a project called **Alaskool** which helps preserve and protect the state's indigenous culture, says the Inupiat believed that "in ancient days, the boundaries established by physical properties, time and spirit were not sharply distinct and strictly categorical. The world was more fluid and within that world there was potential for movement across physical, spiritual and temporal dimensions."

> "THE INUPIAT BELIEVED YOU COULD ONCE MOVE BETWEEN PHYSICAL, SPIRITUAL AND TEMPORAL DIMENSIONS."

CITTÀGAZZE

Two Venices have inspired Cittàgazze (which means "city of magpies"). The real city atop the Adriatic and the fictionalized city in Brian Aldiss's novel *The Malacia Tapestry*. Visit Venice with *His Dark Materials* in mind and you find enough strange resonances to suggest the city has had a broader, deeper role in the creation of the trilogy than, as Pullman admits, merely inspiring the charming, tragic, magnificent, deserted city of Cittàgazze, a place with a Mediterranean air where the scent of flowers mingles with the salty smell of the sea and a broad sea boulevard leads to narrow streets with cafés. Like Venice,

Cittàgazze was a trading city though, since it was devastated three hundred years ago, its leading citizens have turned to thievery – something the mercenary Venetians have been accused of. The Guild steals gold, jewels and pencils. Venetian sailors, in the year 828, stole the relics of **St Mark** from Alexandria for their basilica.

> "THE GUILD'S PHILOSOPHERS STEAL JUST AS VENETIAN SAILORS NICKED THE RELICS OF St MARK FOR THEIR BASILICA."

You will also, if you pick the right districts at the right time, find plenty of deserted streets in Venice whose beauty has been compromised by all the ruined, patched up buildings – just like those in the haunted city of Cittàgazze.

In the trilogy and in Pullman's interviews, there are a lot of small allusions to the city famed, not for magpies but for pigeons. The epigraph for chapter 21 in *The Amber Spyglass* is extracted from a letter from Byron to John Murray who was staying in Venice in 1817, a letter that muses on the Doge Marino Faliero, decapitated on the very staircase where he was crowned Duke. Byron, one of the role models for **Asriel**, couldn't, he said, walk around the Piazza San Marco without thinking of the beheading. He even wrote two largely overlooked Venetian plays – one of which, *The Two Foscari*, features characters who seem like Spectres, an often-used Byronian term which influenced William Blake.

Venice was also the city where **Giordano Bruno**, cited in Pullman's history of the alethiometer, sought refuge but was eventually handed over to the Inquisition in Rome to die.

The resonances start in the **Piazzo San Marco**. If you stand facing the golden basilica, then turn to your left and look straight ahead, you will see the glorious **Torre dell'Orologio** (Clock Tower). The tower's extraordinarily elaborate timepiece displays the time

VENETIAN LITERATURE

There are three books on Venice which Pullman has definitely read. Apart from Brian Aldiss's *The Malacia Tapestry*, the other novel set in the city he admires is *Pandora's Galley* by **Macdonald Harris**, one of his favourite authors. The novel is set in Venice in 1797, the year the city lost its independence to Napoleon, and imagines the story of a little known American who fought for the Venetians. The book is full of sumptuous – sometimes, says Pullman, too sumptuous – descriptions of Venice. In one lecture in April 2003, he quoted **John Ruskin**'s *The Stones Of Venice*, a masterful analysis of Venetian art and architecture which could have helped him imagine Cittàgazze.

Venetian time: many public clocks, like this one near Canareggio, have echoes of the alethiometer

Compromised beauty: the deserted streets of Venice — and Cittàgazze — have been patched up

of day, the dominant sign of the zodiac and the current phase of the moon and is one of several clocks on display in Venice which, in shape, style and complexity, recall Lyra's alethiometer.

Turn around and you face the mighty **Campanile**, the tallest structure in Venice. The tower has had a golden angel on top since 1515, making it a likely inspiration for the **Torre degli Angeli** (Tower of Angels) where Will learns to use the subtle knife. The Campanile is relatively new. The old one fell to the ground in 1902 but remarkably only killed the caretaker's cat.

If you stroll from the Campanile towards the Grand Canal and quickly turn left you will find the queue for the **Doge's Palace**. Inside, apart from some visions of Hell by **Hieronymus Bosch** that are as horrific as Pullman's land of the dead, you will be ushered through the hall of the compass (though the compass the room is named after is wooden, not golden). It was in Venice, in 1609, that a Dutchman called Fleming demonstrated a spyglass that prompted **Galileo** to perfect his telescope. The scientist's letters don't specify the colour of the spyglass.

Walk around the city and you find other strange echoes of the books. There are more angels in Venice, albeit stone ones, than in the trilogy and in the church of **San Lio** you will find carvings of two obscene harpies who are much better looking than their compatriots in *The Amber Spyglass*.

VENICE: THE BASICS

The essential rule for the **Doge's Palace**, **St Mark's Basilica** and the **Campanile** is to go early, before the day trips start clogging up the Piazza San Marco. Most of the sights open at 9am and by 10am have attracted long queues. That is now the case most of the year. Do allow several hours for the Doge's Palace, it's worth it and there is a fine, not too pricey cafe attached where you can sip prosecco. There is no bad time to visit Venice but July is hot and crowded. If you want to get the feel of Cittàgazze's deserted streets, head north from the Piazza San Marco to **Canareggio**.

THE FENS

This "wide and never fully mapped wilderness of huge skies and endless marshland in eastern Anglia" ruled by the **gyptians** differs substantially between Lyra's world and Will's world. In Will's world, they have been drained and tamed. In Lyra's world, as Pullman has noted: "it's still a complicated maze of rivers. Somehow, I had a feeling that the gyptians would have a lot of Dutch in them – perhaps because there has always been a lot of commerce between the Fens and the Low Countries. And so their language contains Dutch words and speech rhythms."

The wild Fens of Lyra's world is a place of slithering eels, flickering marsh fires, waylurking criminals, bogs and swamps where the gyptians, through human indifference, exert some sovereignty.

In the books, the wetlands of the Fens seem to fill East Anglia, the region where Pullman was born and spent some happy years as a boy. The landscape has appealed to other novelists – notably Graham Swift (*Waterland*) – but also **C.S. Lewis**. *The Silver Chair* features Puddlegum the marshwiggle, a stereotypically gloomy Fenlander who lives on eel and pike. In contrast, Pullman's gyptians are plucky, resourceful, loyal and tight-knit, though regarded as second-class citizens by the Gobblers. The gyptians' fondness for eels is so great they have named one of their few permanent structures Eelmarket, an obvious echo of **Ely**, the Fens town so named because it was situated on a marshy island where the silvery fish were plentiful.

> "THE BLACK SHUCK MAY BE AS LARGE AS A HORSE OR A BIG DOG AND HAVE EYES LIKE SAUCERS OR ONE CYCLOPS EYE."

Pullman's description of the Fens brilliantly captures the landscape's capacity to blend folklore and truth much as it blurs the boundaries between water and dry land. The most famous surviving wild fen of the kind Pullman conjures up is **Wicken Fen** in Cambridgeshire, the home, so local legend has it, of the **Black Shuck**, the phantom black dog the fen-dwellers in *Northern Lights* tell stories about. East Anglia is full of tales of the phantom hound – the myths probably reached Pullman's part of Norfolk. The beast may be as large as a horse or only the size of a big dog and has two flaming eyes like saucers (which are red or green) or one Cyclops eye in the middle of its forehead.

Waylurkers tempting careless travellers to their doom are not unknown in Wicken Fen. In 1855, a 24-year-old policeman called **Richard Peake** went missing from his beat in the early hours. His body was never found and foul play, by a local gang, was suspected.

Today, Wicken Fen is a National Trust nature reserve which is open all year (times vary – see *www.wicken.org.uk*). In the summer you can take a boat through the Fen. If you stand in the middle of the nature reserve, you can see nothing but water, fen and woodland. It's probably as close as you can get to seeing what the Fens were like before they were drained or as they are in Lyra's world.

The Wild East: Wicken Fen is the last remnant of the Fens as Lyra would know it

GENEVA

A jaundiced traveller once said of **Geneva** that everything good in the city comes from somewhere else. Italian cooks, French girls, white wine from Lausanne. In *His Dark Materials*, this wealthy Swiss city imports the papacy, after an initiative by **Pope John Calvin**. In our world, the real city is home to many global institutions. In the books, the city hosts the **Magisterium** and the **Consistorial Court of Discipline**. On the beautiful lake nearby, the **Swiss Guards** – imported, with the papacy, from Rome – have their very own zeppelin docking area.

In Pullman's Geneva, the clerics bitch, fret about Dust (the torture of **Boris Mikhailovitch Rusakov** was ordered from here) and plot. At **St Jerome's College**, the austere, unpleasant building where the Consistorial Court meets, Father Gomez is granted pre-emptive absolution for his planned murder. In our world, **Saint Jerome** (342–419) was notorious for his polemics against critics of the Roman Church and his craven submission to the Pope.

> "IN THE BOOKS, GENEVA IS THE 16TH-CENTURY CITY OF CALVIN, KNOWN AS THE PROTESTANT ROME."

The real Geneva is home to **CERN**, the world's largest particle physics laboratory, but in the books the city is an enemy of science. Geneva, as imagined by Pullman, is essentially the 16th century city of Calvin, so dominated by religious totalitarianism it was known as the Protestant Rome.

If Pullman's portrayal hasn't turned you against the place, you will find Geneva pleasant, rich, expensive, self-satisfied, laissez-faire and dead after 11pm. But the lake and **St Pierre** cathedral are worth an afternoon of anyone's life.

HIMALAYAS

The world's most iconic mountain range has a small, if telling, part to play in *The Amber Spyglass*. Here, in a cave, **Mrs Coulter** hides **Lyra** after abducting her from Cittàgazze. The range is never named but Pullman gives us an unusually precise, vivid and long description of the valley where Lyra is hidden. Lush, windy, misty, with a river running through rhododendrons and pine trees, the

War cry: the Himalayas were fought over, in our world, by the US and Japan in 1941–45

valley is, at its head, always enveloped with rainbows. The only settlement is a few herdsmen's houses and prayer flags mark a shrine near a glacier. An illustration of the prayer flags – meant to carry prayers to the wind in Himalayan custom – provided the woodcut for Chapter 1 in *The Amber Spyglass*.

The Himalayan valley in Lyra's world has a counterpart in ours. **Yumthang Valley**, a grazing pasture in the state of Sikkim in northern India surrounded by the Himalayan mountains, has a river running through it, is lush enough in the summer for cattle to graze and is home to the Shingba rhododendron sanctuary, which contains 24 species of the flower. Sikkim is more famous for its monasteries and for being disputed by China and India.

LAPLAND

Pullman's reimagined Lapland largely, but not completely, excludes the Finnish part of the region which is now sadly synonymous with over-priced day trips to see **Santa Claus**. In the books, Lapland roughly coincides with Norway with some strategic additions. The seaport of **Trollesund**, where the gyptians sail to in search of their abducted children, is on the Norwegian coast and, in John Parry's map (published as an appendix to the tenth anniversary edition of *The Subtle Knife*), is near Lake Enara, which Serafina Pekkala's witch clan call home. Enara surely owes something to **Inari**, a lake in the very north of Finland which was, in pagan times, a place where human sacrifices were offered.

Lapland's reputation for magic and witchcraft predates Pullman and Milton. The tradition stretches back to at least two millennia. In 992, a king of Norway called **Eric Bloodaxe** met a daughter of the aristocracy who had been sent to Lapland to learn sorcery. In 1584, **Ivan The Terrible** asked Lapp magicians to explain the meaning of a comet. **Joannes Scheffer** in his book *The History Of Lapland* (1674) suggested that the Lapps' melancholic constitution gave them the power to see the future in dreams.

The 1796 painting, *The Night-Hag Visiting Lapland Witches* by **Henry Fuseli** (1741–1825), is a remarkable gothic nightmare which touches on many themes in *His Dark Materials*. Seeking a child's body to contain her demon lover, the night-hag finds a virgin-child being prepared for sacrifice by the cruel, repulsive Lapland witches. As 47 of Fuseli's paintings were suggested by themes in Milton – and the *Night-Hag* painting was shown at an exhibition Pullman opened in Grasmere – it seems reasonable to assume the novelist was familiar with the artist's oeuvre.

> "LAPLAND'S REPUTATION FOR WITCHCRAFT PREDATES PULLMAN, GOING BACK TO 992 AND ERIC BLOODAXE."

Trollesund, the largest seaport in Pullman's Lapland, will seem familiar to anyone who has travelled much in northern Scandinavia and Russia. Smelling of fish, pine resin and earth, beneath a sky full of gulls, the town consists of a few wooden houses mainly grouped around the harbour, a single oratory, a few concrete warehouses, a smoke-filled café and a tavern for sailors to drink in. The fact that the priest's house is made of brick, an expensive material in this region, is one of Pullman's subtler digs at organized religion. Four days' march from Trollesund is **Bolvangar**, the experimental station where children are cut, which seems, from its description, to be inspired by various forms of institutionalized wickedness, from Josef Mengele's lab at Auschwitz to such secretive research establishments as Los Alamos and Porton Down.

Today, Lapland is more correctly known as **Sapmi**. This region spreads across Norway, Sweden, Finland and Russia and is usually said to include the Norwegian counties of Finnmark, Nordland, Nord-Trondelag, Troms; the Swedish counties of Jämtlands Län, Norbottens Län and Västerbottens Län, Lapland province in Finland and part of the Murmansk oblast in Russia.

DEATH OF AN AËRONAUT

Some explorers tried to ski to the poles, others relied on sledges and dogs, but the reckless Swedish aëronaut **S.A. Andrée** (1854–97) tried to drift there in his balloon.

Andrée was so confident his hydrogen-filled balloon, the **Eagle**, would fly over the North Pole in a few days and land near the Bering Straits, that he took precious little supplies, didn't bother to test the newly manufactured balloon and ignored warnings that it was leaking hydrogen faster than had been predicted.

The balloon lifted off from Svalbard on 11 July 1897 but, by 13 July, the Eagle had landed, unexpectedly in pack ice. With precious little food and clothing, Andrée and his companions **Nils Strindberg** and **Knut Fraenkel** trekked south, just made it to **Kvitoya** (White Island) near Svalbard and died there. Nobody knew what had happened to them. Their remains were found, by accident, 33 years later. The last coherent entry in Andrée's diary, recovered with the bodies, began: "Morale remains good".

The disaster has already inspired one novel, **Per Olof Sundman**'s *The Flight Of The Eagle* (later made into a film). Fortunately for Lyra, Lee Scoresby proved to be a much more thoughtful kind of aëronaut, the anti-Andrée if you will.

To most tourists, Lapland is defined by the Finnish province. This enchanting, strange region, where the repeated juxtaposition of snow and forest somehow never becomes monotonous, has its own capital, **Rovianemi,** best reached by the fantastic overnight train from Helsinki.

The Sami city's roads are laid out to resemble reindeer's antlers from the sky. On the road north east, as you enter the Arctic Circle and head towards the charming village of **Sodankyla**, the wilderness begins to envelop you.

To head straight to Inari, the likely inspiration for the witches' home lake, just fly from Helsinki to **Ivalo**. The lakeside village of Inari is just along the E75 highway and has a fine Sami museum. The lake is best seen between May and July when it isn't frozen and the sun never sets. If you want to see the Aurora, travel between November and March and head to the resort of **Saariselka**, where you have a 75 percent chance of seeing the lights.

London

Pullman's capital is a contradictory city. Sometimes contemporary yet mainly Victorian, intoxicating and scary, pretty and ugly, rich and poor, his London is Dickensian in its diversity and in the sense that it represents, for Lyra, a test of character and nerve.

BOOKS FOR GLOBETROTTERS

In Lyra's Oxford, Smith and Strange Ltd publish "books on travel, archaeology, and related subjects". Here is a list of the books with any notes that seem relevant.

Bronze Clocks Of Benin Marisa Coulter Benin does get a fleeting reference as a country in the world of Cittàgazze, but it's also possible that Pullman is referring to Nigeria.

By Zeppelin To The Pole Lt. Col. J.C.B. Carborn.

Fraud: An Exposure Of A Scientific Imposture Professor P. Trelawney, Ph.D., F.R.A.S., F.B.A. the Palmerian professor at Jordan. An intriguing title. In *Northern Lights*, Trelawney is accused of plagiarism by Jotham Santelia.

From Novgorod To Cairo: An Alternative Trade-History Ricardo Pontoppidan.

A Guide For The Traveller In The Realms Of The Witches Karel Powers.

Lamaseries Of Bhutan Jasper Wetzel.

Optical Phenomena Among The Glaciers Of The Alps T.G. Hammersley.

Phrase Book For The Levant James Verity, who is also the author of *Phrase Book For The Nordic Lands* and *Phrase Book For The Oceanic Lands*. The Levant phrase book would not have been of use to anyone in *His Dark Materials*, so it must either be a red herring or a clue to *The Book Of Dust*.

Polymathestatos: A Festschrift In Honour Of Joscelyn Godwin Edited by Athanasius Kircher. Godwin (1945–) is a musicologist and writer whose many works often focus on hermeticism, the occult and music. Kircher (1602–80) is a mysterious Renaissance scholar who could not have edited a book in Godwin's honour without the gift of time-travel.

Prisoner Of The Bears, A Professor Jotham D. Santelia. Presumably a heroic memoir of his incarceration.

Proto-Fisher People Of L'Anse Aux Meadows Leonard Broken Arrow.

Some Curious Anomalies In The Mathematics Of Palladio's Quattro Libri Nicholas Outram. Pullman's original name was Philip Nicholas Outram. In 1570, the Italian architect Andrea Palladio published a four volume – hence the *Quattro Libri* – treatise which set down various systematic rules for architecture and was much admired by Thomas Jefferson who called it his "bible" and used these principles when designing his Monticello house.

Star-Maps Of The Yenisei Region D.V. Mikuschev.

Treatise On The Use Of The Sextant Giovanni Battista Kremer.

Where The Reindeer Run Lars Unsgaard.

With Gun And Rod In The Hindu Kush Capt. R.T.G. Collins. Surely, in part, an homage to Eric Newby's classic *A Short Walk In The Hindu Kush*.

Dickens could draw on the city he lived in. Pullman's sources are more varied. His capital owes something to Dickens, Sir Arthur Conan Doyle (whose stories so inspired Pullman he spoofed them in his play *Sherlock Holmes And The Limehouse Horror*) and the massive amount of historical research he did for the Sally Lockhart novels.

Even before she reaches London, Lyra is intoxicated by the very idea of the city. As described by Mrs Coulter, the city is a fabulous place of soirees, intrigue and ballrooms. For Lyra, Mrs Coulter's perfect flat – in the fashionable district of Falkeshall – and her dizzying shopping trips, only add to the allure.

Falkeshall is one of the old names for Vauxhall. Falkes de Breaute was a French mercenary who fought for King John, with courage and cruelty, and acquired, through marriage, a house in London which was known as **Fawkes Hall**. The area definitively acquired its present name when the local **Vauxhall Pleasure Gardens** opened in the 1660s. Dickens, in *Sketches By Boz*, describes a visit where the fireworks and the lights left him mortified and astonished. The gardens closed in 1859 and the area, though its gentrified enclaves are home to many MPs and civil servants, is now best known as a stop off on London's public transport system.

> "MRS COULTER'S LONDON IS SIMILAR TO MRS PULLMAN'S: A DAZZLING WORLD OF CRAVATS AND SPORTS CARS."

Though it's clear we are meant to equate Falkeshall and Vauxhall, Pullman might be using language and history to throw us off the scent. Mrs Coulter's plush London, with its grand mansion blocks and beautiful shops, seems to have more in common with Chelsea, where Pullman's mother rented a flat for a year or so. In an interview with *New Yorker* magazine, Pullman admitted to being dazzled by these "men with pipes and cravats and sports cars". This milieu is surely the basis for Mrs Coulter's social world and the cocktail party at which Lyra makes her escape.

Fleeing the luxurious imprisonment of Falkeshall, Lyra is soon on the run in a very different London. The adjectives change – brilliant, pretty and glamorous are replaced by raucous, cold and clangorous. Even the air takes a turn for the worse: the clear air they gazed through at the cityscape from the zeppelin is now murky, laden with fumes and soot.

Lyra passes ugly houses with gardens as small as dustbins, great gaunt factories and the occasional "dismal oratory" before reaching the grim slums of **Limehouse** where poor children are snatched away by Gobblers and spirited abroad from Hangman's Wharf and King George's Steps, in a manner reminiscent of "white slavery" panics – the fear that young girls were being lured to brothels in Europe – that gripped London in the late Victorian era.

On the northern bank of the Thames, opposite Rotherhithe, Limehouse has, at different times, been associated with explorers (like Martin Frobisher) and opium dens. The area's name springs from its association with the sea – Limehouse is probably inspired by the lime juice given to sailors to prevent scurvy – but, in the 19th century, it was such a hotbed of crime that lurid pulp novelists like **Sax Rohmer** used it as a backdrop. Pullman's Limehouse is less sensationalized than Rohmer's but it is still essentially Victorian.

> "THE ABDUCTION OF CHILDREN RECALLS THE WHITE SLAVERY PANICS THAT GRIPPED LONDON IN VICTORIAN TIMES."

Other parts of London have supporting roles in *Northern Lights* – notably **Clerkenwell** (where the Gobblers also do their worst), **White Hall** and **Wapping** (which he used to great effect in his Lockhart novels) – but Pullman wisely uses only as much of London as is convenient and essential for his story. **Mortlake** is mentioned in passing, allowing Pullman to allude to the Elizabethan magician, astrologer and spy **John Dee**, who is a significant figure on the margins of the novels (see p.205) and was an associate of Humphrey Gilbert, an explorer and would-be alchemist who lived in Limehouse.

The metropolis all but disappears from the story after *Northern Lights*, although the notes in the tenth anniversary edition of *The Subtle Knife* say that **John Parry** found it 'harder to live in the streets I thought I knew than in the wilds of Siberia". Did Pullman feel something similar as boy when he was taken up to Chelsea to see his mother in her chic apartment?

MUSCOVY

In Lyra's world, the city or principality that experimental theologian Boris Mikhailovitch Rusakov hails from seems to equate with the principality of the grand duchy of Moscow – aka **Muscovy** – which lasted from 1340 to 1547.

Moscow was burned by the Mongols – or **Tartars** as they were once known in the 13th century – but recovered and became, under **Ivan III** (1462–1505), the core of the country we now call Russia. But Pullman's Muscovy transcends time and history. This city or principality is also known as the **Soviet Union** (which didn't exist until 1917) and has been in conflict with **Nippon** (Japan) as the Russian empire was, disastrously, in 1904–1905. It is hard, from the novels' passing references, to gauge Muscovy's power. Though menaced by Tartar troops, it has unleashed weapons containing naphtha (a carcinogenic petroleum ether) on Nippon, has an observatory on Nova Zembla and sends its troops in pursuit of Lee Scoresby and Stanislaus Grumman.

SIBERIA

One of the most famous, yet misunderstood, regions of the world, **Siberia** makes a memorable entrance in the first novel as the land, we are told, where heads are scalped so badly they look "hardly human". Scalping has, through Westerns, always been linked in the public mind with Native Americans but nearly a decade after this scene was written, four 2,500-year-old skulls from southern Siberia were found to have been scalped. Archaelogists still debate how widespread the practice might have been but the discovery reinforces the Siberia's stereotypical image as the **Wild East**, a vast, lawless, often sparsely inhabited region where anything bad can happen and often does.

His Dark Materials encompasses most of Siberia, alluding to the Kamchatka peninsula in the east, the Urals and the Ob river in the West, the Lena and Yenisei rivers which feed into Lake Baikal and such obscure townships as Kholodnoye and Turukhansk and **Tunguska**, the last being the site of a huge, mysterious explosion in 1908 that has figured in the fiction of Thomas Pynchon, Stanislaw Lem and Isaac Asimov and inspired an episode in *The X Files*. But a narrower strip of Siberia, bounded by the Ob in the West and the Yenisei in the east, is the backdrop for two quests: the journey by Will and the panserbjørne to the Himalayas to find Lyra; and Lee Scoresby's search for Stanislaus Grumman.

The narrative in *The Amber Spyglass* is consistent – writer Laurie Frost has shown in detail – with the bears sailing from Svalbard to the mouth of the Ob river, stopping near **Kholodnoye** where they meet Will and then continuing down the Ob to the Altai mountains. From there, with much luck, a master navigator's knowledge of minor rivers and some lake-hopping it is conceivable, says Frost, that they really could reach the Tibetan foothills of the Himalayas by boat.

Scoresby's quest takes him to a Tartar village near the **Yenisei** and the river's winding progress is celebrated in Pullman's woodcut illustration for Chapter 10 of *The Subtle Knife*. The novels – and the various appendices – show that Grumman has probably roamed more freely across Siberia than Scoresby or the bears. He learned how to make an ointment in the region of Turukhansk, a town on the mouth of one of the Yenisei's tributaries, and first met Asriel at the delta of the river Lena, the tenth longest river in the world.

The **Samoyeds**, a native Siberian people now better known as the Nenets, have a fleeting role in the trilogy. Samoyed hunters ambush the gyptians and abduct Lyra to sell her for silver. They seem to know just how much she would be worth to the Gobblers, so the child-selling racket is obviously not new to them. Lyra later spots Samoyed photos and artefacts when visiting the Pitt Rivers museum in *The Subtle Knife*.

"THE NENETS, CHILD-SELLERS IN NORTHERN LIGHTS, ARE, IN REALITY, AN ENDANGERED RACE, EXPOSED TO NUCLEAR TESTING."

The **Nenets** are, in reality, an endangered race. Once nomadic reindeer herders, they are now scattered between the Kola peninsula, that part of Siberia that lies between the White Sea, the Yenisei and the Ob, and Novaya Zemla, where they were shipped to stop Norwegians from settling and later exposed to the side-effects of hundreds of nuclear tests. Their numbers are now growing – up to 35,000 in 1989 – but, like many native peoples, they are being culturally marginalized in their own towns and villages.

Siberia is not all arctic wastes and former penal colonies. The West is often flat, the centre well-forested and the East wonderfully wild and mountainous. In many parts of Siberia, what impresses travellers most is not the quality of the scenery, but the quantity of it. The sheer scale of the place can unnerve.

If you're tempted to see for yourself, you could take the Trans-Siberian Railway from Moscow and stay on to Vladivostok or get off at Irkutsk and see **Lake Baikal**, a banana-shaped lake in the middle of nowhere, a mile deep and so large it's bigger than Belgium. Even in the Siberian winter, only half of Baikal freezes over.

You might find it easier to go with an independent travel company like Steppes Travel (*www.steppestravel.co.uk*), Russia Experience (*www. trans-siberian.co.uk*) or RusAdventure (*www.rusadventure.com*) as booking compartments or seats on the Trans-Siberian is a bit of a black art.

Landscape art: Siberia is so vast, the sense of infinite space can unnerve tourists

Monumental puzzle: a Soviet memorial to the miners of Barentsburg in Svalbard

THE OTHER ARCHIPELAGO

Nova Zembla, the island Iorek Byrnison came to in search of armour while in exile, is modelled on Novaya Zembla, an archipelago where the Soviets tested their nuclear armoury. Both names mean "new land". The extra 'b' in the name subtly nods to Vladimir Nabokov: the fictional land in his masterpiece *Pale Fire* is Zembla.

North of Russia – and on the very northeastern tip of Europe – this archipelago was a haven, for a winter, to Willem Barents. Until the 1950s, fishing was a major industry (as it is in Nova Zembla in the books) but then the island became a nuclear test-bed and an airforce base, with little thought for the effects on the indigenous Nenets people (as the Samoyeds, who kidnap Lyra, are now known). After 224 explosions – equivalent to 130 times the explosive power unleashed in World War II – testing finally stopped in 1990. The Imperial Muscovite Academy's Observatory in *His Dark Materials* may be a distorted reflection of the Soviet observatories that studied the science of destruction here.

The Novaya Zemla effect, as it is known, is a natural phenomenon no sci-fi writer would dare invent. One of Barents' colleagues, Gerrit de Veer, noticed a polar mirage that makes the sun look like it's rising earlier than it should or, more scarily, turns the familiar orb into a line or a square.

SVALBARD

Pullman wanted to see **Svalbard** for himself but couldn't get a grant. "It didn't matter very much," he said in an email. "I'm inclined to think that travel is overrated but that might be because I dislike all forms of it. I can find out most of what I need from the Bodleian Library. I chose Svalbard because I liked the sound of it. I built up a picture of the Arctic in general, especially the inhabited edge of it, which is all I need. But remember I'm writing about another Arctic in another world so I'm allowed to take liberties."

One book that could have helped Pullman was the *Account Of The Arctic Regions And Northern Whale Fishery* (1820), written by William Scoresby, the explorer who visited these islands and gave his surname to Lee Scoresby.

Though the archipelago is so remote that its name means, in Norse, "cold edge", Svalbard has exerted a surprising pull on the literary imagination. **Sir Arthur Conan Doyle** set his short story *The Captain Of The Polestar* off Amsterdam Island in northwest Svalbard. In the 1970s and 1980s, the archipelago was the setting for two cold war thrillers: *Orion's Belt* by Norwegian novelist Jon Michelet and Geir Finne's *The Svalbard Passage*.

But it was Pullman's depiction of Svalbard as a land ruled by armoured

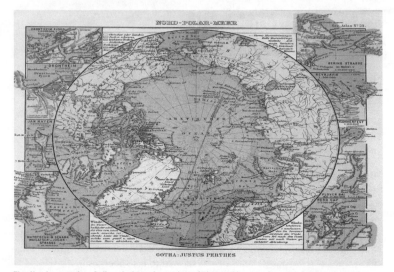

The North countries: Pullman's favourite region of the world, even though he's never been there

bears that really put the archipelago on the map. Even his warnings about environmental decay are prescient. By the end of this century, the sea ice around the north pole may vanish every summer, in which case the 500 real polar bears that currently live in the archipelago may struggle to survive.

If your literary imagination is fired by all things northern, as Pullman's would seem to be, it would be almost impossible to neglect Svalbard. The settlements on the archipelago are the northernmost permanently inhabited spots on the planet, far more northerly than Alaska and most of Canada's Arctic islands. Possibly discovered by Vikings in the 12th century – and reached by Dutch explorer **Willem Barents** in 1596 – the archipelago is slightly larger than Croatia but most of the 3000 or so permanent residents live in two settlements, Longyearbyen and Barentsburg, on the most famous island, Spitsbergen.

Officially part of Norway, the archipelago has mineral reserves which are jointly exploited by the Norwegians and the Russians (who mostly live in Barentsburg). The steady trickle of tourists who arrive by cruise ship (from Tromso) or plane (from Oslo or Tromso) want to see the rugged, desolate landscape. Pullman accurately describes the interior as "mountainous with jumbled peaks and sharp ridges deeply cut by ravines and steep-sided valleys". Some mountains look like slag heaps. There is not one tree on any of the islands. But if you like snowy peaks, glaciers, exotic Arctic flowers, seabirds, bears and brown moss that looks like dead grass, Svalbard is well worth a visit between June and August, the tourist high season when the sun seldom sets.

The capital **Longyearbyen**, named after the American industrialist John Longyear who founded the town and the nearby mine, is the best base for any visit.

Tourism has already begun to reshape this town – it now has its very own Radisson hotel – but the transformation is partial and inconsistent. The shops in the Lompensert shopping mall often only open for three hours on Saturdays and there is no public transport.

> "IF YOU FANCY A STROLL OUTSIDE THE CAPITAL LONGYEARBYEN TAKE A RIFLE AS POLAR BEARS ARE A REAL THREAT."

Apart from the obligatory snow safaris, there are day trips to abandoned coal mines, the remains of a Russian settlement and a cruise to the Esmarkbreen glacier. If you fancy a stroll outside city limits, you are advised to take a rifle or an armed guide as polar bears are a real threat. As the

THE OTHER MR SCORESBY AND MR PARRY

Two of the explorers in *His Dark Materials* share part of their name with real explorers of the Arctic. Lee Scoresby gets his surname from **William Scoresby** (1789–1857), the Yorkshire explorer and whaler's son.

He was given his own ship by his father when he was 21 and made the most of his legacy. His journals on the Arctic are still regarded as landmark texts even today, almost 190 years after they were first published, and a sound off the east coast of **Greenland** which he mapped with remarkable accuracy in 1822 is named in his honour. After Scoresby retired as an explorer

and joined the clergy, he helped the Admiralty to improve its compasses.

Will's father, Colonel John Parry, vanishes on an expedition to find a gateway to another world.

The rear admiral and explorer **Sir William Edward Parry** (1790–1855) returned to England in triumph in 1820 after having sailed more than half the distance between Greenland and the Bering Strait, proving that there was a gateway for ships between the Atlantic and the Pacific oceans.

Like Scoresby, he knew Spitsbergen pretty well, sailing from there in one attempt to reach the North Pole.

bears are protected, if you do shoot one you will be investigated by the police.

If you do decide to visit Svalbard, be sure to save up – it's slightly cheaper than mainland Norway, but only just. The Radisson hotel in Longyearbyen will typically cost at least £120 ($235) a night per room but you can camp in the summer for less than £8 ($15) a night. To get a fuller picture of what Svalbard can offer, go to *www.svalbard.net*.

TEXAS

Though the United States doesn't exist in the trilogy, Texas, homeland of **Lee Scoresby**, does. Between 1836 and 1846, Texas was a sovereign republic between Mexico and the US, an independence won, in part, by the mythologized defence of the Alamo and it is to this Texas, mainly, that Pullman refers.

Scoresby grew up near enough to this legendary mission in present-day San Antonio to play there and his defence of **Alamo Gulch** is worthy of Davy Crockett, William Travis and Jim Bowie. Pullman's Alamo is the heroic myth of the **John Wayne** movie, not the revisionist theory which suggests that some defenders, notably Crockett, surrendered and were executed.

When he retires, Scoresby dreams of booking passage to Port Galveston – which must be the city made famous by Glen Campbell's hit version of the Jimmy Webb song *Galveston* – and buying a small cattle farm there. Homesickness may partly explain why the mulefa world reminds Scoresby of the prairies and sagelands of Texas.

Scoresby would be stunned to hear that the 4.2 acres officially known as **The Alamo** now attract over 2.5 million visitors a year. The best way to enjoy it, in this crush, is not to restrict yourself to the serene old church which may, on first sight, seem disappointingly smaller than you imagined.

The other traces of the old Alamo are harder to spot yet worth the look. Much of the fighting occurred in Alamo Plaza, where you can, roughly, discern the outline of the old mission and fort. A plaque marks the spot where Jim Bowie's Low Barrack stood. The palisade, that part of the defences manned by Crockett and his volunteers, is marked by paving stones on the plaza. Less romantically, the spot where commander William B. Travis gave his life for Texas is under a post office building. For more info see *www.thealamo.org*.

··✝··

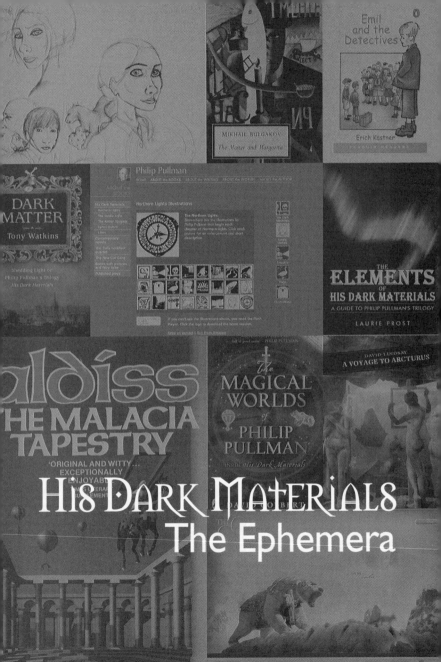

His Dark Materials

The Ephemera

MATERIAL BENEFITS

Check out Philip Pullman's favourite reads and the websites that cut a window into the world of *His Dark Materials*

The Hollywoodization of any great novel can be a mixed blessing for fans of the book. But the filming of *The Golden Compass* has already brought undiluted joy to many *His Dark Materials* fans because, with the merchandizing that will precede and accompany the movie, they will finally be able to buy themselves an armoured bear.

Granted, the bear in question will be an action figure, rather than a living, breathing panserbjørne – it may even come with a McDonald's Happy Meal – but you can't have everything. Fans may also be able to purchase battery-powered toy **alethiometers** and **subtle knives** but, stripped of their powers to tell children whether their new friend has murdered anybody or to cut holes into parallel universes, these may disappoint all but the most imaginative children. But cometh the movie cometh the computer game from **Sega**, various trump cards and much more besides.

Devotees have had, till now, to largely make do with collecting books and browsing websites so this harvest of toys, games and posters will come as a boon to many. The Sega computer game, available on Playstation 3, will enable thousands to take on the characters of Lyra or Iorek Byrnison as they trek across the frozen north in pursuit of a friend – presumably Roger – abducted by the Gobblers. And there's always the hope that, in years to come, the occasional movie prop will reach the market. It happened after the play at the National Theatre. In 2005, the actor **Alistair Petrie**, who played Iorek Byrnison, sold his bear head and claw on **eBay** for charity.

If you feel there's not enough *His Dark Materials* in your life, this chapter is here to help, pointing you to the best books and websites relating to the trilogy, the themes raised in the novels and its creator.

COLLECTING BOOKS

Lucky the reader who had the foresight to pick up a few copies of Pullman's first novel, *The Haunted Storm*, back in 1972. Although Pullman won't even say the book's name in interviews, a hardback first edition can fetch £850, while even the 1973 paperback is worth £200. Pullman wrote many books before *His Dark Materials* and these early works are an important area for the serious collector: the earlier the better – although Pullman's willingness to sign means the serious collector will only buy their copies inscribed.

> "THE ROGUE FIRST IMPRINT OF THE TIGER IN THE WELL, WHICH LACKS ITS FINAL PARAGRAPH, SOLD FOR £5000."

After *The Haunted Storm* came another now out-of-print adult novel *Galatea* (1978) which is extremely collectable. The spine of the hardback suffers from fading, but a good, signed first edition will go for at least £500. Even a ragged 1979 American copy will fetch £30. Pullman's 1982 children's book *Count Karlstein* was reprinted in 1991, but a first edition often makes more than £200, whereas a first edition of *The Ruby In The Smoke* – the first in the Sally Lockhart series – has been known to reach ten times that, and a signed copy of the rogue first imprint of *The Tiger In The Well*, which lacks its final paragraph and was recalled by the publisher, sold recently for £5000!

But the real Pullman collectables are *His Dark Materials*. The trilogy's popularity has introduced desirable qualities beyond scarcity, condition and inscription. Those with money will aim for the 1995 first edition of *Northern Lights* – identified by the publisher's Pratt Street address – which,

PHILIP PULLMAN'S FAVOURITE READS

As you might expect, Pullman is scarily well read. The books that seem to have most significance to *His Dark Materials* or to him have been reviewed elsewhere in this section. But if you fancied stalking him – in a purely literary sense – you could also read the following: Marcel Proust's *Remembrance Of Things Past*, the novels of Jane Austen, George Eliot's *Middlemarch*, Mary Shelley's *Frankenstein*, Arthur Ransome's *Swallows And Amazons*, Tove Jansson's Moomin stories, Lionel Davidson's *Kolymsky Heights*, Jamila Gavin's *Coram Boy*, Peter Dickinson's *The Kin* and *Angel Isle*, Jan Mark's *The Eclipse Of The Century*, the collected novels of **Macdonald Harris** (see p.264), Prosper Mérimée's novella *Carmen*, Italo Calvino's Italian folk tales, Adèle Geras' *Silent Snow, Secret Snow* and Joan Aiken's *The Wolves Of Willoughby Chase*.

Pullman thinks Aiken is severely underrated: "She was prolific (which I always admire – energy both of productivity and of vigorous and imaginative language), hugely inventive, and very funny," he told Rough Guides.

in some cases, has already appreciated by a thousand percent. Those with less disposable income might be drawn to the 2001 *His Dark Materials* **gift set**, which includes no additional features, but is an attractive collectible, while those with more interest in the books' content should turn to the 2005 **Deluxe Tenth Anniversary** editions, whose tempting additions include sixteen pages of scientific information, letters written by Lord Asriel, Magisterium archival documents, notes from Stanislaus Grumman, a ribbon bookmark and, in *The Amber Spyglass*, the wood-cuts Pullman had intended to illustrate this novel.

The most obvious grab for fans in recent years has been *Lyra's Oxford*, which is beautifully presented as a cloth-bound hardback, with lavish illustrations, wood-cuts by John Lawrence and annotated fold-out maps. It only costs £9.99 and it's a pretty good present while you're waiting for *The Book Of Dust*.

MATERIAL EVIDENCE

Many – even most – writers protect their sources and are reluctant to shed light on their inspirations. Pullman isn't like that. In the acknowledgements at the end of *The Amber Spyglass*, he admits: "My principle in researching for a novel is 'Read like a butterfly, write like a bee' and if this story contains any honey, it is entirely because of the quality of the nectar that I found in the work of better writers." His openness in naming sources does mean that any serious aficionado of *His Dark Materials* can spend years reading good books that inspired the trilogy.

PARADISE LOST

John Milton (Oxford University Press, 2005)

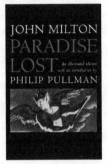

This fine edition of the 1667 poem that has enthralled, bored and intimidated generations of schoolchildren, comes complete with a foreword by Pullman in which he sensibly encourages the reader not to worry, initially, about the sense of the poem but to surrender to the music of Milton's verse.

THE COMPLETE PROSE AND POEMS

William Blake (Anchor, 1997)

The 18th-century mystic English poet, author, printer and visionary is one of the writers who has influenced Pullman most. You can find echoes of Blake throughout *His Dark Materials*. This scholarly edition of his complete works includes a critical commentary by Harold Bloom and the latest thoughts on variants of Blake's work. The poems "My Spectre Around Me Night and Day", "The Smile", "The Little Girl Lost" and his essay *The Marriage Of Heaven And Hell* are especially relevant to *His Dark Materials*. You might also enjoy delving into the large Blake archive, maintained by the University of North Carolina and the Library of Congress on *www.blakearchive.org/blake*.

ON THE MARIONETTE THEATRE

Heinrich von Kleist (Hackett, 2004)

This essay, along with Milton and Blake, is cited by Pullman as one of the three great influences on his trilogy. You can download it online from various sources, read it at the end of Nicholas Tucker's book on *His Dark Materials* or find it and another anecdotes and stories by the German Romantic author in his *Selected Writings* (Hackett, 2004), edited and translated by David Constantine. The essay's premise – that mankind might, through wisdom, cease to be part-animal and part-god and act with the confidence and grace of a marionette dancing on stage – was never experienced in life by its author. Kleist's short fiction has a surprising affinity with – and was a major influence on – the work of Franz Kafka. The two authors – one a Prussian officer, the other a

Jewish agnostic – both had short unhappy lives, with Kleist shooting himself and his dying lover, when he was 34 and Kafka dying of tuberculosis when he was 41.

GIORDANO BRUNO AND THE HERMETIC TRADITION
Frances Yates (Routledge, 2002)

Answering questions for Rough Guides, Pullman admitted that Yates's book, which highlights two characters (Giordano Bruno and Rudolf II) who feature in his fictional history of the alethiometer, just blew him away. This is not a biography of Bruno – an Italian intellectual who found the 16th century so uncongenial he almost seemed to accept his fiery end at the stake – but a fascinating attempt to place him in the context of the ancient mystic hermetic beliefs, which, when rediscovered in Renaissance Europe, caused much intellectual ferment. The historian's two other great works, *The Rosicrucian Enlightenment* and *The Art Of Memory* – the latter being one inspiration for the alethiometer – are worth reading too. None of the books are for those who like to consume their history in easily digestible chunks.

THE MALACIA TAPESTRY
Brian Aldiss (Harper Collins, 1990)

Pullman has acknowledged that this baroque, picaresque entertainment, set in a 17th-century Italian city that is cursed never to change, partly inspired Cittàgazze. This novel, first published in 1976, also features a zahnophone – a device which has certain similarities with Asriel's photograms – hydrogen balloons and an aristocratic figure who wants to do something with the sky that the authorities don't approve of. This charming, intelligent, tale of a struggling young actor whose illusions about love and society are cruelly exposed, has been republished but some of the 1970s covers, like the one on p.262 from Triad Granada, are worth the price of admission themselves.

ODYSSEY
Homer, translated by Richmond Lattimore (Harper Collins, 2002)

Lattimore's translation set a new standard for the accuracy, flow and verve it gave to Homer's classic, which hasn't, in the last 2,800 years, always been well served by its publishers and translators. His version of the *Iliad* (University of Chicago Press, 1951) is even better. Both of Homer's masterpieces influenced *His Dark Materials* and taught Pullman a lot about the art of storytelling.

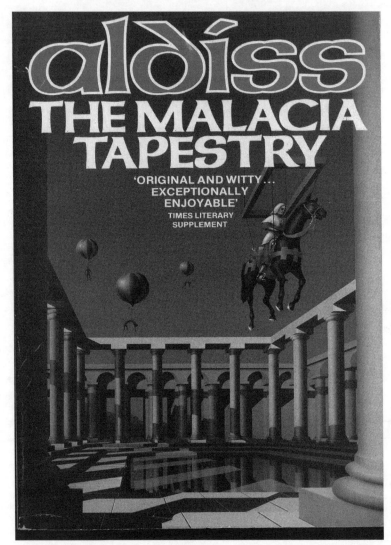

Source material: Aldiss's inventive novel, seen here in the Granada Triad edition with a superb cover illustration by Philip Tonkyn, inspired the creation of Cittàgazze

THE MASTER AND MARGARITA

Mikhail Bulgakov (Penguin, 2001)

Pullman hasn't actually read this great novel from 1940. One look at the jacket was enough to tell him that it fell so squarely in his fictional territory that he might be tempted to borrow ideas. But if you're not intending to write a fantastic novel of your own, Bulgakov's masterpiece is a treat. An ambitious triumph set in three worlds, an entertaining variation on *Faust*, this dark, satirical romp and weird novel of protest features one of literature's most charismatic Lucifers since Milton.

A VOYAGE TO ARCTURUS

David Lindsay (Gollancz, 2003)

If you ignore the obvious shortcomings – cardboard characterization, stilted language, some lapses in style – you will discover why Colin Wilson called this "the greatest novel of the 20th century". It's not quite that great, but this 1920 sci-fi novel brings philosophical depth to a familiar scenario – a man stranded on a planet – in a story which at times reads almost like a Gnostic parable. Scottish novelist David Lindsay (1876–1945) believed, like the Gnostics, that this world was only an illusion. That idea informs *Arcturus* and

COMIC INSPIRATION

Pullman's appreciation of the narrative power of illustration started when, as a boy in Australia, he fell in love with the superhero comics.

In an email, he told Rough Guides: "I liked the early *Batman* because it was so unself-conscious. It didn't know how good it was. It thought it was catchpenny comic-book trash so it could be honest about its imaginative extravagance. I loved it passionately when I was nine or ten. Later, I grew to love the more sophisticated **Marvel** comics (*Dr Strange* was my favourite) but nothing will surpass my exultant bliss when a new *Batman* or *Superman* comic arrived when I was nine or ten."

Later, in the 1950s, Pullman discovered the joy of **Dan Dare** and his great, green, bald enemy the Mekon.

his second novel *The Haunted Woman*. Lindsay never wrote a work of fiction this influential again, with C.S. Lewis, Pullman and Alasdair Gray all owing a debt to this compelling tale. The American critic Harold Bloom's only novel *The Flight To Lucifer* was a sequel to Lindsay's masterpiece, though Bloom later disowned the book. *A Voyage To Arcturus*, arguably the most influential underground novel of the 20th century, can be downloaded online at Project Gutenberg. Lindsay's life story reads like a comic novel by Malcolm Bradbury. His hopes of running a bed and breakfast in Brighton were scuppered when the first German bomb to land on Brighton in World War II struck his house. Lindsay was in the bath at the time and never recovered from the shock, though he didn't die until he was 69, from an infection caused by an abscess in his tooth.

EMIL AND THE DETECTIVES

Erich Kästner (Red Fox, 2001)

Pullman admits this "marvellous" novel, first published in 1929, with worldwide sales of over two million and an obvious source

for the children detectives novels of Enid Blyton, is one of the books that has significantly inspired his fiction. The boy in the title, Emil Tischbein,

THE LOST GENIUS

Philip Pullman would most like the world to rediscover an American novelist called **Macdonald Harris** (1921–93). "I have a particular bee in my bonnet about him," Pullman admitted to Rough Guides.

"He wrote sixteen novels, none of which was a best-seller, none of which gained him much recognition, except for *The Balloonist* (1977). But he was immensely intelligent, a witty and very subtle stylist, a writer of great variety – which was his undoing, really: each of his books was quite different from all the others. Publishers, booksellers, and readers didn't know how to place him, or what to expect next, so he never built up a loyal and growing readership.

"Various themes do emerge: his typical protagonist is a man who's lost control of his life, or who decides to abandon control, or who is defeated by circumstances; and that didn't play with an American readership, which loves above all a successful defiance of fate and not an existential resignation to it. None of his books is in print."

Macdonald Harris was the pseudonym for **Donald Heiney,** a Californian who gave up engineering to write fiction. His first novel, *Private Demons*, about a fantasist scheming to restore the Emperor Franz Josef's royal yacht, was published in 1961. He is remembered fondly by Pullman and on this website *www.physics.upenn. edu/~heiney/harris/side.html*.

gets robbed while asleep on a train but tracks down the thief who turns out to be a bank robber. *Emil And The Detectives* broke new ground because it was set, not in some enchanted fantasy land, but in the suburbs of Berlin. Hero and villain have joky surnames – Tischbein means "table leg" while the robber's name, Grundeis, means "ground ice". Pullman has scattered similar jokes throughout his fiction. Kästner's life was more eventful than his novels. A lifelong pacifist, he watched his books being burned by the Nazis in the 1930s, arrived in Dresden shortly after its destruction by Allied bombs and was rediscovered as an author in the 1970s, by which time he had become an alcoholic. He died in 1974, aged 75, still best known for the Emil books – he also wrote a 1933 sequel called *Emil And The Three Twins* – although his memoir *When I Was A Little Child* is very moving. Pullman is also a big fan of Kästner's *The Thirty-Fifth Of May* in which: "A little boy called Conrad has to do an essay about the South Seas; he grumbles about this to his uncle who takes him to the back of a wardrobe and there they find themselves magically transported to the South Seas. I wonder if that gave C.S. Lewis the idea of wardrobes as an entrance to another world?"

A Hundred Million Francs

Paul Berna (Bodley Head Children's Books, 1957)

Pullman discovered this in a library in Battersea and was quickly intrigued by this "exciting novel about a gang of working class Parisian kids who had a wooden horse on wheels which they could sit on and ride down the hill". Pullman fell in love with Richard Kennedy's illustration of a "very tough scruffy girl called Mariana, aged about eleven, with blonde hair and big dark eyes, wearing a leather jacket" and it was one of the images that inspired Lyra. (The milieu may have inspired his New Cut Gang books too.) Berna's novel still stands up. If you like this, try *The Horse Without A Head*, another tale of street urchins. His *Threshold Of The Stars*, an engrossing, sensitive novel about boys watching a rocket being built, is a good read too.

The Picture History Of Painting

H.W. Janson and D.J. Janson (Thames & Hudson, 1968)

"I bought this with a book token when I was 15", Pullman recalled once. His interest in illustrations and pictures, for their own sake and as a way of telling stories, can be traced right back to his early love of superhero comics. This hard-to-find book, which goes back to the first cave paintings, was his artistic bible, inspired him as a youngster to draw – and learn to love – the landscape around Llanbedr, in north Wales.

THE ALTERATION

Kingsley Amis (Vintage, 2004)

In *His Dark Materials*, John Calvin becomes Pope. In Amis's strange alternative history novel (published in 1976), the Reformation was stymied when Martin Luther was co-opted into becoming Pope. The Church Militant which, in this novel, has kept England in a quasi-medieval state, is even more ruthless than Pullman's Authority, using Nazi tactics to discriminate against the Jews and plotting the castration of the novel's boy hero Hubert Anvil so his voice remains pure

– another possible inspiration for intercision? This isn't the kind of fiction that made Amis' name but it is, despite some terribly stilted dialogue, an intriguing novel, full of "what if?"'s.

PULLMAN'S INFLUENCES

In interviews, Pullman often fervently enthuses about books that have no obvious connection to *His Dark Materials* but have made a big impression on him. Let's take a look at the most significant or interesting of his enthusiasms.

ALICE'S ADVENTURES IN WONDERLAND

Lewis Carroll (Macmillan, 2005)

This unforgettable tale of a girl who accesses another world through a rabbit hole, has all sorts of psychedelic adventures and meets some of the most beautifully grotesque characters in English children's literature, is restored to its original glory in this edition which features John Tenniel's illustrations and a foreword by Pullman. This was so successful that it was soon followed by a Pullman/Tenniel/Carroll edition of *Through The Looking Glass And What Alice Found There*.

GRIMM'S FAIRY TALES

The Brothers Grimm (Gramercy, 1993)

At a whopping 704 pages, this edition of 215 stories may be for completists only (you may prefer to test the water with the Penguin Popular Classics edition), but this is probably the best single volume of the tales which have influenced so much of

Pullman's fiction, especially his modern fairytale *Clockwork*. These tales are, Pullman says, one of the books that has made the biggest difference to his life.

THE MAGIC PUDDING

Norman Lindsay (New York Review of Books, 2004)

This edition, featuring Lindsay's own superb illustrations and a foreword by Pullman, is probably the definitive edition of a story Pullman calls "the funniest children's book ever written". The pudding in question is truly magic: it is everlasting, can turn into anything its owner wants it to be and is so bad-tempered it's a wonder Bunyip Bluegum, Barnacle Bill and Sam Swanoff, members of the Noble Society of Pudding Owners, don't just bury it as they roam across Australia. This stands, as the blurb says, somewhere between *Alice In Wonderland* and *The Stinky Cheese Man* as one of the craziest books ever written for young readers. Legend has it that Lindsay wrote this as a bet to prove his contention that all a book needed to entertain children was "food and fighting".

THE NEW ANNOTATED SHERLOCK HOLMES

Sir Arthur Conan Doyle, edited by Leslie S. Klinger (Norton, 2004)

All 56 stories, lavishly annotated and illustrated, are collected here and supported with enough material to satisfy even the most ardent Holmesian and brilliantly place the detective in his Victorian context. Pullman wrote a play about Holmes and, after reading this expensive, exhaustive tome, you begin to understand the stories' influence on him.

GEORGE BERNARD SHAW'S COLLECTED LETTERS

(Viking Books, 1955)

As a young man, Pullman loved reading the playwright's letters. A cracking read.

BOOKS ABOUT *HIS DARK MATERIALS*

Pullman's bestselling trilogy has inspired a slew of guides, anthologies and companions. The array of intellectual issues raised in *His Dark Materials* means there is plenty for other authors to write about. But many of the books are of the same ilk, dwelling on favourite themes like science and religion. What's still missing after all these years, is a more literary appreciation of the novels. American novelist **Michael Chabon**, in an article which can be downloaded for a small fee from the *New York Review Of Books*, has championed the trilogy, but few of Pullman's literary peers have offered much enlightenment.

Those journalistic sibling rivals Christopher and Peter Hitchens have weighed in on either side of the debate about Pullman. Sadly, Christopher's characteristically entertaining appreciation in *Vanity Fair* is not available online, whereas Peter's right-wing demolition job, which does raise a few good points among all the invective, can be found by a quick Google search. Laura Miller's superb *New Yorker* article on Pullman, *Far From Narnia*, has been archived at *www.newyorker.com*.

There is also a DVD called *Inside His Dark Materials* (Artsmagic, 2006) which features an extensive interview with Pullman, insight from friends and acquaintances, and animations and illustrations to tell the story of the books.

DARK MATTER

Tony Watkins (IVP, 2004)

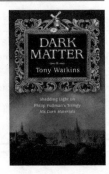

A sympathetic, serious investigation into the trilogy by an author who doesn't let his Christian faith blind him to the novels' considerable merits but rightly challenges Pullman's treatment of Christianity, scrutinizes some of the scientific concepts underpinning the books and explores the novelist's faith in "accumulated human wisdom". As Watkins points out, if the human race was amassing wisdom as Pullman suggests surely the "moral foundation of our society" should be improving. Perhaps too academic in tone for the general reader, this is an intelligent study.

DARKNESS ILLUMINATED

Edited by Lyn Haill (Oberon Books, 2004)

The entertaining transcripts of the discussions on the books and the play between Pullman, the Archbishop of Canterbury Rowan Williams, director Nicholas Hytner and members of the cast and crew of the National Theatre's dramatization of the trilogy can be found in various online shops for a bargain price.

DARKNESS VISIBLE

Nicholas Tucker (Wizard, 2003)

Easier to read than Tony Watkins' tome, this intelligent, thoughtful guide to the fictional world of the trilogy is especially valuable for the light it sheds on his life and work before the trilogy and how that influenced *His Dark Materials*.

THE DEVIL'S ACCOUNT

Hugh Rayment-Pickard (Darton, Longman & Todd, 2004)

A more bite-sized, sarcastic alternative to Tony Watkins' guide, focusing on the theme of Christianity, this isn't in the same class, possibly because the author just doesn't seem to like the novels that much.

THE ELEMENTS OF HIS DARK MATERIALS

Laurie Frost (The Fell Press, 2006)

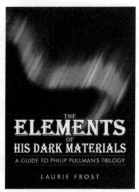

To call this the trainspotter's guide to the trilogy is definitely intended as a compliment, not an insult. You can find almost any aspect of the books discussed and annotated here – from the source of the many Biblical allusions to the differences between the many worlds, even the food characters eat. It's easy to imagine Pullman doing as he says on the blurb and keeping this for reference as he completes *The Book Of Dust*. The only question raised by the sheer exhaustiveness of Frost's research – one every reader will have their own answer to – is whether, if you spend too long delving in this treasure trove, it increases or diminishes your enjoyment of the books. Sometimes, it's more satisfying if novels retain a bit of mystery.

EXPLORING PHILIP PULLMAN'S HIS DARK MATERIALS

Lois Gresh (Griffin Press, 2006)

This decent guide to the trilogy's themes and issues is designed to be read by young adults but is probably not quite in the same league as David Colbert's *The Magical World Of Philip Pullman* (see p.270).

His Dark Materials Illuminated

edited by Millicent Lenz and Carole Scott (Wayne State University Press, 2005)

An intriguing, if sometimes overly academic, anthology of critical essays that considers the trilogy from a literary, historical, linguistic and theological perspective.

The Magical Worlds Of Philip Pullman

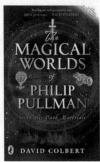

David Colbert (Puffin, 2006)

A superb, clear, concise, entertaining, intelligent guide to the books that packs a lot into its 145 pages and, as all such books should do, leaves you wanting to dive back into the novels again.

Navigating The Golden Compass

Sarah Zettel and Glen Yeffeth (BenBella, 2006)

This title in the SmartPop series doesn't quite press all the buttons, probably because it focuses a tad too intently on the Pullman versus Christianity theme.

Philip Pullman, Master Storyteller

Claire Squires (Continuum, 2006)

Don't be put off by the childish cover foisted on some editions of this book, this is an intelligent, informed, insightful guide to the trilogy and to Pullman as an author, polemicist and professional big mouth.

The Science Of Philip Pullman's His Dark Materials

Mary and John Gribbin (Hodder Children's Books, 2003)

No *His Dark Materials* fan should be without this. The Gribbins have the scientific understanding to appreciate Pullman's conceits and ideas and have a very readable way of explaining the science that underpins them. The chapter on science in Tony Watkins' *Dark Matter* raises a few issues with the theories expounded in this book.

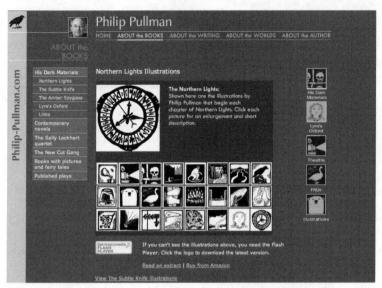

Author, author: Pullman's website is one of the most intriguing author sites on the Web

WEBSITES

If you Google *His Dark Materials*, you get 2.7 million mentions, so it is no surprise to find the books popping up in some very unusual parts of cyberspace. Interviews with Pullman are scattered across the Web. Two of the best are Jeanette Winterson's (go to *www.jeanettewinterson.com* and follow the links from the journalism tab) and his debate with the Christian magazine *Third Way* (go to *www.thirdway.org.uk* and click on the WayBack tab). You can also download some influential texts (notably *Paradise Lost*) from Project Gutenberg.

Here you will find the websites that fans keep returning to and a few others that seem significant or entertaining. *The Guardian* has a decent archive of Pullman's own journalism, book reviews, opinion pieces and interviews and some intelligent reviews of the books and the play.

Wikipedia has a decent amount of material on the trilogy and Pullman (the best place to start is by searching the site for *Northern Lights*), complete with synopses and notes on the major characters and controversies. But there are some superb fansites and plenty of sites that refer to the fantastically diverse range of themes touched on in the books.

PHILIP PULLMAN

www.philip-pullman.com

The only real complaint fans have about this site is that Pullman doesn't add his thoughts to it as often as they'd like. Others see the infrequency as a small price to pay for the completion of *The Book Of Dust*. But there's more than enough here to delight and intrigue any fan of *His Dark Materials*, including some moving reminiscences by the author, and his thoughts on many of his books plus his opinions on almost everything else. The gallery of illustrations he drew for the books is a delight. You get a real feeling of connection with Pullman and, through the wealth of material, with the books.

HIS DARK MATERIALS

www.bridgetothestars.net

After Pullman's own site, this is probably the first port of call for *His Dark Materials* fans on the Web. This site is packed with news, a glossary, a character guide, columns and essays (of varying quality and tone), some educational resources and a bit of fan fiction. The site is so influential that Chris Weitz, director of *The Golden Compass*, asked to be interviewed on it, to assuage fans after he had been hired, to much disquiet among aficionados, to make the movie. Bridge To The Stars also held the poll to decide how fans of the books would collectively refer to themselves. They chose "sraffies" which combines "sraf", the mulefa word for Dust, with the last syllable of "Trekkies".

HIS DARK MATERIALS: AN UNOFFICIAL FANSITE

www.darkmaterials.com

A dated fansite with some decent material. The foreign covers are worth a look and there's an essay comparing Lyra to Little Red Riding Hood.

HIS DARK MATERIALS.ORG

www.hisdarkmaterials.org

Does a similar job to Bridge To The Stars with a cool design, good forum, access to an online encyclopaedia, a dæmon name generator (this author's was axioleya – she was a female dæmon by the way) and the opportunity to download a version of the alethiometer so you can practise your truthometer reading skills.

THE REPUBLIC OF HEAVEN

republicofheaven.blogspot.com

A blog inspired by the finale of *The Amber Spyglass* which often touches on Pullman themes. Contributors have given themselves the IDs Mrs Coulter (who is really a American woman in her thirties living in Columbus, Ohio) and Lee Scoresby. The FAQ is quite interesting. The pseudonymous Mrs Coulter says she didn't name herself after a heroic character in literature because she felt that was "a form of hubris". She is so keen on the books she named her daughter, born in May 2004, Lyra.

THE FICTION OF CERES WUNDERKIND

www.cereswunderkind.net

Don't be put off by the pale purple homepage. This is a collection of half-decent fan fiction set in the worlds of *His Dark Materials*. To some Pullman fans, the very idea of fan fiction seems sacrilegious. The ten commandments of fan fiction Wunderkind has posted here make for amusing reading.

Commandment No.1 – "Thou shalt not reunite those whom Philip Pullman hath parted" – sounds a bit Stalinist but his commandment No.5 – "Thou shalt give Elaine Parry an even break" – should be heartily applauded. As Wunderkind says, her five functions in the books are: "To be bonkers, to be loved by her husband, to be loved by her son, to have that love superseded by Lyra Silvertongue, to be bonkers." There are a few thought-provoking articles on the books too. Wunderkind seems to take something of a proprietary interest in the novels.

DAKOTA BLUE RICHARDS

dakota.skyefairy.net

It didn't take long for the girl who is to be Lyra to acquire her own, not bad, fansite. The homepage in which Dakota/Lyra is twinned is a bit spooky but don't let that deter you.

The Golden Compass

www.goldencompassmovie.com

This official movie site started off low-key but has gradually accumulated an impressive amount of material. As you might expect from New Line Cinema, it's tastefully done, with some nifty features. And few fans could resist the chance to see the trailer and production visualizations of some key scenes. Pity it forces you to have Flash though.

Other Sites

Nikolai Medtner

www.granta.com/extracts/1469

After saying that he can't really explain why he is so moved by the piano music of Russian composer Nikolai Medtner (1880–1951), Pullman goes on to prove himself triumphantly wrong in an endearing piece first published in the literary magazine *Granta*. Though sometimes compared unfavourably to better known composers like Rachmaninov and Scriabin, Medtner is a subtle genius whose reputation would be a lot higher if his music was easier to perform. The Russian maestro's work was not built for the age of easy listening smooth classics radio. If you're so convinced by Pullman's eloquent appreciation you want to hear some of Medtner's music, you can download some pieces for free. Go to *http://pianosociety.com/cms* follow the composers menu for Medtner or listen on the relaunched official website *www.medtner.com*.

Pullman On Storytelling

www.newhumanist.org.uk/issues/0203/pullman.htm

The author's views on the storyteller's responsibility to his tale, audience and mortgage. The essay begins with the fine phrase: "Ethics is a big subject of which I know little." Later on, he sounds like he's back in the classroom as he declares: "If we're rhyming, let's rhyme properly, and get the metre right while we're about it; if we're telling a detective story, we shouldn't cheat by withholding information from the reader; if we're writing a film script set in the past, let's make sure the dialogue is at least as authentically in period as the costumes."

THE DARKSIDE OF NARNIA

www.crlamppost.org/darkside.htm

Pullman takes C.S. Lewis severely in hand for, among other sins, "reactionary sneering, misogynism, racism" and the "sheer dishonesty" of his narrative method. For the counterblast go to *The Golden Bough* (on *http://dedulysses.wordpress.com*) and see *For Love Of Narnia*. You might want to bookmark this anyway, for the fascinating discussion between Pullman and Tony Watkins, author of *Dark Matter*, on religion, God and science.

ROBOT WISDOM

www.robotwisdom.com/jorn/pullman.html

Don't be put off by the oddness of the home page, Robot Wisdom's entries for its authors offer a quirky timeline on the likes of Pullman, Peter Dickinson and Tom Wolfe.

WILLIAM BLAKE

www.newstatesman.com

In similar vein to the Medtner piece, Pullman's article for *New Statesman* celebrates Blake with the delightful admission: "I can't be objective about Blake. In fact, I love him."

THEMES IN *HIS DARK MATERIALS*

The sheer intellectual sweep of Pullman's trilogy is impressive and to suggest a website relevant to every theme he touches on would fill this book, so what follows is a handpicked selection that might increase your enjoyment of the books.

AURORA BOREALIS

www.gi.alaska.edu/ScienceForum/aurora.html

You can find Aurora Borealis sites all over the Web, but this compact collection of jargon-free articles on the phenomenon touches on such fascinating ideas as whether you can hear it, whether it can be predicted and which ones are bad for your eyes. Even Galileo got the Aurora Borealis wrong, believing it was sunlight reflecting off the Earth's high atmosphere. Still, he was distracted by the Roman Inquisition.

EMBLEM BOOKS

www.netnik.com/emblemata
These illustrated books – in which a common phrase or moral was expressed in a picture with a brief explanation – were very much the rage in the 16th and 17th centuries and, Pullman has revealed, were one of the inspirations for the alethiometer. The most famous of these books, Andres Alciati's *Emblemata Liber* (1531), which literally means Emblem Book, is reproduced on this site.

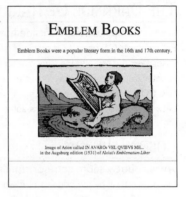

EMBLEM BOOKS

Emblem Books were a popular literary form in the 16th and 17th century.

Image of Arion called IN AVAROs VEL QVIBVS ME... in the Augsburg edition (1531) of Alciati's *Emblematum Liber*

EVIL MONKEYS

www.classicreader.com/booktoc.php/sid.1/bookid.2551
Mrs Coulter's evil monkey dæmon was drawn in part from *Green Tea*, a chilling ghost story by Joseph Sheridan le Fanu, which can be read here.

THE GNOSTIC ARCHIVE

www.gnosis.org
Pullman is not a Gnostic but some of the views in *His Dark Materials* could be described as postmodern Gnosticism. If you want to know more about this still much misunderstood strand of religious thought, this is a pretty good place to start.

PARALLEL UNIVERSES

http://www.slate.com/id/2087206/
Disappointingly, many of the sites and articles devoted to the theory of parallel universes require you to register, or part with cash, or are attached to now dated TV series. This article on *Slate* is a good place to get to grips with the issues.

His Dark Materials
The Glossary

These harpies, created for an edition of Dante's Inferno by Gustave Doré, one of Pullman's favourite artists, are ancestors of his harpies in the world of the dead

MATERIALS WORLD

Your alphabetized rough guide to the instruments, characters, places and creatures in Pullman's trilogy

ALETHIOMETER

Alethia is Greek for "truth", making an alethiometer a "**truth-meter**". A disc of brass and crystal – in appearance like a large watch with 36 images instead of numbers – it has three short hands with which the user can ask a question, and a single long hand through which **Dust** responds. Pullman says the instrument was invented by a 17th-century scholar in Prague, but it largely fell out of use two centuries before the events in the books, partly because it is so difficult to use. Like **tarot** or the **I Ching** (to which the alethiometer is compared), its images are ambiguous and normally require great knowledge to interpret. Thanks to "grace" and an unusual ability to make her mind "go clear" Lyra can use hers instinctively. The Master of Jordan College says there are only six alethiometers in existence, though others give different numbers.

AMBER SPYGLASS

An instrument devised by **Mary Malone** in the mulefa's world, the amber spyglass allows humans to see **sraf** (or Dust). It consists of two discs of amber lacquer smeared with wheel seedpod oil and held "a hand-span apart" by a bamboo tube.

ANBARIC

The new power source that is replacing naphtha is from the Arabic word "anbar", the root of our word "amber". Ninety percent of our world's amber comes from Russia's **Kaliningrad** enclave on the Baltic Sea.

ANGELS

Spread throughout "a million universes", angels are winged luminous beings composed of **Dust**, although – in contrast to the Biblical story – their leader, the **Authority**, is an angel himself. Their status is reflected in their brightness. Balthamos is near-invisible in daylight whereas Mrs Coulter compares Metatron to the Sun. To humans, angels appear in human form because their eyes "expect" it, but some, such as Baruch and Metatron, were once humans themselves. Angels can live for thousands of years, see deep into the human mind, and travel between worlds without windows.

AURORA BOREALIS

In our world, the Aurora Borealis – **Northern Lights** – is an atmospheric phenomenon mainly seen in the polar regions, the result of charged solar particles trapped by the Earth's magnetic field. In *His Dark Materials*, it has "the property of making the matter of this world thin" – revealing other worlds faintly behind it.

THE AUTHORITY

The Authority was the **first angel** ever to come into being, but he told "those who came after him that he had created them". His deceit resulted in the notion of **God** – a lie that has persisted, despite the first angelic rebellion, when **Xaphania** and others discovered the truth. Among the Authority's early exploits was the creation of the world of the dead but, confined in a crystal litter by his Regent, **Metatron**, he has since become "demented and powerless".

BOLVANGAR

Known among witches as the "fields of evil", Bolvangar is an **Experiment Station** in the snowy wastes of Norroway where the General Oblation Board performs **intercision** on kidnapped children. It consists of "brilliantly lit" metal and concrete buildings – some subterranean – and is surrounded by Tartar guards and an electric fence.

POPE JOHN CALVIN

In Lyra's world, Calvin was not a great religious reformer. As the last Pope, he moved the seat of the **papacy** to **Geneva**, established the **Consistorial Court of Discipline** and made the authority of the Church "absolute". In other words, he's not one of Pullman's heroes.

CITTÀGAZZE

The city seen by Lord Asriel through the Aurora, Cittàgazze (**City of Magpies**) is a beautiful place of boulevards and palm trees, inhabited by **Spectres**, which have eaten the adults' dæmons, leaving only "wild scavenging children". It is here that Will and Lyra first meet, and, in the **Torre degli Angeli**, that **Will** receives the **subtle knife**. Although Cittàgazze has much in common with Venice, according to Pullman a greater influence was Brian Aldiss's *The Malacia Tapestry*: a novel about an ancient European city whose inhabitants have followed a separate evolutionary line and grown wings or become satyrs.

CHTHONIC RAILWAY

The Chthonic railway is the equivalent of the **Underground** in Lyra's London. Described by the Margaret Thatcher-like Mrs Coulter as "not really intended for people of their class", it does not appear in the books since Lyra decides she is safer in the open streets. The word "Chthonic" comes from the Greek **"khthon"** ("earth") and means "beneath the earth" or "in the Underworld".

CLIFF-GHASTS

"Half the size of a man, with leathery wings and hooked claws, a flat head with bulging eyes and a wide frog mouth", these scary monsters have personal hygiene issues and like to shriek a lot or go "yowk-yowk-yowk". They have been around a long time – they claim to have witnessed the angels' rebellion against the Authority – but don't like anyone very much (apart from arctic foxes which they eat) and look forward eagerly to the coming war between Asriel and the Church, primarily because they can't wait to see all the casualties.

Clouded Mountain

This giant mountain fortress, home to the angels who haven't rebelled, can move under its own power and might be Pullman's homage to the mighty Harlech Castle, in the shadow of which he studied as a boy. The Clouded Mountain is only mentioned once, when Mrs Coulter tricks the Regent to his death, and is assumed, after the final battle, to have been destroyed or taken by the rebels.

Consistorial Court of Discipline

This is a branch of the **Magisterium**, responsible for investigating and punishing acts of heresy. Established by **Pope John Calvin**, it is "the most active and the most feared of all the Church's bodies" – **torturing** or **assassinating** anyone who challenges its authority. The Court is based at the College of St Jerome in Geneva and consists of twelve members, under **President Hugh MacPhail**. Among its closely guarded doctrines is **pre-emptive absolution**, which allows **Father Gomez** to repent before setting out on his mission to kill Lyra. By the end of the books, the Court has become "confused and leaderless".

Dæmons

Essentially, a dæmon is a person's soul manifested as an animal. It is usually of the opposite sex to its human and, for children, changes shape continually to reflect his or her emotions – although at puberty it "settles" in the form that best reflects the person's deeper character. So, **Lord Asriel** has a **snow leopard** – cold and lone – whereas servants normally have dogs. The connection with a dæmon is a bond of near-atomic strength. Straying a few feet too far apart can send both parties "mad with grief and terror" – it is this power that Asriel harnesses when he severs **Roger** from Salcilia and blasts a hole to Cittàgazze.

In 2003, Pullman was asked if dæmons were born at the same time as their humans. "The gynaecology of dæmons is a closed book to me," he replied, saying that he had never really had to think about it because he'd never written a scene in which a human character was born. "What I do know is about how they get their names: the parents' dæmons choose the name of the child's dæmon."

DUST (SRAF, SHADOWS, RUSAKOV PARTICLES)

According to the angel Balthamos, **Dust** is "a name for what happens when matter begins to understand itself". It is an elementary particle, discovered by the experimental theologian **Boris Mikhailovitch Rusakov**, responsible for "everything good" in the universe and constantly renewed "by thinking and feeling and reflecting, by gaining wisdom and passing it on". When Lyra visits the **Pitt Rivers Museum** in Will's Oxford, she discovers that Dust has existed for 33,000 years. Having established that Dust is drawn only to adult humans, the Church believes that it is the result of **original sin** – the coming to knowledge in the **Garden of Eden** – and must be destroyed. By following her alethiometer, which responds to Dust, Lyra stems the golden flood of Dust passing away into the abyss and secures the future of the universe. As Lord Asriel says, the word Dust comes from Genesis, Chapter 3: "for dust thou art, and to dust shalt thou return".

GALLIVESPIANS

Gallivespians are creatures from an alternate universe: human in appearance, but small enough to ride insects the size of dragonflies. They seem to be **part-insect** themselves. Although the Chevalier Tialys and the Lady Salmakia both look like people, Lyra is surprised by how easily Tialys can lift the relatively large lodestone resonator, while both Tialys and Salmakia have very short lifespans (nine or ten years) and poisonous spurs in their heels, which can stun or kill, and require at least 24 hours to return to full power after use. The name Gallivespian seems to have been inspired by the gall-wasp ("vespa" is the Italian for wasp): a very small variety, typically six to eight millimetres long. The size, honour and bravery of the Gallivespians, who have joined Lord Asriel in the war against the Authority, make them ideal spies.

GENERAL OBLATION BOARD

The General Oblation Board is a **"semi-private initiative"** – a branch of the **Magisterium**, but almost independent of the Consistorial Court of Discipline. It was founded by **Mrs Coulter** ten years before the events of the books, to investigate Dust, and its members are engaged in abducting children and smuggling them to their **Experiment Station** in Bolvangar, to be severed from their dæmons. Among their many other names, the Board is known among the witches as the "Dust-hunters", and among the children of Oxford as the "**Gobblers**". In our world, the word "oblation" has two relevant meanings: during the **Middle Ages**, "oblates" were children given to the Church by poor families to become monks and nuns, while an "oblation" is the action of giving something to God.

Gyptians

Waterfarers of the Eastern Anglian fens, the gyptians are a "tight-knit" people, whose six extended families are led by **King John Faa**. They have allies "in all sorts of places you wouldn't imagine" – Lord Asriel and Serafina Pekkala among them – but they are outsiders in Brytish society and, staying only briefly in cities like Oxford, they are natural targets for the General Oblation Board. Gyptian society is loyal and courteous. To rescue their missing children, 170 gyptian men sail fearlessly for Bolvangar, and when Faa and Farder Coram retrieve Will, Lyra and Mary from the world of the mulefa they present their hosts with such ornate gifts as "silver tapestries from Turkestan". Many of the gyptians in *His Dark Materials* have **Dutch** names, but the word "gyptian" is an archaic word for gypsy – gypsies being once thought to have come from Egypt.

Harpies

Stinking and caked in blood and slime, harpies are **vulture-sized birds** with a woman's head, breasts and "matted, filthy black hair". They have lived in the land of the dead for millennia – since the arrival of the first ghost – and can "see the worst in everyone", which makes them adept at psychological torture. They persecute Lyra for her lying, and Will for leaving his mother, but prove partial to true stories. Their main reason for resisting Will's idea to cut a window into another world is fear that it will render them redundant. Harpies have their forebears in classical mythology. The Greek word **harpazein** means "to seize". The original harpies were vicious spirits who carried people to their deaths.

I Ching

In our world, the *I Ching* (or *Book Of Changes*) is an ancient Chinese text – possibly dating from 2800 BC. It is a system of divination to find order in chance events, and expresses the wisdom and philosophy of ancient China. In *The Subtle Knife*, Lyra discovers that, like her alethiometer, it is a means of communicating with Dust. **Mary Malone** packs her poster of the *I Ching* symbols before she leaves her Oxford laboratory and uses it to guide her through Cittàgazze and the world of the mulefa, where she enters a state of "calm and concentrated attention" and casts with yarrow sticks.

Intercision

The process of severing a person from his or her dæmon – intercision – was devised by **Mrs Coulter** after she encountered African **zombi**: men "who will work night and day without ever running away or complaining". In theory, the General Oblation Board are "cutting" children to stop them from attracting Dust as adults. An earlier means of intercision was the **Maystadt scalpel,** which was so traumatic that many children died of shock, even under general anaesthetic. This is largely replaced by the **silver guillotine** which is regarded as more efficient and less harrowing – for the cutters. Intercision is of great interest to Lord Asriel because of the enormous blast of energy that it releases, which allows him to blow a hole through the Aurora Borealis to Cittàgazze. He does though admit, to Lyra, that the process is harrowing, much worse than the agony of any physical operation.

Intention Craft

So advanced that some readers speculate that it is powered by **anti-gravity,** yet so basic that it uses leather and string, this bizarre variation of a **helicopter** owes something to illustrator Heath Robinson, H.G. Wells and Jules Verne. The craft, as the name suggests, is driven by the pilot's intentions – but only if the pilot has a dæmon with them. The craft's weaponry is so advanced it may be using lasers or particle beams to shoot down the enemy. It proves invaluable when **Mrs Coulter** needs to escape Asriel's fortress to reach the Clouded Mountain.

Jordan College

"Like some enormous fungus whose root-system extended over acres", Jordan College is the **Gothic** Oxford institution where Lyra was sent to live by Lord Asriel. A labyrinth both above and below ground, it was built between the early

Middle Ages and the 18th century and provides her with endless tunnels, vaults, staircases, roofs and gardens to explore. Jordan's layout and location in Lyra's Oxford are very much like that of **Exeter College** (the alma mater of Pullman and Tolkien), but Jordan is the oldest, the most academically prestigious, "the grandest and richest" of the 24 Oxford colleges in Lyra's world, whereas Exeter is merely the fourth oldest in "our" world, founded in 1314 by **Walter de Stapledon**, a professor of law, bishop of Exeter and a chaplain to **Pope Clement V**. At the end of *The Amber Spyglass*, Lyra returns here "because this used to be my home and I didn't have anywhere else to go."

LAND OF THE DEAD

The land of the dead was created by the **Authority** as "a prison camp" where ghosts would be tormented eternally by harpies. The land has grim, stinky, extensive suburbs where Will and Lyra spend a night with a family who came there some time ago and must now wait until their deaths say it is time to die. The land is entered by a ferry from a "foul and dismal shore", then by a battered wooden door. The unnamed ferryman owes a lot to **Charon** who, in Greek myth, ferried the dead across the river Styx (aka Acheron) to **Hades**. Inside is an "immense and oppressive" plain, where everybody who has ever lived is standing, sitting or lying down. Together Lyra, Will, Tialys and Salmakia resolve to free them, although it is only when one of the harpies, **No-Name**, shows Will a place where he can cut through to the world of the mulefa that they finally succeed. According to Tialys, this is "the greatest blow you could ever strike" against the Authority.

LODESTONE RESONATOR

A communication device used by the **Gallivespians**, the **lodestone resonator** resembles a "short length of pencil made of a dull grey-black stone, resting on a stand of wood". It is operated by stroking the end with a bow and pressing points along its side, whilst messages can be received via a pair of headphones. The principle of the lodestone resonator has its roots in quantum physics and sympathetic magic. As Tialys explains, the particles of a "common lodestone" are first entangled and then divided into two halves, so that "whatever happens to one happens to the other at the same moment". Messages can even be sent between different universes but not to the world of the dead.

Magisterium

The Magisterium arose after the death of **Pope John Calvin**, and essentially took over the duties of the papacy. A "tangle of courts, colleges and councils", its branches include the General Oblation Board, the Consistorial Court of Discipline and the College of Bishops. Despite constant internal machinations, the power of the Magisterium is immense. In some countries, it even has authority over the army, with the **Swiss Guard** and the **Imperial Guard of Muscovy** under its command. In our world, magisterium is a technical term used by the **Roman Catholic Church** to describe its authority as a teacher.

Mulefa

Invertebrate antelope-like creatures with trunks, the **mulefa** have claws which have evolved to grasp cylindrical seedpods, allowing them to travel on "wheels". Intellectually, the mulefa are the "people" of their particular world – having become conscious, they relate, about **33,000 years** earlier – roughly about the time that Dust came into existence. They can speak, inflecting their words with movements of the trunk, and, although illiterate, have a rich story-telling tradition. These chilled-out creatures inhabit small villages, where they work cooperatively, love monogamously and live in harmony with their environment: a suitably Edenic context for Will and Lyra to fall in love.

Muscovy

A Moscow princedom and forerunner of **Tsarist Russia** in our world, in *His Dark Materials* Muscovy is a country equivalent to modern Russia (or the **Soviet Union**), with enormous financial and military clout. It is under the sway of the Church, and members of its Imperial Guard hunt Lee Scoresby and Stanislaus Grumman into a gorge in Cittàgazze, where Scoresby is killed. The Muscovite Boris Mikhailovitch Rusakov discovered Dust (Rusakov Particles).

Naphtha

An oil used for illumination in *His Dark Materials*. The word **naphtha** may have Greek, even Persian, roots but it is also derived from napthalene, a hydrocarbon discovered in 1819. In our world, **napalm** – the flammable liquid used so extensively and horrifically in Vietnam – springs from the word naptha which does rather tie in with its predicted use as a weapon by the Imperial Army.

NEW DENMARK

A North America-like continent across the ocean, New Denmark includes **Texas** among its countries, as well as the land of the **Skrælings** and certain French territories. The Texan aëronaut **Lee Scoresby** remembers a battle between the French and the New Danes at the **Alamo**. New Denmark is famous for exporting smokeleaf.

OXFORD

Lyra's **Oxford** is both recognisable and fundamentally different from our own. Many of these differences are minute. In Lyra's world, the **Bodleian Library** (restored by Thomas Bodley in 1598–1602) has become Bodley's Library, while **"the Broad"** is the name normally given to Broad Street by Oxford students. Arriving in Will's Oxford, Lyra is at first like a Victorian time-traveller. She knows St John's College but is confused by the traffic lights outside – then she comes to the Pitt Rivers Museum, which doesn't exist in her world at all. The two cities seem to have evolved differently from the same source. In Lyra's world, for instance, Durham and Cardinal's Colleges were never changed to Trinity and Christ's Church – suggesting either that **Henry VIII** didn't exist, or else that there was no schism with the **Catholic Church**.

PANSERBJØRNE

The panserbjørne are **armoured bears** from **Svalbard** – ten feet tall, loyal and warlike, with yellow-white fur, small black eyes, opposable thumbs and the power of speech. They wear armour made from **sky iron** (Iorek Byrnison compares its importance to a human's dæmon) and they are extraordinary metalsmiths, working with dagger-like claws. Although King Iofur Raknison has begun to acquire human characteristics and has built himself a stone palace, traditionally the panserbjørne live in ice forts, avoid contact with humans and, as animals, cannot be tricked. The name panserbjørne means "armoured bears" in Danish. In early British editions, the bears were called panserbjørne. They have much in common with **polar bears** of our own world, which also move both legs on one side simultaneously and have been spotted using tools. Iofur Byrnison's victory over the usurper may be a plea for a more sustainable way of life.

SIBERIA

Siberia is "the **dusty brown-green emptiness**" where Will arrives from Cittàgazze in *The Amber Spyglass*, and soon meets Iorek Byrnison, who is leading his panserbjørne to the Himalayas, in search of lower temperatures. It is also the homeland of the **Tartar** troops patrolling the **Bolvangar Experiment Station**, and of the **Yenisei Pakhtars** – among whom John Parry became the shaman Jopari. On the Siberian island of **Nova Zembla**, Lee Scoresby looks for Stanislaus Grumman and Iorek Byrnison finds sky iron to make his new armour.

SKY IRON

Sky iron is the name given to **meteorite iron** by the panserbjørne, who prize it highly for use in their armour. It can be found in Svalbard and on the island of Nova Zembla. In our own world, **Inuits** in Greenland have been known to use meteorite iron in the construction of tools.

SKRÆLING

Norse explorers of **Greenland** and **Newfoundland** in the 10th century called the native people "Skræling". The word may derive from their habit of wearing clothes made from skin (for which the old Norse word was "skra") or scrawny ("skral" in old Norse) but in Iceland the word now means "barbarian". That is pretty much how this ethnic group, primarily found in New Denmark, is regarded by the scholars of Jordan College when they ponder the head that has, allegedly, been scalped by the Skrælings. **Tony Makarios**, abducted by the Gobblers, is part Skræling and the censor at **Nova Zembla** is known only as "the Skræling" which would suggest that, in Lyra's world, they have had a lot of contact with other races.

SPECTRES

Spectres are evil, translucent beings, given to eating both Dust and the Dust-attracting dæmons of adults – accounting for the dominance of children in

Cittàgazze, where Spectres are rife. The only direct defence against them is the **subtle knife**, although Mrs Coulter does manage to pass among them by directing them to other victims. As **Kirjava** explains near the end of *The Amber Spyglass*: "Every time we open a window with the knife, we make a Spectre." The relationship between Spectres and the knife is not as straightforward, say, as that between Superman and Kryptonite. The knife isn't simply their enemy; by cutting windows, it also gives birth to them. Ultimately, only the end of travel between worlds can guarantee the future of the universes – meaning that Will and Lyra must part forever.

SUBTLE KNIFE/ÆSAHÆTTR

The subtle knife is "the **one weapon in all the universes** that could defeat the tyrant, **the Authority**". It has a rosewood handle inlaid with golden angels, one side sharp enough to cut the bonds between matter, and the other sharp enough to cut matter itself, while its tip can slice windows into other worlds. **Giacomo Paradisi** says it is "a subtle knife, not a heavy sword", and its use depends on the concentration of the knife bearer. **Will**, who is destined for the role, uses the knife to free Lyra from the Himalayan cave, release the ghosts from the land of the dead, and let the Authority break out of his crystal litter. But the knife has its own agenda. Its use through the centuries has produced **Spectres** and caused the exodus of **Dust**. Ultimately, Will has to think about Lyra whilst using the knife – disrupting his concentration – in order to break the blade for good.

SVALBARD

The kingdom of the panserbjørne, Svalbard is an island in the **Arctic Circle**: a place of "**slow-crawling glaciers**", "jumbled peaks and sharp ridges", surrounded by **cliff-ghasts** and thousand-foot cliffs. At its heart is **Iofur Raknison**'s stone palace and the prison/palace of exiled Lord Asriel. When Asriel makes a hole in the sky, the climate changes and the bears head to the Himalayas – although they later return because they "can live more easily by the sea, even if it is warm".

TARTARS

Tartars are natives of Siberia – specifically, the region between the rivers **Ob** and **Yenisei**, although they have also conquered Muscovy. With their "broad Asiatic" faces and ferocious reputation, they owe much to Genghis Khan's **Mongols**. Mrs Coulter has chosen Tartars to protect the Experiment Station at Bolvangar. There are many legends of Tartar atrocities. They are reputed to pull out the lungs of their enemies. Yet the Tartars **John Parry** meets are an intriguing shamanistic people, who trepan themselves to allow Dust into their brains.

Tokay

The Master of Jordan College uses a bottle of this "rich golden wine" to try to poison Asriel – specifically, one of 36 bottles remaining of the famed 1898 vintage. In our world, Tokay is an Anglicized spelling of **Tokaji**, the wines of the Tokaj-Hegyalja region of Hungary.

Windows

The passageways into worlds are usually described as windows, though sometimes they are doors or doorways. Mary Malone refers to them as a "square patch of difference". When Will first spots a window, he has to look hard before finally spotting a square patch that looks as if it has been cut from the air. It is, though, only visible from certain angles.

Small passageways, only large enough for a person to stoop through, can be cut with four swift movements while the knife bearer is standing up. But the window Will finally cuts to release the ghosts from the world of the dead must be much larger.

There were windows between worlds even before the **Guild of the Torre degli Angeli** invented the subtle knife three hundred years ago. The witches of the North and the shamans in the Arctic made use of them. You have to know where to find them because they can be anywhere but are not everywhere, otherwise Will would always be able to cut one. In the world of the dead, he cuts several windows but they only open to the underground of another world, until a harpy agrees to show him a place where he can cut a window and escape.

There seem to be no hard and fast rules about who goes through windows, in what circumstances and why. A cat disappears through one in Sunderland Avenue, Oxford, attracting Will's curiosity. His father walks from one world into another in Alaska through a blizzard. Mary Malone strolls through the same window as Will and the cat, even though it is guarded, on the instructions of the shadow particles.

Dust leaks through the windows into emptiness, threatening the physical and geographical balance of worlds. This is why all but one window has to be shut. Through the self-sacrifice of Will and Lyra, the remaining window links to the world of the dead.

WITCHES

Witches look like young women dressed in **thin black silk,** but they can live a thousand years, fly on branches of cloud-pine, make themselves invisible (though this spell takes a physical toll) and travel far from their bird-dæmons. They have no interest in worldly gain, living in forests and other remote areas. They feel the cold, but prefer not to insulate themselves against "the star-tingle and the music of the **Aurora**". The great tragedy of witches is that they can fall in love with ordinary men, who "die so soon that our hearts are continually wracked with pain". Only their daughters become witches. When the news of Asriel's rebellion against the **Authority** spreads, the witch clans quickly rally to his support.

$$\cdot\dagger\cdot$$

PiCTVRE CRЕӘit8

COVER CRЕӘit8

Outer cover **Front cover: polar bear, Churchill, Canada © Kevin Schafer/Alamy; Oxford spires © Alamy; Back cover: Northern Lights, Denali National Park, Alaska © Johnny Johnson/Getty**

Inner cover **Standing polar bear © Miles/Zefa/Corbis**

ILLVStRAtiOΠ8

Press Association 69, 73, 80, 83, 86, 90, 304

Catherine Ashmore 45, 59 75, 77

His Dark Materials, National Theatre 2004, based on the novels by Philip Pullman, adapted by Nicholas Wright, directed by Nicholas Hytner with Matthew Wilde, photographs © Catherine Ashmore

Getty Images 13, 16, 95, 107, 1 17, 122, 125, 162, 168, 181, 193, 197, 201, 205, 210, 223, 241, 252, 277

Agence France Press 167

Lesley Turner 7, 35, 93, 217, 235, 236

Paul Delma 107

Roger Viollet 115

Maclellan Don/Corbis Sygma 23

Jack Simpson 219

Ceres Wunderkind 273

Triad Granada/Philip Tonkyn 262

Time-Life Pictures 159, 181

The Art Archive/The Princes Czartoryski Museum, Krakow 40

Galileo by Justus Sustermans (1639) 64

Thomas Huxley's Evidence As To Man's Place In Nature (1863) 156

Colin M. L. Burnett 155

Library of Congress 202

Wikipedia users JW1805/Chris O. 129

Toby Ord 228

Darren Bradrick 239

His Dark Materials
Index

INDEX

INDEX

My readers are intelligent: I don't write for stupid people. Now mark this carefully, because otherwise I shall be misquoted and vilified again; we are all stupid, and we are all intelligent. The line dividing the stupid from the intelligent goes right down the middle of our heads. Others may find their readership on the stupid side: I don't. I pay my readers the compliment of assuming that they are intellectually adventurous.

Philip Pullman